USING

mac os® x
snow leopard®

Yvonne Johnson

800 East 96th Street, Indianapolis, Indiana 46240 USA

Using Mac OS® X Snow Leopard®

Copyright © 2010 by Pearson Education, Inc.

ISBN-13: 978-0-7897-4326-8
ISBN-10: 0-7897-4326-4

Library of Congress Cataloging-in-Publication Data:
Johnson, Yvonne.
  Using Mac OS X Snow Leopard / Yvonne Johnson.
    p. cm.
  Includes index.
  ISBN 978-0-7897-4326-8
  1. Mac OS. 2. Operating systems (Computers) 3. Macintosh (Computer)—Programming.
I. Title.
  QA76.76.O63J6394 2010
  005.4'465—dc22
                    2009050183

Printed in the United States of America
First Printing: April 2010

Trademarks

All terms mentioned in this book that are known to be trademarks or service marks have been appropriately capitalized. Que Publishing cannot attest to the accuracy of this information. Use of a term in this book should not be regarded as affecting the validity of any trademark or service mark.

Mac OS and Snow Leopard are registered trademarks of Apple Inc.

Warning and Disclaimer

Bulk Sales

Que Publishing offers excellent discounts on this book when ordered in quantity for bulk purchases or special sales. For more information, please contact

U.S. Corporate and Government Sales
1-800-382-3419
corpsales@pearsontechgroup.com

For sales outside of the U.S., please contact

International Sales
international@pearson.com

Associate Publisher
Greg Wiegand

Acquisitions Editor
Laura Norman

Development Editor
Kevin Howard

Managing Editor
Kristy Hart

Senior Project Editor
Lori Lyons

Copy Editor
Bart Reed

Indexer
Ken Johnson

Proofreader
Debbie Williams

Technical Editor
Matthew David

Publishing Coordinator
Cindy Teeters

Book Designer
Anne Jones

Multimedia Developer
John Herrin

Senior Compositor
Gloria Schurick

Contents at a Glance

Media Files Table of Contents

To register this product and gain access to the Free Web Edition and the audio and video files, go to **quepublishing.com/using**.

Table of Contents

About the Author

Yvonne Johnson has been writing computer books and teaching computer classes since 1982. She has written more than 60 computer books and college texts for well-known publishers on practically every type of software that exists—from operating systems to desktop publishing, from word processing and spreadsheets to databases, from programming to graphic design and web design. Her most recent Mac projects include doing the technical editing for *Easy iLife 09* (Que) and *Switching to Mac OS X Snow Leopard* (Pearson Education).

She started the first proprietary computer-training school in Kentucky and operated it for 12 years, serving local clients such as Brown & Williamson Tobacco and General Electric, and sending out trainers to locations all over the country for the Department of Defense, the IRS, and Fortune 500 companies. During that time, she wrote the curricula for all the software programs taught at the school. After selling the school, she worked as a freelance computer curriculum developer, writing a large percent of the curricula offered by a national computer-training company headquartered in Chicago. She also wrote computer-training material and trained extensively for a computer-training and consulting subsidiary of the *Washington Post*. Ultimately, she took the position of Vice President of Curriculum Development with this company.

Although she has a tremendous depth and breadth of computer knowledge, she has never forgotten how to communicate with beginning learners. She is known for the simplicity of her writing and her ability to explain complex topics in understandable terms. This ability comes from years of delivering classroom training on computer applications to thousands of employees of large and small businesses, military and government personnel, teachers, attorneys, secretaries, and, yes, even Microsoft software support engineers.

Dedication

To my son Todd, who insisted I get a Mac.

Acknowledgments

Writing a book is a team effort, and I appreciate all the people who made this book possible. Thank you Laura Norman, acquisition editor; Kevin Howard, development editor; and Lori Lyons, production editor—I've never worked with a better group of editors. I'm also grateful to my copy editor, Bart Reed, and my technical editor, Matthew David. Many of the people on the team worked "namelessly" behind the scenes to get this book into print, and I want to thank them as well. I do know at least one of these people by name: John Herrin—thanks for all your help with the guidelines for the media elements in the book.

We Want to Hear from You!

As the reader of this book, *you* are our most important critic and commentator. We value your opinion and want to know what we're doing right, what we could do better, what areas you'd like to see us publish in, and any other words of wisdom you're willing to pass our way.

As an associate publisher for Que Publishing, I welcome your comments. You can email or write me directly to let me know what you did or didn't like about this book—as well as what we can do to make our books better.

Please note that I cannot help you with technical problems related to the topic of this book. We do have a User Services group, however, where I will forward specific technical questions related to the book.

When you write, please be sure to include this book's title and author as well as your name, email address, and phone number. I will carefully review your comments and share them with the author and editors who worked on the book.

Email: feedback@quepublishing.com

Mail: Greg Wiegand
Associate Publisher
Que Publishing
800 East 96th Street
Indianapolis, IN 46240 USA

Reader Services

Visit our website and register this book at quepublishing.com/register for convenient access to any updates, downloads, or errata that might be available for this book.

Introduction

The subject of this book is the newest operating system for the Mac, OS X Snow Leopard, including the applications in the iLife '09 suite. The book's divided into three parts:

- Part I, "Introducing Mac OS X Snow Leopard," covers installing the software and getting comfortable with Snow Leopard's many features, installing printers and setting preferences for your hardware, customizing your desktop, getting help, and managing your applications and files.

- Part II, "Getting Busy," covers the applications that you use most often to get things done: the web browser Safari, iCal, Address Book, Mail, iChat, TextEdit, iPhoto, Widgets, and several applets. It also covers security settings, updating applications, and backing up and restoring files with Time Machine.

- Part III, "Having Fun and Getting Creative," covers the fun and creative side of your Mac: listening to music and podcasts with iTunes and Front Row; watching DVDs and videos with DVD Player, Front Row, and QuickTime Player; playing games; creating slideshows, photo books, greeting cards, photo calendars, and comic strips; producing your own movies with iMovie; producing your own musical recordings with Garage Band; and designing websites with iWeb.

Although the book is written for beginner-to-intermediate users (people who have purchased a Mac for the first time or people who have upgraded to Snow Leopard from an earlier version), I waste no space on basic computer skills and knowledge that most people have. For example, instead of teaching you how to surf the Internet, I focus on how to use the web browser securely and efficiently.

Using This Book

This book allows you to customize your own learning experience. The step-by-step instructions in the book give you a solid foundation in using Snow Leopard, while rich and varied online content, including video tutorials and audio sidebars, provide the following:

- Demonstrations of step-by-step tasks covered in the book

- Additional tips or information on a topic

- Practical advice and suggestions

- Direction for more advanced tasks not covered in the book

Here's a quick look at a few structural features designed to help you get the most out of this book.

Notes: Important tasks are offset to draw attention to them.

Let Me Try It tasks are presented in a step-by-step sequence so you can easily follow along.

Show Me video walks through tasks you've just got to see—including bonus advanced techniques.

Tell Me More audio delivers practical insights straight from the experts.

Special Features

More than just a book, your USING product integrates step-by-step video tutorials and valuable audio sidebars delivered through the **Free Web Edition** that comes with every USING book. For the price of the book, you get online access anywhere with a web connection—no books to carry, content is updated as the technology changes, and the benefit of video and audio learning.

About the USING Web Edition

The Web Edition of every USING book is powered by **Safari Books Online**, allowing you to access the video tutorials and valuable audio sidebars. Plus, you can search the contents of the book, highlight text and attach a note to that text, print your notes and highlights in a custom summary, and cut and paste directly from Safari Books Online.

To register this product and gain access to the Free Web Edition and the audio and video files, go to **quepublishing.com/using**.

Introducing Mac OS X Snow Leopard

This chapter walks you through the initialization process on a new computer to ensure you have set up Snow Leopard correctly and steps you through an upgrade, as well.

1

Setting Up Snow Leopard

I'm assuming that you wouldn't have bought this book about Apple's newest operating system unless you already own a Mac. Either you just bought a new Mac with the Snow Leopard operating system, or you already own a Mac and you upgraded to Snow Leopard.

If you just bought a new Mac, you've probably already gone through the process of initialization that I'm going to outline next, and I'm sure you got through it just fine. However, if you are a true beginner with the Mac, you may have some nagging reservations in your mind. "Did I do everything right?" "Is something going to go wrong later because of a choice I made?" If this describes you, this chapter should help allay your misgivings. If you've already been using a Mac for a while and you are upgrading to the new operating system, the last section in this chapter, "Upgrading to Snow Leopard," walks you through the upgrade step by step.

Whether you're a new Mac user or an established "Mackie," I think you're going to like Snow Leopard, the latest version of the operating system, Mac OS X (pronounced oh-ess-ten). Snow Leopard has a very cool vibe; its graphics are gorgeous and it's fast and streamlined like a sleek sports car—no waiting at startup, no braking for curves. It shuns even the thought of viruses, worms, and spyware, so you can actually use the Internet without fear of losing your identity or your bank account. The applications just plain work; there are no mystifying quirks, no ifs, ands, or buts. Snow Leopard has a very human, even humorous quality that makes you very comfortable. You also get the feeling that no matter what you do wrong, Snow Leopard has some graceful way to rescue you.

Initializing a New Computer

The thought of getting a new computer and setting it up can be a little intimidating. Fortunately, Apple really does make things as simple as possible. So let's review the process starting from the point of opening the box. After you have all the hardware out of the box, you need to plug the pieces together and then plug the Mac into an electrical outlet. Depending on the particular Mac you bought, you may have different things to plug (or not to plug) together.

Following the Prompts

After your Mac is assembled and ready to go, it is a simple matter of pressing the power button and following the prompts to get your Mac software initialized. This initialization process, which sets up the operating system with your user information and preferences, has to be done only once. In general, these are the tasks in the initialization process:

1. Select the language.

2. Select the country or region you are in.

3. Select a keyboard layout.

4. Import data from another Mac.

5. Select your network.

6. Register your Mac.

7. Answer some questions of interest to Apple.

8. Create your user account by supplying your full name, a nickname, and a password, and then taking a picture of yourself or choosing an icon.

> Snow Leopard names your Home folder with your nickname, so to be consistent with the names of other folders on the Mac, I recommend that you capitalize your nickname. (For more information about folders, see Chapter 6, "Managing Applications and Files.")

9. Select your time zone.

Now let's see how you fared with the steps in the initialization process and if there is anything you need to change or complete. By the way, if you had made an appointment with Apple to set you up with a Personal Shopper when you bought your Mac from an Apple store, you could have had your Personal Shopper go through the whole process with you at the time of purchase.

Selecting the Language

The Mac OS X operating system comes in several translations. Since you bought this book, I'm assuming that you read English perfectly well, but if you are more comfortable working on your Mac using a different language, you can select the language that you want to use. The Menu bar, menu options, help articles, and so on, appear in the language you select.

 **LET ME TRY IT**

Setting the Language Preferences

I'm sure you made the right selection for language, but let's suppose for one moment that your practical-joking best friend set up your computer for you and selected French or some other language as your default language. Fortunately, icons look the same in any language so you won't have to know the foreign language to correct this problem. Follow these steps to set the language for English:

1. Click the icon that looks like a set of gears in the row of icons at the bottom of the screen. The System Preferences window opens, as shown in Figure 1.1.

2. Click the blue flag icon in the top row. A list of languages displays.

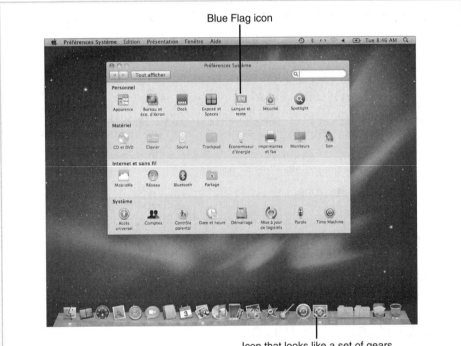

Blue Flag icon

Icon that looks like a set of gears

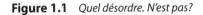

Figure 1.1 *Quel désordre. N'est pas?*

3. Drag English to the top of the list (see Figure 1.2) and then click the red button in the upper-left corner to close the window.

This button closes the window.

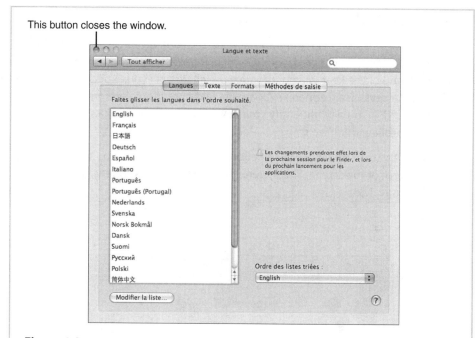

Figure 1.2 *Fortunately, the word for English is written in English so you can readily recognize it.*

4. Click the Apple logo in the upper-left corner of the screen.

5. Click the last option on the menu (or the one above the last option if you see your name in the last option) to shut down the Mac.

6. In the next dialog box, click Shut Down.

7. Restart the Mac by pressing and releasing the Mac's power button.

Selecting a Keyboard Layout

When you got to this point in the initialization process, Mac OS X assumed that you are using a keyboard that matches the language you had already selected. So the correct keyboard layout was probably easy for you to select.

 **LET ME TRY IT**

Selecting a Different Keyboard

When you were asked to identify your keyboard layout, if you clicked Show All and selected a different keyboard layout (German, for example), when you try to type in English, some of the keys will not produce the characters you expect. That's because the keys on a German keyboard are laid out differently from the keys on a U.S. keyboard. If you didn't identify your keyboard correctly, you can rectify your mistake by following these steps:

1. Click the icon that looks like a set of gears in the row of icons at the bottom of the screen. The System Preferences window opens, as shown in Figure 1.3.

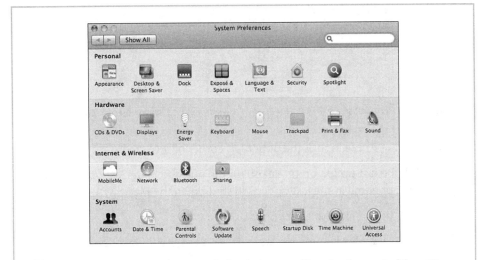

Figure 1.3   *The System Preferences window is the central location for most of the settings that a user is allowed to modify.*

2. Click the Language & Text icon and then click Input Sources.

3. Click the check box for the language that matches your keyboard, as shown in Figure 1.4.

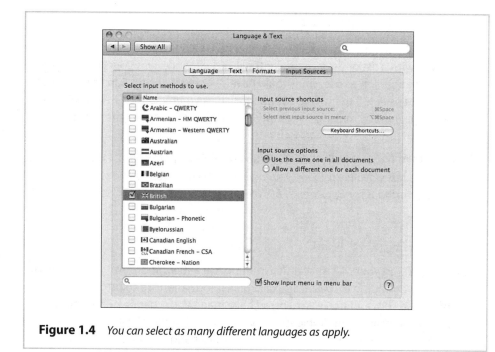

Figure 1.4 *You can select as many different languages as apply.*

4. Click the red button in the upper-left corner of the window.

Importing Data

This step in the initialization process would have helped you transfer data from another Mac to your new Mac. The default option for this feature was *Do not transfer my information now*. Following the rule of when in doubt, use the default, you probably did not transfer any data. If you didn't, it's quite all right. You can still move data from another Mac by using the Migration Assistant located in the Utilities folder. The Migration Assistant can transfer your Home folder, network settings, applications, and more, and it's easy to use. Just follow the instructions on-screen after you start the application. If you have lots of applications on your old Mac that you need to reinstall on your new Mac, use the Migration Assistant to transfer them instead of reinstalling them.

Migration Assistant can't help you move data from a PC to a Mac.

Selecting the Network

If there were wireless networks in the area when you initialized your Mac, you were presented with a list of them. If one of the listed networks was yours or one that you have permission to use, you should have selected it. If you didn't select a network, or you selected the wrong network (such as your neighbor's), you can still make things right by making the proper settings in the Network preferences.

 SHOW ME   Media 1.1—A video about Setting Network Preferences
Access this video file through your registered Web Edition at
my.safaribooksonline.com/9780789743916/media.

Registering the Mac

If you registered your Mac successfully during the initialization, and you would like to change your Apple ID, password, or profile information, go to https://www.myinfo.apple.com and log in. When you have made your changes, click Log Out. If you want to change the Apple ID and your original Apple ID is tied to a MobileMe account or an iChat ID, you can't really change it. You have to create a new Apple ID.

 **LET ME TRY IT**

Registering Your Mac at a Later Time

If you didn't register your Mac during the initialization process, you can do it later, when you have your Internet connection set up. But first, you need to make a note of your Mac's serial number. Click the Apple logo in the upper-left corner of the screen and click About This Mac. Click the Version number twice to display the serial number. Then to register, follow these steps:

1. Make sure you are connected to the Internet and then click the first icon in the bottom row of your screen (the blue, two-faced man).

2. On the left side of the window that opens, click your Home folder (the one with your nickname).

3. Double-click the tuxedoed Send Registration icon that Snow Leopard left for you in your Home folder.

4. When you arrive at the registration web page, follow the prompts to complete the registration.

When you register your Mac, you have to enter your Apple ID, if you have one. If you don't, you have to create one. Your Apple ID contains information about you (your profile) that identifies you to Apple when you want to register another Apple product, make a purchase from the Apple Store or iTunes Store, make an appointment for face-to-face support, and so on.

Answering Demographic Questions

With two questions, Apple collected demographic information about you that goes along with your registration information. The questions identified where you use your Mac (home, business, school, and so on) and the main thing that you do on the Mac (design, music, finance, and so on). Apple assured you that your privacy would not be invaded with these questions. It doesn't really matter what answers you gave for these questions. You'll never hear anything more about them.

Creating Your User Account

When you created your user account, Snow Leopard automatically made you an administrator on the computer. As an administrator, you have special privileges and responsibilities: You have the ability to install software and updates, change system preferences, create other user accounts, change passwords, and do anything else that it is possible to do on a Mac.

The full name you supplied during initialization is your User Account name. You will log in with it when you start your computer and use it to unlock System Preferences and give permission to install application updates. For more information about installing application updates, see Chapter 13, "Keeping Your Mac Safe, Updated, and Backed Up."

The name you supply for your nickname is the name that Snow Leopard gives to your Home folder. You cannot change the name of the Home folder, so I hope you created an appropriate nickname.

The password that you created should be a strong one—that is, one that is difficult to guess.

SHOW ME   Media 1.2—A video about Changing Your User
Account Password
Access this video file through your registered Web Edition at
my.safaribooksonline.com/9780789743916/media.

 LET ME TRY IT

Changing Your User Account Password

If you used your name, any word, a date, or simply a string of numbers, then you
need to change your password. A strong password has at least eight characters
with both letters and numbers, and it never hurts to throw in a capital letter somewhere.

Follow these steps to change your password:

1. Click the icon that looks like a set of gears in the row of icons at the bottom of the screen. The System Preferences window opens.

2. Click the Accounts icon in the bottom row of icons in the window. Your
   account is selected by default.

3. Click Change Password to open the dialog box shown in Figure 1.5.

4. Type your original password in the Old Password field.

5. In the New Password field, type a new password and this time use a combination of letters, numbers, and, for good measure, throw in a punctuation mark as well as a capital letter. There is an art to creating a password
   that is strong yet easy to remember.

 **TELL ME MORE**   Media 1.3—A discussion about Creating Strong
Passwords
Access this audio recording through your registered Web Edition at
my.safaribooksonline.com/9780789743916/media.

6. Type the password again in the Verify field.

7. If you want to (recommended), type a hint to remind yourself of the password and then click Change Password.

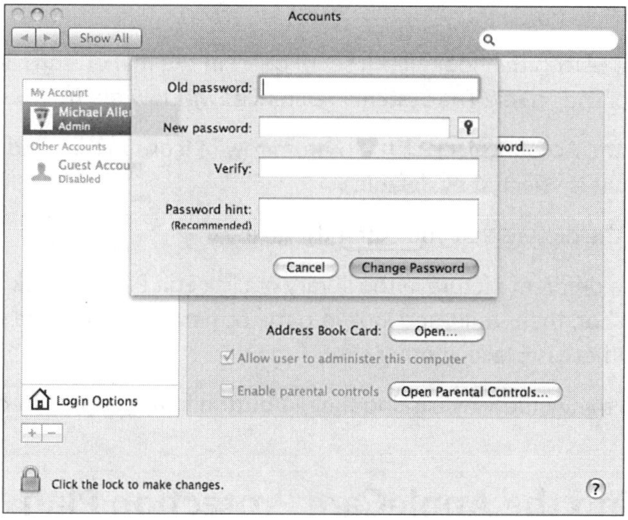

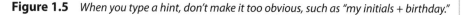

Figure 1.5   *When you type a hint, don't make it too obvious, such as "my initials + birthday."*

8. Click OK for the alert that tells you that your new password is going to replace your current login keychain password.

A keychain is a file that stores your passwords for you so you don't have to remember them all. Snow Leopard created your first keychain for you automatically, called the "login" keychain, when you created your user account. By default, your login keychain password is the same as your account password. For more information about keychains, see Chapter 13.

9. Click the red button in the upper-left corner of the window to close it.

 **LET ME TRY IT**

Changing Your Account Picture

If you chose an icon from the picture library or took a photo of yourself to include as your User Account picture, you may want to change it from time to time. For example, if you change your hair color frequently, you can take new photos of yourself to keep your account current. Likewise, you can select a new icon for yourself from the library if you prefer not to use a photo.

To choose a new icon to represent you or take a new picture of yourself, follow these steps:

1. Click the icon that looks like a set of gears in the row of icons at the bottom of the screen. The System Preferences window opens.

2. Click the Accounts icon in the bottom row of icons in the window. Your account is selected by default.

3. Click the picture that you currently have.

4. Click a different picture in the library or click Edit Picture. Click Take Photo Snapshot, then smile, and look into the camera. If you like the photo, click Set; otherwise, take another shot.

5. Close the window by clicking the red button in the upper-left corner.

Purchasing the AppleCare Protection Plan

To save a little money when you purchased your new computer, you may have decided to forego the AppleCare Protection Plan that was undoubtedly offered to you. If you said no to this option at the time of purchase, you need to reconsider. The plan adds two years to your existing one-year warranty as well as two years to your existing 90-day telephone support. Fortunately, Apple lets you purchase the Protection Plan after the fact, any time within the first year. The effective date of the plan, regardless of when you purchase it or register it, is always the purchase date of the hardware.

Even *Consumer Reports*, which says, "Just say 'no' to extended warranties," makes an exception for the AppleCare Protection Plan—not because Apples are trouble-prone, but because of the valuable telephone support.

With the Protection Plan, you can literally be worry-free for three years. You can call Apple Support any time you have a question—no matter how small. Because Apple is not only the software manufacturer, but the hardware manufacturer as well, you'll never be caught in the loop where the hardware manufacturer blames a problem on the software and the software manufacturer blames the problem on the hardware. Apple is your one resource for problems or questions.

If any part of your computer or software fails due to defective parts or workmanship, Apple replaces it at no cost. Thanks to my AppleCare Protection Plan, I just received a free, brand-new battery for my almost-out-of-warranty, three-year-old

MacBook Pro. You gotta love it! If you spill coffee in the keyboard, however, you're going to have to foot the bill yourself. The plan doesn't cover carelessness.

If you purchase AppleCare, you must register it to activate your plan. One crucial piece of information that you need to have before registering is the number assigned to your plan. This number may be referred to as "the registration number," "the enrollment number," "the serial number," or the "AppleCare agreement number." The number is located just above a barcode on an instruction card or booklet that comes inside the AppleCare box.

Once you have the number, go to https://www.selfsolve.apple.com/Agreements.do and click Get Started. Then follow the prompts.

Purchasing a MobileMe Account

In its simplest form, a MobileMe account is an email account. Instead of getting a free Gmail address from Google, you can buy an email address from Apple. What a deal, huh? But wait, with a MobileMe account, you get much more than an email address. MobileMe keeps your email, contacts, and calendar up to date and in sync on all your devices—Macs, iPhones, iPods, and even PCs (with no physical docking). Email is entirely ad free and includes spam and virus protection. You get plenty of storage space on the MobileMe server for email, backup files, photos, and your own personal website—20GB for an individual account or 45GB for a family account. You can access the files you store on MobileMe from any Mac or PC web browser, and you can even use a Public folder to make your files available to others and to allow others to upload files to you. MobileMe also includes a Photo Gallery feature that allows you to create albums and slideshows for the viewing pleasure of your friends and family.

A MobileMe account is well worth the money ($99 per year for an individual account or $149 per year for a family account). Even if you already have an email account, I highly recommend purchasing a MobileMe account just for the convenience of being able to sync your email, contacts, and calendar and then access that information from any computer anywhere as well as for the online storage space that allows you to keep a backup copy of your critical data.

Once you purchase a MobileMe account, you need to activate your membership. To do this, you need the activation key that is printed on a card inside the MobileMe box. Once you have located this character string, go to http://www.me.com/activate to enter it and follow the prompts to set up your account (see Figure 1.6).

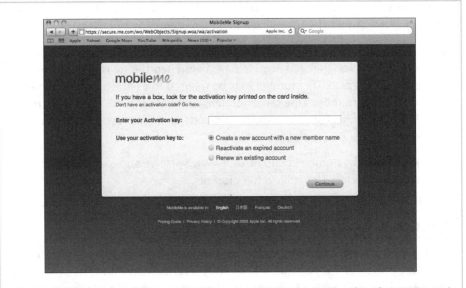

Figure 1.6   *The Go Here link goes to a page that allows you to sign up for a free 60-day trial.*

Keeping Records

Keeping records of your serial numbers, IDs, user names, passwords, and so on can certainly save you some time and headaches in the future. How many times have you fallen for that trick your mind plays on you that says, "I'll remember *that*"? You have to write these things down, but the minute you do, you have to think of some way to safeguard your information, such as hiding it in the freezer.

I have a sturdy little spiral-bound book that I record all my information in. I don't need to hide it in the freezer because I write any sensitive information in a cryptic way. For example, for a login name or password, if I use a number string that is one of my former street addresses, I don't record the actual number; I record the street name. If I use the letters in my cat's name (I don't really have a cat), I don't write down the cat's actual name, I write "Cat" or "cat," depending on the capitalization. So, for example, if I created a password of "502Fancy" (502 for 502 Orchard Avenue and Fancy for my fictitious cat's name), I would enter the password in my book as "orchardCat." To make the password more secure, I would replace the *a* in Fancy with @. To remember that substitution, I would make it a rule that I always use @ for *a*.

Recording Apple ID Information

The Apple ID information that you need to record is the ID itself and the password. Generally, if you followed Apple's recommendation, you used your email address for the Apple ID.

If you didn't record this information and you have forgotten your Apple ID or your password, go to https://www.iforgot.apple.com. If you have forgotten your password, you can supply your Apple ID, and Apple will email you a link to your account where you can enter a new password. Alternatively, if you can verify the month and day of your birth and answer the security question that you provided when setting up your profile, Apple will allow you to change your password immediately.

If you have forgotten your Apple ID, you can supply your first and last name and up to four email addresses. If any one of the email addresses is the one you originally supplied in your profile, Apple will be able to find your account and will email you a link to your account or allow you to verify the month and date of your birth and answer the security question that you provided when setting up your profile. Whether you follow the link from an email or answer the security question, Apple will display your Apple ID online. At that point, write it down and then click Cancel.

Recording User Account Information

When you created your user account, you supplied Snow Leopard with three pieces of information: your full name, a nickname, and a password. Hopefully you wrote these down and put them in a secure place (not on a note stuck to your screen). If you didn't make note of them, then we can at least look up your full name and your nickname.

- **Full name**—To look up the full name that you supplied, click the icon that looks like a set of gears in the row of icons at the bottom of the screen. Click the Accounts icon in the bottom row of icons in the window. Your full name is shown on the left under My Account and on the right in the Full Name field. Click the red button in the upper-left corner of the window to close it.

If you want to change the full name that you originally supplied, simply type a new name in the Full Name field and enter your password when prompted.

- **Nickname**—To look up the nickname that you supplied, click the icon of the blue, two-faced man in the row of icons at the bottom of your screen. It should be the first icon. Your Home folder is selected in the left pane, as shown in Figure 1.7. The name of this folder is the name you selected for your nickname. Click the red button in the upper-left corner of the window to close it.

Figure 1.7   *Hopefully your Home folder's name is* not *something embarrassing like "Sugar Pie."*

- **Password**—Unfortunately, if you didn't write down your password and you forget it, there is no way to find it on the computer. If this happens, before you start creating files, importing pictures, making entries in your address book, and so on, the easiest thing to do is back up as much as you can of the work you have already done and then do a "clean install" of Snow Leopard. The clean install erases your hard drive before installing the operating system. This wipes out your User Account and requires you to set up a new one.

Recording AppleCare Protection Plan Information

For the AppleCare Protection Plan you can record the agreement number that is given to you and the expiration date. You can look up this information by going to https://www.selfsolve.apple.com/Agreements.do and clicking Get Started. Next, sign in with your Apple ID and your password.

Recording MobileMe Information

The MobileMe information that you need to record is your MobileMe email address and your password. If you forget your email address, call Apple support for help. If you forget your password, you can set up a new one.

 **LET ME TRY IT**

Setting Up a New Password on Your Apple ID

When you initially set up your Apple ID password, you had to supply a security question. You will have to give the answer to this question to change your password. If you forget the password for your Apple ID, follow these steps to set a new password:

1. Open Safari and go to http://www.me.com.

2. Enter your Apple ID and click Forgot Password.

3. Click Answer Question.

4. Select the month and day of your birthday and click Continue.

5. Answer the security question and click Continue.

6. Type the new password in both fields and click Change Password.

7. Click Continue when finished. This returns you to MobileMe.

If, in the course of events, you got your MobileMe email address before it was necessary to create your Apple ID (you'll remember that the Apple ID is required when you register your Mac), then the MobileMe email address and the Apple ID should be the same. If you get a MobileMe email address after you have already created an Apple ID, your MobileMe address will be associated with your existing Apple ID, but it will not change the Apple ID to your new MobileMe email address. If you want one less login and password to keep up with, though, you can create a new Apple ID using your MobileMe email address and password, and just ignore your old Apple ID.

Upgrading to Snow Leopard

Okay, so you're the "upgrader." If you're reading this section, I'm going to assume that you haven't pulled the trigger yet. If you have already installed the upgrade, you probably have nothing to gain by reading this part unless you just want to relive the experience.

If you've never upgraded a Mac operating system before, you will be pleasantly surprised. It is a fairly painless process, and when you are finished, you will find that all of your previously set personal preferences and settings have been retained, your email is still intact, your Safari bookmarks are still there, and all of your data is right where it was before.

 **LET ME TRY IT**

Performing the Install

Just for safety's sake, you should perform a full backup of your computer before upgrading in the unlikely event that something goes wrong. As an experienced user, you probably make backups all the time, so I'm going to trust that you know how to back up your computer and that you will do it. After backing up your computer, follow these steps to upgrade:

1. Start your Mac and insert the upgrade disc in the optical disk drive. The Mac OS X Install DVD window opens, as shown in Figure 1.8.

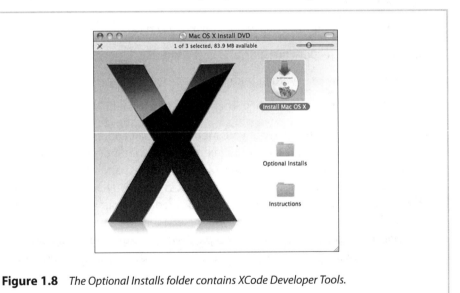

Figure 1.8   *The Optional Installs folder contains XCode Developer Tools.*

2. Open the Instructions folder and open the Installation Instructions file. Print the document to refer to in case you have a problem with the installation. A second document in this folder, called Welcome to Snow Leopard (which is 73 pages long), gives you detailed information about the features of Snow Leopard. After the installation, you may want to come back to this file and read it onscreen.

3. Disconnect the printer, any external drives, and any other external devices.

4. Double-click the Install Mac OS X icon. A Welcome screen displays.

5. Click Continue. The License Agreement displays.

6. Click Agree.

7. A new screen displays that tells you that Mac OS X will be installed on the "Macintosh HD" (or whatever you have named your hard drive).

8. Click Customize. The screen shown in Figure 1.9 appears.

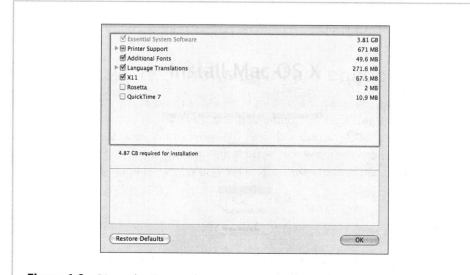

Figure 1.9 *Dimmed options on the screen cannot be changed.*

9. Select or deselect optional software and click OK.

If you want to conserve disk space, you can deselect many of the Language Translations options, which are all selected by default, and the Additional Fonts option. If you have an uncommon printer, you might want to select All Available Printers, and if you have some older applications, you should consider selecting the Rosetta option.

10. Click Install.

11. A dialog box opens asking if you are sure you want to install. If you are ready for the installer to quit all open applications for you and install Snow Leopard, click Install.

12. Enter your password and click OK. A progress bar displays and Time Remaining continually updates—but don't rely on the accuracy. It could take 35 to 60 minutes.

13. When the installation finishes successfully, a screen with a big green circle with a check mark in the middle displays. If you're not right in front of your Mac at the moment the installation finishes, you might not see this screen because the Mac restarts after about 20 seconds.

14. When Mac OS X restarts, log in if necessary, and a big Thank You displays.

15. Click Continue. You should now see your desktop—just like you left it.

16. Open and read the Welcome to Snow Leopard PDF file in the Instructions folder if you want.

17. Eject the Install DVD.

Troubleshooting the Installation

If Snow Leopard detects a problem with the DVD drive that you are using or with the disc itself, it will "back out" of the upgrade, leaving your original operating system intact. To check for issues with your DVD drive or the Snow Leopard disc, use the Disk Utility program to verify the drive and to verify the disc. If neither has a problem, then it's time to make a trip to the Apple Store or Apple Authorized Service Provider.

Settling In

Even though you have merely upgraded your system, and all your preferences are retained, some things do start over again. For example, the first time you open some applications, you will get the dialog box that says, "You are opening the <name> application for the first time. Are you sure you want to open this application?"

The first time you start some of your older applications (those that were not written specifically to run on an Intel-based Mac), you may see a dialog box that says you need to install Rosetta. Rosetta is an install option on the Snow Leopard Install DVD, but if you didn't do a custom install, you missed it. It isn't selected by default. If you get this message and click the option to install Rosetta, Mac OS X finds Rosetta on the Internet and installs it for you. If you aren't connected to the Internet, you can install it from the Mac OS X Snow Leopard Install DVD.

If your printer doesn't seem to function properly, it's probably because the pre-10.6 printer driver doesn't work in Snow Leopard. Most likely, Snow Leopard has the new, correct driver. You can delete the printer and add it back again so that Snow Leopard will install the correct driver. Refer to Chapter 3, "Getting Familiar with Your Hardware," for instructions on installing a printer.

Getting Comfortable with Snow Leopard

If you just upgraded to Snow Leopard from Leopard, you will see a desktop that looks very similar to your old one. This is because, as Apple says, Mac OS X Snow Leopard is "refined, not reinvented." Although there are some features that do have a new look, Apple design engineers really focused on making Snow Leopard faster, more reliable, and easier to use. If you are a new Mac user, it's all new to you, so let's look at some of the basic features you are presented with when you start your Mac.

Starting Up

The first thing you see after pressing the power button is a gray screen with the Apple logo in the middle. After logging in, Snow Leopard's dazzling, yet uncluttered screen displays itself before you, and it all happens in less than a minute.

In this chapter, I will be helping you get familiar with the default appearance and behavior of your Mac—that is, with the original settings that come with a new Mac. In Chapter 4, "Tailoring the Desktop to Your Liking," I will show you how to customize the appearance of the screen components and the Finder window by setting System Preferences, options that determine the way things look and act on a Mac in general. You may have already used some of the System Preferences if you performed some of the activities in Chapter 1, "Setting Up Snow Leopard."

Instead of slogging through the legion of System Preferences in a chapter at the back of the book (what a boring chapter that would be), I will discuss specific System Preferences as they are relevant.

Exploring the Desktop

The screen that you see when the Mac starts is referred to as the "desktop." The default desktop has a cool, sort of outer-space-looking graphic as the background and a row of icons at the bottom of the screen called the Dock. Icons may be present in the open space above the Dock if you have any external drives connected or any discs inserted in optical drives. At the top, extending across the width of the screen, is a menu bar.

The left side of the menu bar contains commands for an application called Finder. Each time the Mac starts, it opens the Finder application automatically, and this application remains open until you shut down the computer. The Finder is the application that lists and manipulates all the files and folders on the computer.

The right side of the menu bar contains Menu Extras (or *menulets*, as Mackies call them). These are menus represented by icons, and they generally show the status of your computer or give you quick access to a particular feature, such as the sound volume level. The last icon on the right is the Spotlight. It is an unassuming little icon that looks like a magnifying glass, but, to quote Shakespeare, "Though she be but little, she is fierce." The Spotlight is an unbelievably powerful search tool that is truly amazing. See Chapter 6, "Managing Applications and Files," for more details. Figure 2.1 shows the default desktop.

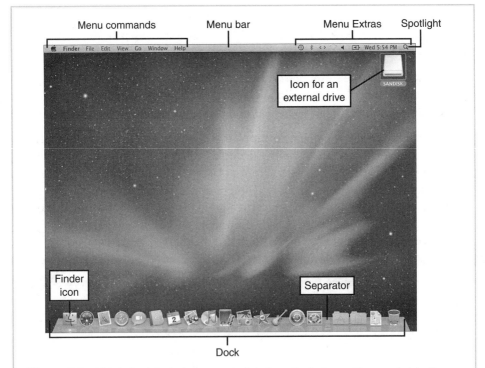

Figure 2.1   *This is the default desktop—straight from the factory with no customizations.*

Using the Dock

The Dock is the flashiest part of the desktop and probably attracts the most attention, so let's look at it in more detail first. Notice that it is divided into two sections
by a line, which looks like the dotted line in the middle of a highway to me, but
technically, it's called the "separator." You can see it in Figure 2.1, under the first
icon.

Launching Applications

The function of the left side of the Dock is launching applications (*applications*
being the official Apple term for software programs). Every icon on the left side of
the Dock represents an application. Until you get familiar with what applications
the icons represent, you can display the name of the application by pointing to the
icon.

Note that the Dock does not contain an icon for *every* application that is available
on the Mac, but you can add or remove icons so that the Dock contains the applications you use most often. See Chapter 4 for details. You can always launch applications that you don't use frequently from the Applications folder, which also
appears in the Dock.

To launch an application, just click the icon. If the application doesn't open instan-
taneously, its icon bounces up and down. Either it's excited because it's been
selected, or it's impatiently waiting on itself to open. I haven't decided which.
When an application has been launched, a glowing blue bubble appears below the
icon. You can see it in Figure 2.1. This bubble remains in place until you quit the
application.

If you launch an application that doesn't have an icon on the Dock, the application displays its icon on the left side of the Dock until you quit the application.
Then it disappears.

Notice the first icon in the Dock—the two-faced, blue man (love this metaphor).
This is the icon for the Finder application that Snow Leopard always launches at
startup. Because it is always the current application when the computer starts, its
menu is the one displayed in the menu bar, and because Snow Leopard never quits
the Finder, there is always a bubble under this icon. I explain more about the Finder
later in this chapter and, in even greater detail, in Chapter 6.

Quitting Applications

You literally cannot quit the Finder, but you can quit any other application that you have launched. If you have several programs running, and you want to quit one of them, just Ctrl-click or right-click its icon in the Dock and click Quit, as shown in Figure 2.2. If you are working in an application that has unfinished business (for example, you failed to save a file), Mac OS X gives you an appropriate warning so that you have a chance to do the right thing instead of making a careless mistake. When an application closes, the glowing bubble under its icon disappears.

Figure 2.2   *Ctrl-click or right-click to get this menu.*

The shortcut keystroke Cmd-Q also quits an application, but you actually have to be in the application at the time to use the shortcut.

Checking Out the Dashboard

Before we move on to a discussion of the icons on the Dock that don't launch applications (the ones on the right side of the separator), we should look briefly at the Dashboard application because it's a little different from other applications. The Dashboard icon looks like a gauge on—you guessed it—a dashboard.

Every other application that comes with a Mac opens in its own window and has its own menu in the menu bar at the top of the screen—but not the Dashboard. The Dashboard has no menu in the menu bar; it doesn't have a glowing blue bubble under its icon in the Dock when it's running; and you can't quit the Dashboard by pressing Cmd-Q or using menu commands.

The Dashboard is actually a collection of mini-applications that perform discrete functions such as checking the weather, monitoring stock prices, and translating phrases from one language to another. These mini-applications are called, not gauges, or even instruments, but *widgets*—so much for the dashboard metaphor.

When you launch the Dashboard, it spreads out a translucent layer over the entire desktop with its widgets floating on top, as illustrated in Figure 2.3. (Now we've switched from a dashboard metaphor to a clear, shallow pool metaphor.) The desktop is visible under the dashboard, which can be very convenient if you are inputting information in a widget that you need to get from a file that is open on the desktop.

Figure 2.3 *Only a few widgets appear on the Dashboard by default, but many others are available.*

You can launch the Dashboard by clicking its icon in the Dock or you can use the function key, F4. You can quit the Dashboard by pressing F4 again or clicking anywhere on the shadowy background of the Dashboard. For more information about the Dashboard, see Chapter 12, "Using Widgets and Other Applications."

Mac keyboards have evolved over the years, so if you have an older keyboard, the Dashboard key may be the F12 function key. On some keyboards, you may even have to press the Fn key in conjunction with the F12 key to launch the Dashboard.

Looking at Stacks

Immediately to the right side of the separator in the Dock are three icons that do not launch applications (see Figure 2.4). These icons actually represent folders that contain multiple items.

In addition to the three default folders, you can add your own folders to the Dock.

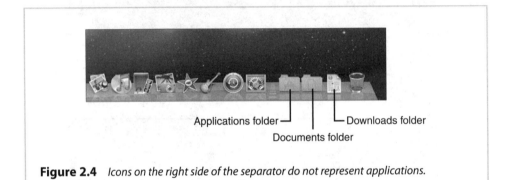

Applications folder —⎤ ⎡— Downloads folder

Documents folder

Figure 2.4 *Icons on the right side of the separator do not represent applications.*

The first icon (looking left to right) is for the Applications folder, which holds all the applications that come with the Mac. Because only a limited number of applications have their own icon on the Dock, the Applications folder gives you instant access to all applications that are available to you. The second icon is for the Documents folder, which is the default folder used by Snow Leopard for saved documents. If you store all your work in this folder or in subfolders of this folder, the Documents stack icon will be a convenient way to access all your work. The third icon is for the Downloads folder, where all files downloaded from the Internet are stored. Let's see; I think Apple thought of everything—quick access to all your applications, all your work, and everything you get from the Internet.

As you learn to use the various applications on your Mac, you will see that the right side of the separator also displays other icons temporarily in certain situations. I'll explain this to you in detail in Chapter 6.

Icons that represent folders have a special name—Apple calls them *stacks*. When you click a stack icon, the individual items in the folder fan out like a deck of cards, as shown in Figure 2.5, or they display in a grid, as shown in Figure 2.6, depending on the number of items in the folder. To open an individual item, just click its icon.

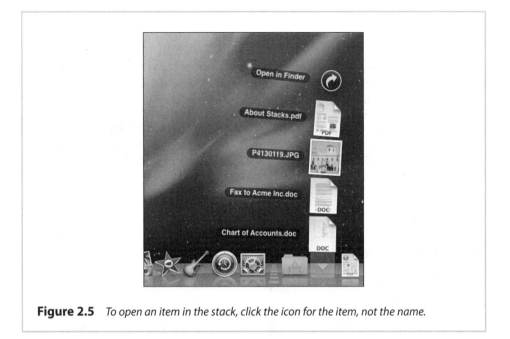

Figure 2.5 *To open an item in the stack, click the icon for the item, not the name.*

Figure 2.6 *The grid displays the items in the folder in a window that pops up.*

After displaying the items in a stack, if you don't really want to open one of them, you can return the items to the stack by pressing Esc or clicking on a blank area of the desktop. In Chapter 4, I'll tell you more about working with stacks.

Going through the Trash

The last icon to the right of the separator is the Trash icon, where deleted files, folders, and applications go until you permanently delete them. On a new computer, the icon for the trash can is empty, but after you have deleted files, the trash can looks like it has crumpled paper in it.

When you click the Trash icon, a window opens with a list of all the items that are "in the trash." You can go through the trash and take things out again or get rid of them for good. For more information about deleting files and folders, see Chapter 6.

Using Menus

Now let's take a look at the menu bar at the top of the screen. Let me begin by saying that there is *always* a menu bar at the top of the screen, but there is never more than one menu bar. Any application you are working in uses this menu bar space to display its menu options.

Notice that the first item on the left is the famous Apple logo. The logo is not just a graphic on the menu bar; it's an actual menu option, as shown in Figure 2.7. Next to the Apple logo is the word *Finder*, which appears in bold text. This is the name of the current application that is open, but it is also the name of a menu that has several commands on it. The words to the right of Finder (File, Edit, view, and so on) are also names of menus.

Figure 2.7   *The Apple menu is always the first menu in the menu bar, regardless of what application you are using.*

You can think of the Finder menu bar as a template for all others. Every application you open on a Mac displays a menu bar that has the Apple logo followed by the name of the application. Figure 2.8 shows you what the menu bar for Microsoft Word looks like.

Figure 2.8   *The Word application menu bar has a dozen menu options!*

The Apple menu always has the same commands on it, no matter what application you are using, but the application menus vary by application, as you would expect. Some commands on application menus, such as the Quit command, are common to all applications, however. The additional menus listed on an application's menu bar usually include some of the same menus as the Finder menu bar, specifically File, Edit, View, Window, and Help, as you can see in Figure 2.9.

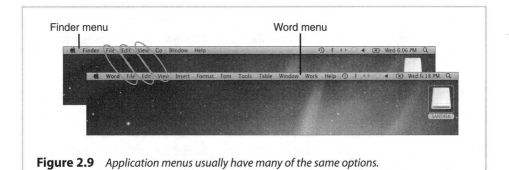

Figure 2.9   *Application menus usually have many of the same options.*

Using the Menu Bar

To use the commands available to you in the menu bar, simply click the menu option to display the menu of commands for that option. Then click the command. Sometimes the command you want may not appear on the first menu. You may have to point to an option with a right-pointing arrow to display yet another menu, referred to as a *submenu*, that has the command on it that you want. Figure 2.10 shows the submenu for the Arrange By command.

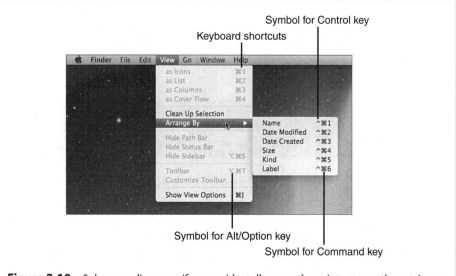

Symbol for Control key

Keyboard shortcuts

Symbol for Alt/Option key

Symbol for Command key

Figure 2.10   *Submenus disappear if you accidentally move the pointer to another option on the first menu while you are trying to click the command that you want on the submenu.*

Notice in Figure 2.10 that several options on the menu are "dimmed"—that is, a light gray. This means that the commands are not relevant at the moment and, therefore, are not available. Additionally, one menu command has three dots after it, an ellipsis. This type of menu command displays a dialog box that contains additional settings or input fields.

One final menu feature you can see in Figure 2.10 is the keyboard shortcut listed beside many of the commands. A keyboard shortcut allows you to perform a command instantly without opening a menu. The shortcuts generally use a regular key (a letter, number, or punctuation mark) in combination with one or more "modifier" keys: Shift, Control, Alt/Option, and Command. To use a keyboard shortcut for a command, first press and hold the modifier keys and then press the regular key.

To see the symbol for the Shift key, look at the Finder's Go menu.

Most people I know don't use many keyboard shortcuts for two reasons: First, many are difficult to remember, and second, it really seems as fast to use the mouse. But…oops! Your 10,000 shares of stock just took a giant nosedive, and you slammed your Mighty Mouse down on the desk, shattering it into pieces! (My husband did this not long ago.) Now what do you do? All you have is your keyboard to control the computer. Table 2.1 shows the keystrokes to use to access the menu bar and make selections so you can get yourself out of this mess. (Of course, my husband had to call me in to get him out of his mess.)

Table 2.1 Keyboard Shortcuts

Action You Want to Accomplish	Action to Take with the Keyboard
Move to the menu bar.	Press Ctrl-F2. (On some keyboards you may have to use Fn with this shortcut.)
Select a menu on the menu bar.	Use the Right or Left Arrow key to move to the menu you want.
Open a menu on the menu bar.	Once the menu is selected, press Return.
Select a command on the open menu.	Use the Down or Up Arrow key to move to the command you want.
Execute a command on the open menu.	Once the command is selected, press Return.
Close a menu.	Press Esc. (This also exits the menu bar.)

If you also need to access the Dock, press Ctrl-F3 (or Ctrl-Fn-F3). Then use the Right and Left Arrow keys to move to the icon that you want and press Return to open the application.

Using Contextual Menus

A contextual menu, also called a *shortcut menu*, is a menu that has a limited number of commands that just apply to a particular item in the current situation. To display a context menu, point to a particular item and press and hold the Ctrl key while you click the item. If a contextual menu is available for the item, it displays; otherwise, nothing happens. For example, if you Ctrl-click the desktop background, a shortcut menu opens, as shown in Figure 2.11. If you Ctrl-click the blank space after the Help menu option in the menu bar, nothing happens.

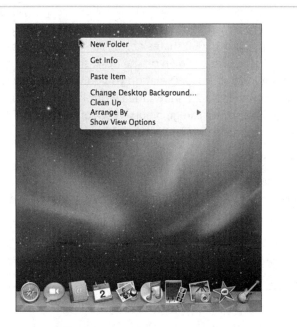

Figure 2.11 *Chapter 4 explains several of the commands on the desktop shortcut menu.*

If you have an Apple Mighty Mouse or a non-Apple two-button mouse, you can display a context menu by clicking the secondary button. By default, the left side of the mouse is the primary button and the right side of the mouse is the secondary button, but if you are left-handed, you can reverse the buttons by changing the Mouse preferences (see Chapter 3, "Getting Familiar with Your Hardware"). For ease of writing, I will use the term *right-click* when I refer to clicking the secondary mouse button. If you are a lefty who has switched the buttons, you'll know what I mean.

Exploring the Finder Window

The Finder application lists and manipulates all the files and folders on the computer. It takes its name from the fact that you can find anything on the Mac with the Finder. Primarily, you use Finder to find and open files, but its other functions also include creating new folders, and copying, moving, renaming, and deleting files and folders.

Identifying Components of the Finder Window

Click the Finder icon in the Dock to open the Finder window, as shown in Figure 2.12. Notice the components of the Finder window pointed out in this figure.

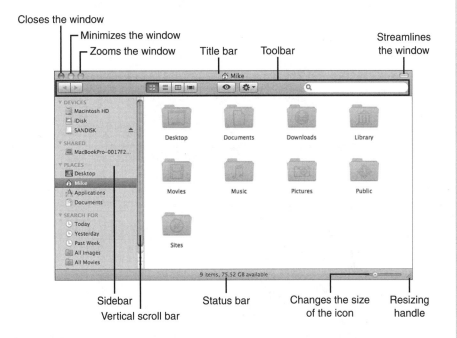

Figure 2.12   *The first time you use the Finder the view is set to the Icon view.*

The Finder window has a title bar with three colored buttons on the left, used to close, minimize, and zoom the window, and a plain little gray button on the right that is used to "streamline" the window. The window has a status bar at the bottom with a resizing handle on the right, used to stretch or shrink the window, and, when necessary, the window has vertical and horizontal scroll bars. The window itself is split into two panes. The pane on the left is called the sidebar; the pane on the right doesn't seem to have a name, so call it anything you want.

Let's take a closer look at some of these components. The title bar, at the top of the window, displays the name of the source that is selected in the sidebar. The status bar, at the bottom of the window, displays the number of items in the selected source and the amount of space still available on the selected drive.

You probably already know that the red button in the title bar closes the window and the yellow button minimizes the window in a disappearing-genie-like swoop to an icon on the right side of the Dock separator. The green button (the Zoom button) makes a window just large enough to display all of the icons inside of it—or if not all, as many as it can, which is dependent on the size of your monitor. Clicking the Zoom button a second time restores the window to its previous size.

Under the title bar is the toolbar. The lozenge-shaped button on the right that seems to have no name (at least not that I can find) is a toggle. Click it once, and it streamlines the window by hiding the sidebar and toolbar and moving the status bar up under the title bar, as shown in Figure 2.13. Click it again, and the Finder returns to its original appearance.

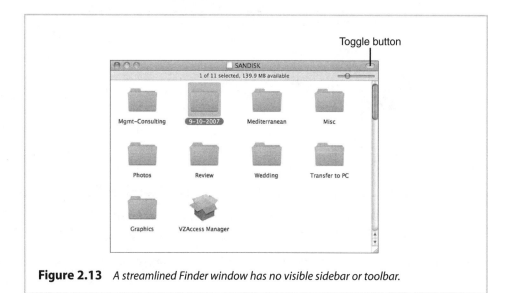

Figure 2.13 *A streamlined Finder window has no visible sidebar or toolbar.*

Exploring the Sidebar

The sidebar has a list of sources that display the content of drives, folders, and files. The sources are categorized as Devices, Shared, Places, and Search For.

By default, the Devices category lists hard disks, any external disks or iPods that are attached to the computer, and any optical drives that have discs in them. Additionally, if you have purchased MobileMe, an iDisk is listed under Devices.

The Shared category automatically lists other computers on your network that you can access. (These are computers that have turned on File Sharing.)

By default, the Places category lists four folders: Desktop, your Home folder, Applications, and Documents. This is not a hierarchical list. In fact, the hard drive contains the Applications folder, and your Home folder contains the Documents folder. The Places category simply lists folders that you tend to use the most. Chapter 6 explains how to add your own folders to Places.

The Search For category lists six different search criteria by default: Today, Yesterday, Past Week, All Images, All Movies, and All Documents. You can add your own searches to this list too. See Chapter 6 for instructions.

Notice the triangle before each of the category names in the sidebar. The technical name for this triangle is the "disclosure triangle." It displays or hides the items listed in that category. When the triangle is pointing down, the items are visible, and when the triangle is pointing to the right, the items are hidden. To hide or display the items, just click the triangle.

When you click a source in any category in the sidebar, the items in that source display in the pane on the right. For example, clicking the external drive called SANDISK in the Devices category shows the files and folders that are on that drive in the pane on the right, as illustrated in Figure 2.14. Clicking Today under the Search For category displays all the files and folders created or accessed today in the right pane. To quickly go back to the external drive again, click the button in the toolbar that has the left-pointing arrow. Then, to go back to Today, click the button that has the right-pointing arrow. These buttons work like the Back and Forward buttons in a web browser. They are pointed out in Figure 2.14.

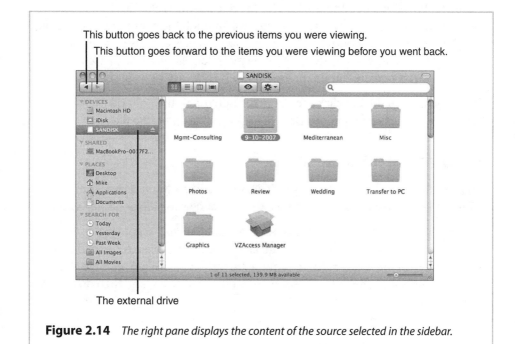

Figure 2.14   *The right pane displays the content of the source selected in the sidebar.*

Using the Icon View

At this point we have been using the Icon view, but Finder provides three additional al views: List, Column, and Cover Flow. In each view, the pane on the right is different. To switch to a different view, click the button in the toolbar for the view you want (see Figure 2.15). When you switch to a different view, that view becomes the new view for all sources that you subsequently view.

The Icon view, as you have seen in previous figures, uses icons in the right pane to represent the content of the item selected in the sidebar. To adjust the size of the icons, use the slider at the bottom-right corner of the window.

You can arrange the icons in this view by dragging the icons to different locations as you wish. For example, you might want to drag all the files that you are currently working on to the top of the window. To realign the icons in a tidy grid again, click View in the menu bar and click Arrange By. Then select Name, Date Modified, and so on.

A Snow Leopard enhancement to the Icon and Cover Flow views allows you to thumb through pages in a PDF file and view certain types of movies (QuickTime formats). When you point to the icon for the document, a set of back and forward arrows appear, and you can use these to scroll through the pages. When you point to a movie icon, a play button appears, and you can play or pause the movie. Because the pages of the document or the movie display in the icon itself, you might want to increase the size of the icon so you can actually see something.

By default, if you double-click a folder in the right pane, the right pane changes to show the content of that folder. Double-clicking a file opens the file.

Using the List View

Figure 2.15 shows the List view. By default, this view lists Name, Date Modified, Size, and Kind. Like the sidebar, this view uses triangles to hide or display subitems.

You can move the columns in this view to rearrange them, except for the Name column, which must remain in place as the first column. To move a column, drag the column title to the left or right. To change the width of a column, point to the right side of the column title until you see a double-headed arrow, and then drag to the left or right.

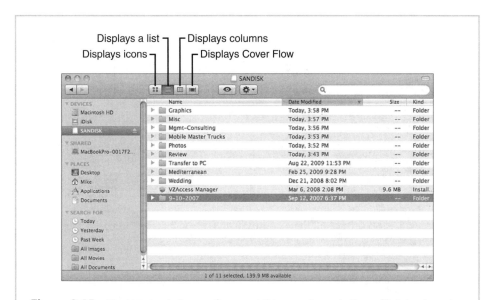

Figure 2.15   *The List view helps you figure out things such as whether a file is too large to email.*

Using the Column View

Figure 2.16 shows the Column view. This view can drill down through nested folders, column by column, until it shows a preview of a file in the last column. In Figure 2.16, for example, the first column shows the content of the source selected in the sidebar. The content of the folder selected in the first column is shown in the second column. The third column shows a preview of the file selected in the second column.

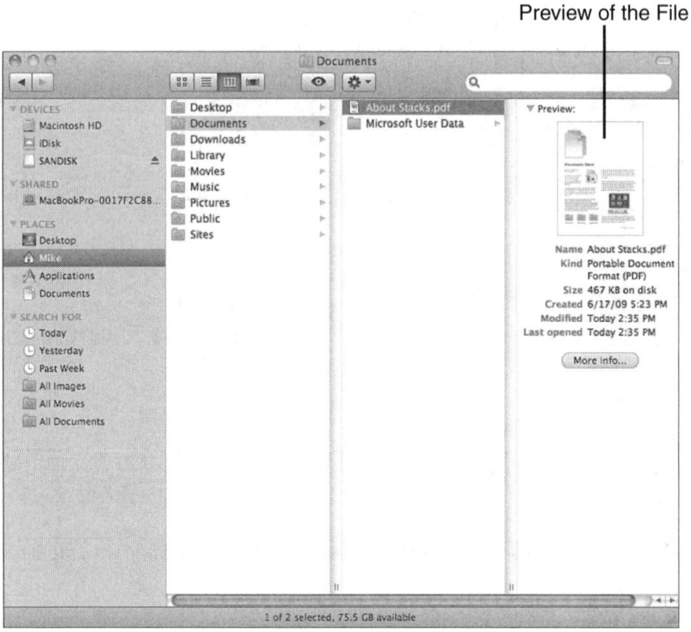

Preview of the File

Figure 2.16   *Use the Column view to keep track of where you are as you move up and down in hierarchical folders.*

Using the Cover Flow View

The Cover Flow view, shown in Figure 2.17, uses the List view in the bottom pane and a graphic 3D view in the top pane. The items contained in the source that you select show as previews in the top pane. If you are an iTunes user, you are already familiar with the Cover Flow view.

Using the scroll bar at the bottom of the graphic pane, you can scroll through the items in the graphic pane. In the Cover Flow view, scrolling through content is synchronized in both panes. In other words, the item previewed in the top pane is the item selected in the bottom pane, and vice versa.

To get the most out of Cover Flow view, make the graphic area as large as possible. Point to the bottom of the pane and drag it down when the cursor arrow changes to a hand.

Figure 2.17 *Use the slider in the scroll bar to scroll items quickly.*

Observing the Default Behavior of the Finder

Each time you open the Finder, it selects your Home folder to display. When you select a different source to view, the Finder replaces what was in the right pane with the content of the new source; it doesn't open a new window. These default behaviors can be changed in the Finder preferences window, as explained in Chapter 6.

As you use the Finder more and more, you may start to notice that the Finder has a memory. For example, it remembers where you last positioned it on the screen and goes right back to that location the next time you open it. It remembers the size you last made its window, and the next time you open it, it opens to that size. It remembers the last view you used and any changes you made to column widths, column order, and so on. It even remembers if you leave its window open when you log out, and it opens the window the next time you log in.

Launching Safari for the First Time

To launch the Mac web browser, Safari, click the Safari icon in the Dock—the one that looks like a blue compass. The first time you launch the application, it welcomes you and displays previews of a dozen popular websites, as shown in

Figure 2.18. At the bottom of the screen, it explains that as you browse the Web, it will take note of your favorite sites and display them above (instead of the ones it has preselected for you).

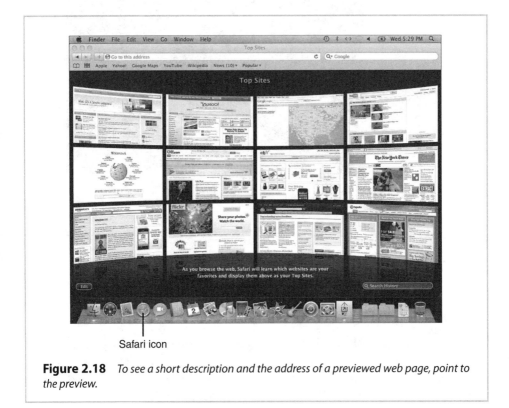

Safari icon

Figure 2.18   *To see a short description and the address of a previewed web page, point to the preview.*

At this point, you can do the following:

- Click one of the website previews to go to that site.

- Type a web address in the box at the top left and press Return to go to a specific website.

- Type a search phrase in the Google search box at the top right and press Return to display Google search results.

Apple's own website is the first preview in the first row. If you are a new Mac user, I recommend that you go there first and familiarize yourself with the site. When you are finished browsing, click Safari in the menu bar and click Quit Safari.

The next time you launch Safari, don't expect to see the 12 previews again. By default, Safari is set up to go straight to "startpage" on the Apple website. If you want to see the previews every time you start Safari, you can, but I'll talk more about that in the chapter devoted to Safari, Chapter 7, "Browsing the Web."

Sharing Your Computer with Another User

If you want to share your computer with someone else (your sister, for example), you could just let her sit down and start using it, but do you really want your sister reading your email or changing the settings you've made to customize the desktop? If privacy or security is an issue, then a better way to share your computer with her is to create a separate account for her. That way, everything you do on the computer is separated from what she does on the computer, and vice versa. After all, she probably doesn't want you reading her email either. If maintaining separate desktops and email accounts is the issue, rather than privacy or security, setting up separate user accounts is still the way to go.

If you need to share your computer only occasionally with people who just want to get on the Internet or use your printer, you don't need to create a separate account for each person; you can let them use the Guest account. Snow Leopard provides a Guest account that is already set up for you to use. All you have to do is enable it.

Setting Up Another User Account

The first account created on your Mac was your own account. Snow Leopard created it during the initialization process described in Chapter 1 and made you an administrator. As an administrator, you can set up and delete additional user accounts on the computer as the need arises.

 SHOW ME   Media 2.1—A video about Creating a User Account
Access this video file through your registered Web Edition at
my.safaribooksonline.com/9780789743916/media.

LET ME TRY IT

Creating a User Account

Even though you have the right to make changes to this part of the system, you will have to unlock the current System Preferences with your account name and password. To set up another user account, follow these steps:

1. Click the System Preferences icon in the Dock and click the Accounts icon in the System row at the bottom of the window. The Accounts page opens, as shown in Figure 2.19.

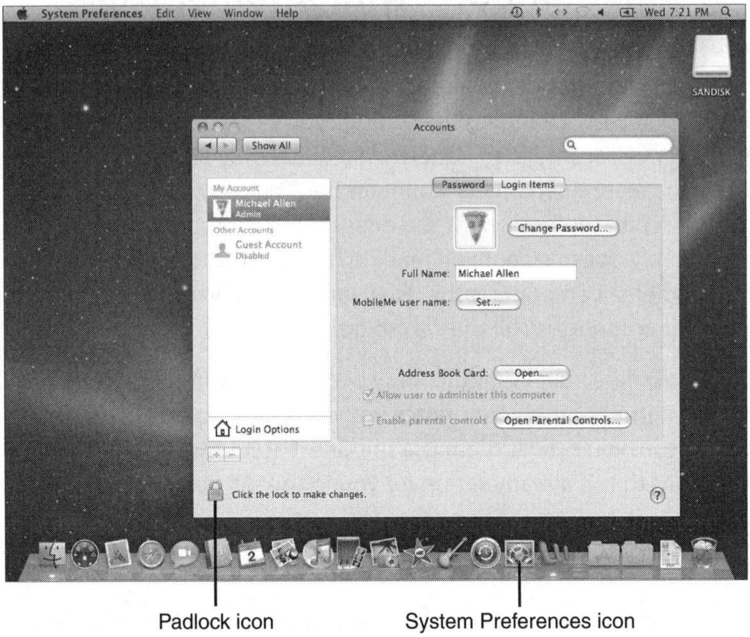

Padlock icon   System Preferences icon

Figure 2.19   *The Guest account is a default account that is standing by waiting to be enabled.*

2. Click the padlock icon in the lower-left corner of the window.

3. Type your password and click OK. The padlock opens.

4. Click the Add button (the one with the plus sign just above the padlock icon) to display the form that you must complete to create a new account, as seen in Figure 2.20.

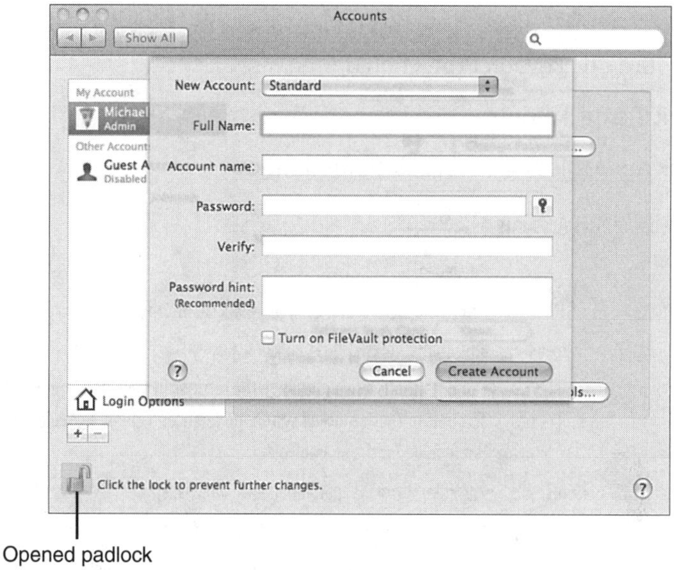

Opened padlock

Figure 2.20   *The New Account type defaults to Standard.*

5. Select the type of account you want from the pop-up menu for New Account. Refer to Table 2.2, "Types of User Accounts" to help you make your decision.

6. Type a full name for the account. This will be the login name.

7. Type an account name. This will be the name of the user's Home folder.

8. Type a password for the account and then type it again in the Verify field.

Make a note of the full name and password you created to give to the user and keep a copy for yourself. Once the account is created, even though you are the administrator, you can't look up the password. You would just have to create a new one if the user forgets his password.

If security and privacy are not an issue, you can actually leave the password fields blank. If security and privacy *are* the issue, you can click the key icon beside the Password field and let the Password Assistant suggest a strong password for you.

9. Type a hint for the password.

10. If you want the user's Home folder encrypted for security reasons, check the Turn on FileVault Protection option.

11. Click Create Account.

12. Lock the padlock icon and close the window.

Table 2.2 Types of User Accounts

Account Type	Privileges
Administrator	Can create, delete, and change user accounts, modify system settings, install software, and change the settings of other users.
Standard	Can install software and change the settings in only his account. Cannot create user accounts or change locked system preferences. Cannot create folders outside of his Home folder or the Shared Folder.
Managed with Parental Controls	Has at least the Standard privileges, which can then be further limited by the settings made under Parental Controls.
Sharing Only	Can access shared files on a network. Cannot run applications or do anything else.
Group	Includes multiple individual users so that you can make global changes to permissions or sharing privileges for these individuals.

Setting Up a Guest Account

Like other user accounts, the Guest account has no access to anything that you or any other user does on the computer with one exception—you can allow the Guest account to access shared folders.

When a guest logs in, he doesn't have to enter a password, and he has his own temporary Home folder to work in called "Guest." When the guest logs out, everything in the Guest Home folder is deleted. Any changes that the user made to the desktop, system preferences, and so on, are reset to the original settings. In other words, Snow Leopard cleans house and gets everything ready for the next guest.

Deleting a User Account

When your sister finally buys a Mac of her own, you can delete her user account. One thing to consider before deleting the account is what should happen to the data in her Home folder. Several options are open to you.

 SHOW ME   Media 2.2—A video about Deleting a User Account
Access this video file through your registered Web Edition at
my.safaribooksonline.com/9780789743916/media.

Logging In and Out

If more than one user account is set up on your Mac, the login process is necessary. To log in when the Mac starts, you click your account name, type the password (if there is one), and press Return or click Log In. If you enter an incorrect password, the dialog box appears to shake its head "no" at you. (Sometimes I enter the wrong password a few times just to see this.) If you fail three times to enter the correct password, your password hint is given.

The first time a new user logs in, the desktop and all the System Preferences are set to the factory defaults regardless of what changes you've made to your own desktop and preferences in *your* user account. Remember, user accounts are like Las Vegas—everything that happens in a user's account *stays* in the user's account.

To log out, you click the Apple menu and click the last option on the menu, Log Out *<User Name>* (where *User Name* is the account name). Logging out does not power down the computer; it shuts down all the user's applications and redisplays the Log In dialog box for the next user to log in.

It can be a bother for one user to log out so another user can log in. If this is a frequent and annoying occurrence on your Mac, you can set up the fast user switching feature.

 SHOW ME   Media 2.3—A video about Setting Up Fast User Switching
Access this video file through your registered Web Edition at my.safaribooksonline.com/9780789743916/media.

 LET ME TRY IT

Turning On Automatic Login

If you are the only user on your computer, you might like the idea of bypassing the login step by using automatic login. Without a required login, however, anyone with access to your computer could start it and peruse your data. If that is a low risk for you, by all means, activate automatic login. Follow these steps to turn on automatic login:

1. Open the System Preferences window and click Accounts.

2. Click the padlock icon to unlock it.

3. Click Login Options.

4. Select your name from the Automatic Login pop-up menu.

5. Type your password and click OK. The results are shown in Figure 2.21.

6. Click the padlock icon to lock it and close the window.

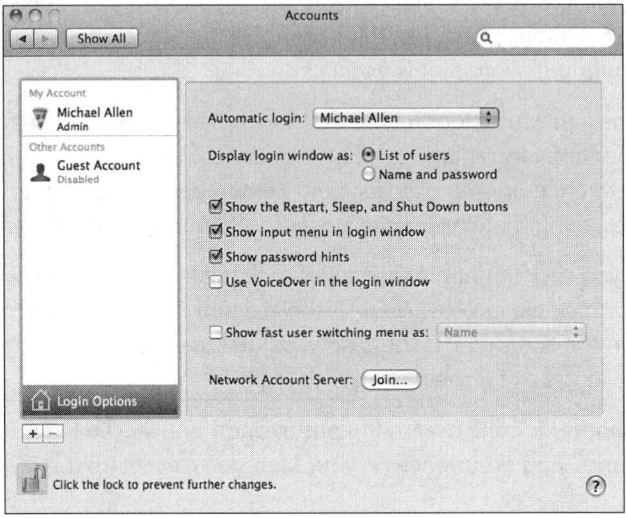

Figure 2.21   *Automatic login allows anyone to use your computer so if your no-good nephew is visiting, you might want to turn this off until he leaves.*

TELL ME MORE   **Media 2.4—A discussion about Inappropriate Use of Automatic Login**
Access this audio recording through your registered Web Edition at my.safaribooksonline.com/9780789743916/media.

Putting Your Mac to Sleep or Shutting It Down

When you finish working on your Mac for the day, you can put it to sleep or shut it down. It's up to you really, but most Mac users I know leave their Macs running all the time. Sleep mode uses very little power, and it keeps all your applications and work open and in memory. The computer wakes up from the sleep mode within seconds after you press a key or click the mouse so you can get back to work much faster than you can if you have to start the Mac, reopen all your applications, and open all your files.

The Mac performs many maintenance routines in the middle of the night, or when it recognizes that you're not using it—another reason to use the sleep mode instead of shutting down.

Putting the Mac to Sleep

To put the Mac in sleep mode, click the Apple menu and click **Sleep**. Alternatively, you can just let the Mac go to sleep on its own. After a period of mouse and keyboard inactivity defined in the Energy Saver preferences, the Mac will put both the hard disk and the screen to sleep. Of course, if the Mac is in the middle of a process that doesn't require keyboard or mouse input, such as playing a DVD movie, playing music in iTunes, doing a Time Machine backup, or downloading files from the Internet, it will not suddenly go to sleep in the middle of the process.

If you have a laptop, you have two sets of sleep options—one for the power adapter and one for the battery. Typically, you want to use shorter time intervals for sleep mode when running on battery to conserve the power.

Shutting Down

Even if you leave your Mac running all the time, you might want to shut it down if you are not going to use it for a couple of days. If you plan to move the Mac, you definitely should shut it down. Moving the computer while the hard disk is spinning could damage the disk.

🖱 LET ME TRY IT

Turning Your Computer Off

By "shutting down," I don't mean pressing the power button—far from it. No, you must follow the proper shutdown procedure. If you simply turn off the power, you will not have a chance to save your work, should you have failed to do so earlier. To shut down correctly, follow these steps:

1. Click the Apple menu and click Shut Down. A dialog box asks you if you are sure you want to shut down your computer now. You have 60 seconds to decide. If you do nothing, the Mac shuts down automatically.

2. Before 60 seconds has passed, click Shut Down.

3. Respond to any prompts that may appear for closing unsaved documents or shutting down applications with unfinished business. When all applications have safely closed, Snow Leopard turns off the power for you.

If you carry your laptop around, you can put it in sleep mode instead of shutting down because sleep mode also stops the hard disk from spinning. A laptop goes into sleep mode automatically when you close the display.

This chapter helps you install or make the optimum settings for your hardware—including the screen, the mouse or trackpad, speakers, disk drives, and printers.

3

Getting Familiar with Your Hardware

In this chapter, we're going to look at some of the settings that control the screen, the speakers, the keyboard and mouse, internal and external drives, and printers. Before reading this chapter you need to familiarize yourself with the components of your own system by reading everything you can about your hardware in your user manuals.

Controlling the Screen Brightness

Two keys on your keyboard control the brightness of your screen: F1 turns the brightness down, and F2 turns the brightness up. Over time, Apple has changed the location of keys on its keyboards, but you can locate the keys by their icons. Look for icons that resemble a sunburst. The one with longer sunrays is the one that makes the screen brighter.

Your screen's brightness automatically adjusts to ambient light by default. To see where this option is set, click the System Preferences icon in the Dock, click Displays in the Hardware row, and click Display to open the Display pane if necessary. When you are finished, close the window.

Mac OS X remembers where you were last and redisplays that pane. So if you last looked at the Color pane, you have to click Display to see those options.

Adjusting the Sound

All Macs have built-in speakers for playing music, listening to videos, and making interface sound effects. Using the speakers, your Mac can even tell you the time or read to you from a file.

Using the Keyboard to Adjust Sound

Three keys on your keyboard control your computer's sound: F10 turns it off, F11 turns it down, and F12 turns it up. Like the brightness adjustment keys, these functions may be located on different keys on older keyboards, but you also can identify them by their icons. One looks like a speaker with many sound waves coming out of it. This one makes the sound louder. The other icons have only one sound wave (for softer sound) and no sound waves (for no sound), respectively.

Setting Sound Preferences

It is possible to set the volume level in the Sound preferences window, but what's the point? It's so much easier to do it with the keyboard. Other preferences in the Sound preferences window are worth looking at, however. They include setting the default alert sound and its volume, turning interface sound effects on or off, and hiding or displaying the volume control in the menu bar.

 **LET ME TRY IT**

Setting Sound Effects

Sound preferences include settings for effects, output, and input. At this point, you probably don't need to make any changes to output or input settings. To set effect preferences, follow these steps:

1. Click the System Preferences icon in the Dock.

2. Click Sound in the Hardware row (second row).

3. Click Sound Effects (if necessary) to display the options shown in Figure 3.1.

4. Click an alert sound in the list to hear it play. When you find the one you want, click it to select it. This will be the sound that plays when you try to do something that is not allowed or the computer needs more information from you.

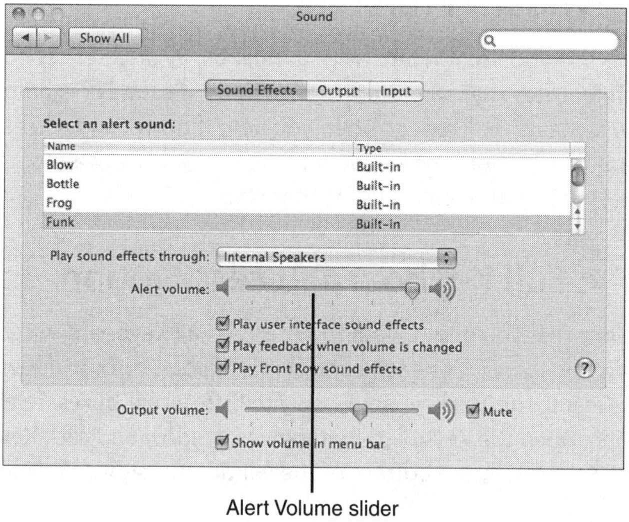

Alert Volume slider

Figure 3.1 *The Sound window has three tabs: Sound Effects, Output, and Input.*

5. Set the volume of the alert by dragging the slider for Alert Volume.

6. Check or uncheck Play User Interface Sound Effects.

7. Check or uncheck Show Volume in Menu Bar. (If you select this option, a speaker icon displays in the Menu Extras on the right side of the menu bar.)

Showing the volume adjustment in the menu bar gives you one more way to adjust the volume without opening the Sound preferences window.

8. Close the window.

Setting Keyboard Preferences

A keyboard is a keyboard. You type with it. How many preferences could there be? What few preferences there are seem almost insignificant. For example, you can change how fast a key will repeat when you hold it down, and you can determine how long you have to hold the key down before it starts repeating. You might use repeating keys in a chat or email, as in "That is so coooool!"

Setting the Full Keyboard Access Option

One preference that you might want to set is the Full Keyboard Access option. This option allows you to move to each control in a dialog box or window by using the Tab key. By default, the Tab key moves only to lists or text boxes. To change the default setting, open the Keyboard Preferences window and click Keyboard Shortcuts. Click All Controls at the bottom of the window, as shown in Figure 3.2.

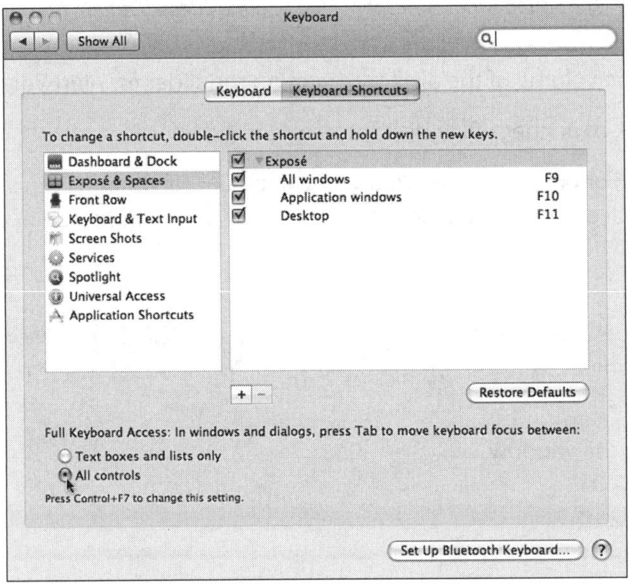

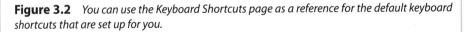

Figure 3.2   *You can use the Keyboard Shortcuts page as a reference for the default keyboard shortcuts that are set up for you.*

Setting Keyboard Preferences for a Laptop

If you have a laptop, there is one very cool keyboard preference for you. You can set a preference to illuminate the keyboard in low light conditions; it's perfect for typing in the car at night on a long road trip (when you're not driving, of course). You also can specify what period of inactivity will turn off the illumination. Once the illumination goes off, though, just touching the keyboard turns it back on. You'll find these settings on the Keyboard page of Keyboard Preferences.

Press F10 to make the keyboard illumination brighter and F9 to dim it.

Operating the Mouse or Trackpad

All new model Macs come with the Apple Magic Mouse—except, of course, the Mac Mini and the MacBooks. The Mac Mini comes with no mouse, and the MacBooks come with a trackpad.

The Magic Mouse is the successor of the Apple Might Mouse, which came out in 2005. Like the popular 1940's cartoon character, the Might Mouse had super powers—it was a "buttonless" mouse with not just one hidden button, but two. It also was the first multibutton mouse produced by Apple, and like the cartoon character's theme song, "Here I come to save the day," it saved the day for all the PC switchers who sorely missed their right-clicking.

Using the Mouse

You might be a new Mac user, but I'm pretty sure you know how to use a mouse. If you need help with pointing, clicking, dragging, and so on, ask any eight-year-old.

Setting Mouse Preferences

Mouse preferences that are available depend on the type of mouse you are using. Generally, you can set preferences for tracking (how fast the mouse moves the pointer on the screen), double-click speed, and scrolling speed. If you have a two-button mouse, you can specify which button is the primary button and which is the secondary button. (Remember, in this book, I use the term *right-click* to refer to clicking the secondary button.)

In Figure 3.3, you can see the default preferences for an Apple Mighty Mouse. The Mighty Mouse has a scroll ball on top between the primary and secondary "buttonless" buttons, and it has a squeezable button on each side. By default, these are set to Off, but the pop-up menus for the two controls offer many useful options.

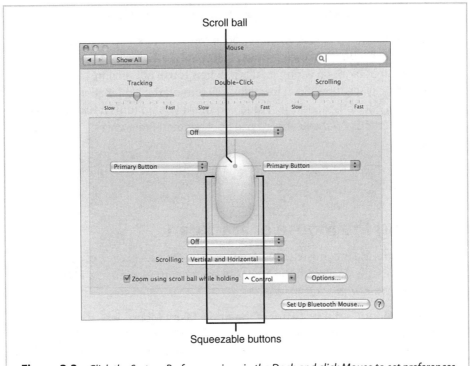

Figure 3.3 *Click the System Preferences icon in the Dock and click Mouse to set preferences.*

Apple released the Magic Mouse just before the printing of this book. This mouse has multi-touch features, many of which were previously available only on a trackpad.

Using the Trackpad

The trackpad on a MacBook moves the pointer onscreen and performs clicking and dragging actions. It can do everything that a mouse can do, and then some. For example, Snow Leopard allows you to input Chinese characters by drawing them directly on a Multi-Touch trackpad!

To move the onscreen pointer with a trackpad, you touch the trackpad with one finger and move your finger in the direction you want the pointer to go. You can set the tracking speed for this action in the Trackpad preferences. To click, double-click, or triple-click, you press the trackpad button once, twice, or three times. You also can adjust the speed for clicking. Other gestures that you can set include scrolling, dragging, and secondary clicking. The newest MacBook Pros have added these additional gestures: pinch, rotate, three-finger swipe, and four-finger swipe.

 TELL ME MORE   Media 3.1—A discussion about Trackpad Gestures
Access this audio recording through your registered Web Edition at
my.safaribooksonline.com/9780789743916/media.

Setting Trackpad Preferences

The trackpad has many possible gestures, but you may not want to use all of them. You can select the gestures you want to use in the Trackpad Preferences window. To set options for the Trackpad, follow these steps:

1. Click the System Preferences icon in the Dock.

2. Click Trackpad in the Hardware row to open the window shown in Figure 3.4.

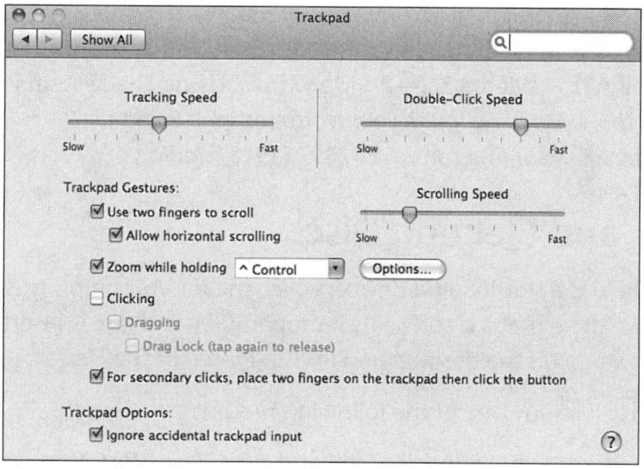

Figure 3.4 *Newer MacBooks offer additional Trackpad preferences.*

3. Set the speed for tracking and double-clicking.

The Zoom While Holding gesture allows you to enlarge what you see on the screen. To zoom in, slide your two fingers forward on the trackpad while holding down the Control key (or the modifier key that you selected). To zoom out, hold down the Control key and slide your fingers back. This gesture is great for enlarging websites that use tiny fonts.

4. Select each gesture you want to use. I especially like the two-fingered-click, which acts like the secondary mouse button, but I don't like the dragging options. It's too easy to drag something by mistake. It's also a good idea to select the option to ignore accidental trackpad input.

5. When you are finished, close the window.

Using CD/DVD Drives

All new Macs, with the exception of MacBook Air, come with a built-in optical drive called a SuperDrive. It reads and writes DVDs (even Double Layer) and CDs at super-fast speeds ranging from 8 to 24 times normal speed. If you have an older Mac, you can see what type of disks your optical drive can write to by opening the System Profiler.

 SHOW ME   Media 3.2—A video about Using the System Profiler
Access this video file through your registered Web Edition at
my.safaribooksonline.com/9780789743916/media.

Inserting and Ejecting Discs

The SuperDrive is a slot-loading device, which means you simply push the disc into a slot and the drive grabs it and seats it properly. Once a disc is inserted, an icon for the disc shows up on the desktop and in the sidebar of the Finder.

To eject a disc, use any one of the following methods:

- Right-click the disc's desktop icon and click Eject *<Disk Name>*.

- Drag the disc's desktop icon to the Trash icon in the Dock.

- Open Finder and click the eject symbol next to the disc in the sidebar (see Figure 3.5).

- Press the eject key on the keyboard. (Look for the same symbol on this key as you see in Figure 3.5.)

Eject symbol

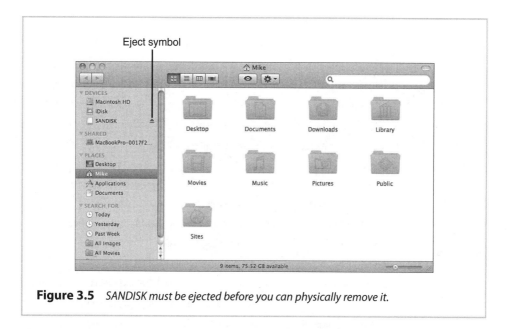

Figure 3.5 *SANDISK must be ejected before you can physically remove it.*

Setting Preferences for CDs and DVDs

The default preferences for CDs & DVDs determine what happens when you insert a particular type of disc in the optical drive. Figure 3.6 shows the default preferences. After you have been using the Mac for a while, you may want to change some of these options, but for now, they are probably just fine. If you are curious about what your options are for each type of disc, refer to Table 3.1.

Figure 3.6 *Click CDs & DVDs in the System Preferences window to see these options.*

Table 3.1   Options for CDs and DVDs

Type of Disc	Options	Use Might Use This Option If...
Blank CD	Ask what to do	You do something different almost every time you insert a blank CD.
	Open Finder	You use Burn Folders. See Chapter 18, "Making Your Own DVDs."
	Open iTunes	You always want to create a music CD when you insert a blank disc.
	Open Disc Utility	You always want to burn a data CD when you insert a blank CD.
	Open other application	You have installed your own disc-burning application.
	Run script	You want to use an AppleScript* that performs a specific routine.
	Ignore	You want to make your own decision about what you want to do in your own good time.
Blank DVD	Ask what to do	You do something different almost every time you insert a blank DVD.
	Open Finder	You use Burn Folders. See Chapter 18.
	Open iDVD	You want to use iDVD to burn a project to the DVD.
	Open iTunes	You always want to create a music DVD when you insert a blank DVD.
	Open Disk Utility	You always want to burn a data DVD when you insert a blank DVD.
	Open other application	You have installed your own disc-burning application.
	Run script	You want to use an AppleScript* that performs a specific routine.
	Ignore	You want to make your own decision about what you want to do with the DVD in your own good time.
Music CD	Open iTunes	You want to play the CD or otherwise manipulate it in iTunes.
	Open other application	You want to use a different application to play or otherwise manipulate the CD.
	Run script	You want to use an AppleScript* that performs a specific routine.
Picture CD	Open iPhoto	You want to archive your photos for viewing in iPhoto.
	Open other application	You want to use a photo-editing application.
	Run script	You want to use an AppleScript* that performs a specific routine.
Video DVD	Open DVD Player	You want to view the DVD in the DVD Player.
	Open other application	You want to view the DVD in a different DVD application, such as Front Row.
	Run script	You want to use an AppleScript* that performs a specific routine.

* AppleScript is a type of programming language that can create routines that use a series of commands to perform tasks.

Using External Drives

An external drive is any storage device connected to the Mac via USB or FireWire cable. The drive could be a flash drive, an additional DVD drive, a hard drive, an iPod, and so on.

Connecting a Drive

Connecting an external drive is a simple matter of plugging the cable or device into the correct port on the Mac. That's it. The Mac recognizes the drive and places an icon for the drive on the desktop and in the sidebar of the Finder.

Ejecting a Drive

Never unplug an external drive without properly ejecting it first. Data could be lost.

To eject a drive, use one of these methods:

- Right-click the drive's desktop icon and click Eject <*Disk Name*>.
- Drag the drive's desktop icon to the Trash icon in the Dock.
- Open Finder and click the eject symbol next to the drive in the sidebar (refer to Figure 3.5).

If you properly eject the drive, its icon no longer shows as a device in the Finder window. Then you can physically disconnect it.

Installing and Managing Printers

While perusing a question-and-answer Mac forum one day, I found this post from a PC switcher: "I feel happy and giddy all the time. Also, I have too much free time because I didn't have to figure anything out when I installed my printer and mouse. What should I do?"

This answer was posted: "Enjoy your Mac."

Like everything else, Apple has streamlined printer installation.

Connecting and Using a Printer

Generally, you can connect a new printer to a Mac and use it right away because Snow Leopard comes with the most common printer software and selects it automatically when it senses a printer has been connected. Additionally, Mac OS X keeps the software updated automatically via the Internet. The only time you will have to do any extra work to install a printer is if you buy an "uncommon" printer.

 SHOW ME   Media 3.3—A video about Installing a Printer
Access this video file through your registered Web Edition at
my.safaribooksonline.com/9780789743916/media.

 **LET ME TRY IT**

Installing a Printer

To verify that Mac OS X recognizes the printer or, if necessary, to install one, follow these steps. In most cases, you will probably have to complete only the first four steps in these insructions.

1. Open any document.

If you don't have any documents to open, click the Documents stack icon in the Dock and then click the icon for the file named About Stacks.pdf. The document opens in the application called Preview.

2. Click File in the menu bar and then click Print to open the Print dialog box, as shown in Figure 3.7.

3. Click the Printer pop-up button to display the list of printers installed on your Mac.

4. If your printer's name is there, you are good to go.

Click here to display the pop-up menu that lists printers.

Printer:	○ HP Officejet J4680 series
Presets:	Standard

(?) (PDF ▼) (Preview)   (Cancel) (Print)

Click here to display more print options.

Figure 3.7   *The Print menu has more options that are currently hidden.*

5. If you don't see your printer on the list, click the Add Printer option in the pop-up list, as shown in Figure 3.8.

Figure 3.8   *Currently installed printers are listed at the top of this pop-up menu.*

6. Click the More Printers button. (If you don't see this button, this could mean trouble. You'll have to contact your printer manufacturer for more information.)

7. Choose your printer type from the pop-up menu (for example, Epson USB).

8. After you choose your printer type, it will appear in the Printer Name column. Click it and then click the Add button.

If you upgraded to Snow Leopard and now your printer doesn't work, unplug it. Then open the Print page of the Print & Fax preferences window and delete the printer. Plug it back in and follow the preceding steps.

Setting a Default Printer

Setting a default printer means that every time you send a document to print, the default printer will be the printer that is selected to print the document. To set the default printer, click the System Preferences icon in the Dock, click Print & Fax, and then click Print, if necessary. Figure 3.9 shows the Print pane. Click the padlock, enter your password, and then select the printer that you want for the Default Printer option. Close the window when you are finished.

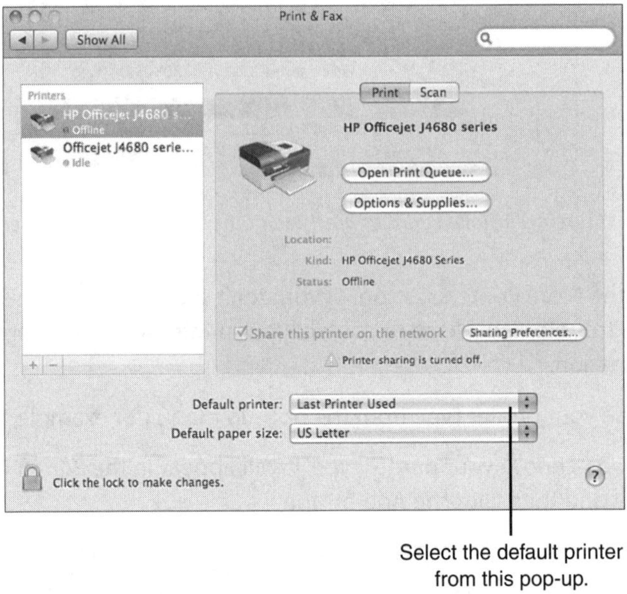

Select the default printer
from this pop-up.

Figure 3.9   *The Last Printer Used setting means that you don't really specify a default printer.*

Setting Up a Simple Network

If you have more than one Mac at your location, you probably have times when
you wish the computers could share data. The subject of setting up a full-blown
network is a little too advanced for this book, but setting up a wireless, computer-
to-computer network between two AirPort-enabled Macs is well within the range
of even a beginning Mac user. For instructions, look up Network Setup in the index
of the Finder Help file, and then click Creating a Computer-to-Computer Network.

From the menu bar to the Dock, this chapter shows you how to customize the desktop, including the Finder.

4

Tailoring the Desktop to Your Liking

The Snow Leopard desktop is fabulous as it is, straight out of the box, but we all have different ideas about exactly how we want our computers to look and behave. Mac OS X throws the door wide open for customizations. In this chapter, we will look at some of the ways you can customize your desktop.

Setting System Preferences

Although this chapter is not about setting system preferences, per se, you are going to be spending a lot of time in the System Preferences window. Before we dig into the real topic of this chapter, I want to give you several hints about working with the System Preferences window.

The System Preferences window is like a large department store with so many departments and so many items in stock that you need an information counter you can walk up to and say, "Where would I find…?" The Spotlight search box in the top-right corner of the System Preferences window is the information counter you are looking for. If you are having a problem with something or just want to make a change and you suspect there is a system preference that governs it, try typing a relative word or phrase in the Spotlight box. For example, if you want to make text larger on your screen, you could type "resolution." If you want your Mac to talk to you, type "speak." As you type, Mac OS X lists topics related to the words, and it highlights the appropriate icons in the window, as shown in Figure 4.1. You can choose an item from the list, and the appropriate window opens, or you can click a highlighted icon in the window.

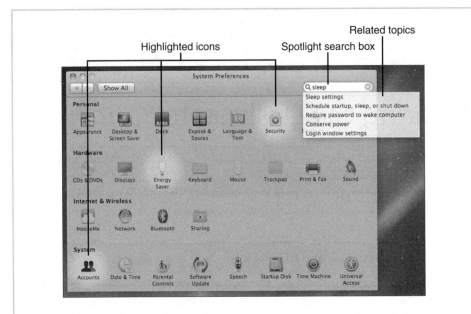

Figure 4.1   *Use the Spotlight to find what you are looking for in the System Preferences window.*

After you open a specific preferences window and make settings, you do not have to close the window if you want to make modifications to other system preferences. You can click the Show All button in the top left (see Figure 4.1) to go back to the System Preferences window.

Because you might be reading this book as a reference instead of sequentially, every set of instructions for setting preferences includes the step to close the window as the last step. Just remember that it is not necessary to close the window if you want to set other preferences.

Most preference windows have more than one pane. To access the pane you want, click the appropriate tab at the top of the window. When you close a preference window with multiple panes, Mac OS X remembers the last pane you looked at so when you open the same preferences window again, it displays the last pane that you viewed. Because of this "sticky behavior," I always include a step to click the appropriate tab, but I include the caveat "if necessary."

Keep these hints in your back pocket as you customize your desktop. Okay, here we go!

Customizing the Desktop Background

Mac OS X provides numerous pictures for you to display on the desktop, from colorful graffiti to Van Gogh and Monet, from the Snow Leopard himself to a ladybug, from black and white to color and pattern. Each graphic is stunning, but you can use one of your own favorite photos instead—that vacation photo in the Swiss alps, your new sports car, your son in his T-ball uniform. Do you have too many favorite photos to select just one? No problem. Select as many as you want and display them in order, or randomly, at an interval that you specify. Your desktop becomes a perpetual slideshow—a virtual digital picture frame.

Using a slideshow-type background will use more system resources, but you won't really notice any sluggishness unless you are running a large number of applications simultaneously.

 LET ME TRY IT

Changing the Desktop Background

Before you get too carried away with such a rich graphic desktop, you need to know that the desktop can be a very important work area if you want it to be. You probably will have numerous icons on the desktop that you use frequently. If that's the case, you might want to use a solid color or muted pattern for the desktop so that the icons don't get lost in the graphics of the background. Alternatively, you can select a photo that has some neutral space in it and group all your icons in that space. To change the desktop picture, follow these steps:

1. Ctrl-click or right-click an empty spot on the desktop to open the shortcut menu and then click Change Desktop Background. The Desktop & Screen Saver preferences window opens, as shown in Figure 4.2.

Figure 4.2   *As soon as you get photographs in iPhoto, iPhoto will be added to the list as a source along with Apple and Folders.*

Using the familiar interface of the Finder, the sidebar lists categories of sources of graphics, and the right pane shows the graphics available in the selected source. Click the triangles (to the left of each category) to hide or display the sources under each category.

2. Click a source in the sidebar and then click the picture you want to use from the right pane.

To use one of your own photographs, click a source under iPhoto or click the Pictures folder. To create a slideshow with all the pictures in a selected source, choose Change Picture and then specify a time interval. Choose Random Order if you want to mix it up a bit.

3. Close the window and see if you like what you selected.

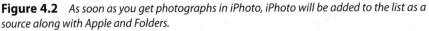

TELL ME MORE   **Media 4.1—A discussion about Creating Neutral Space in a Photo**

*Access this audio recording through your registered Web Edition at **my.safaribooksonline.com/9780789743916/media.***

Working with Icons on the Desktop

The desktop really has two roles on the Mac. It functions as the background on your screen, and it is a folder in your Home folder. In its role as background on your screen, it can use a graphic background, as you've seen. Additionally—and this is where it gets a little confusing—the Finder can display icons for discs on the background. In its role as the Desktop folder, it displays icons for any files or folders you store in your Desktop folder. Remember that any icons for discs that may appear on the desktop are really not located in the Desktop folder.

Showing Icons for Disks

By default, Mac OS X hides icons for some type of disks, but you can display these icons by clicking Finder in the menu bar and then clicking Preferences. (If you've been looking around in this window before, you may have to click the General icon at the top to get to the right place.) Figure 4.3 shows the default options on the General pane in the Finder Preferences window. I recommend showing external disks and CDs/DVDs/iPods so that you can eject them easily by dragging their icons to the Trash. You really have no business with the hard drive, so why put it in harm's way?

Select each type of disk that you want to display as an icon on the desktop. Note that no icon will display for a CD or DVD drive just because it is connected. The icon only displays if a disk is inserted. Unlike the Windows operating system, Mac OS X does not show a CD drive or DVD drive if it is empty.

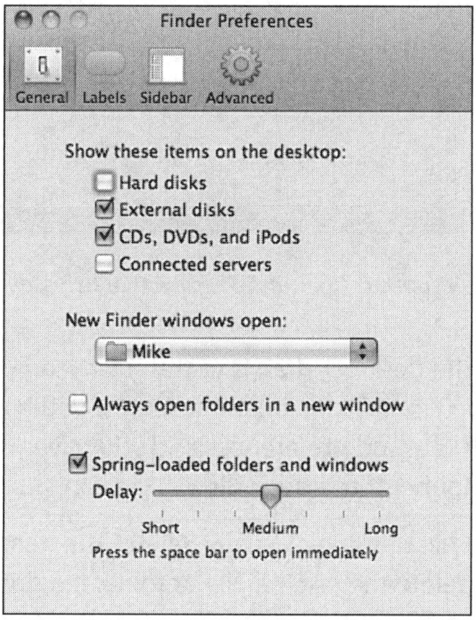

Figure 4.3 *The Finder Preferences window has three more tabs with additional preferences.*

Adding and Deleting Icons on the Desktop

I've already told you that the desktop displays icons for any files or folders you store in your Desktop folder, so you've probably already figured out that adding or deleting icons on the desktop is the same as adding or deleting files and folders in your Desktop folder. It also works the other way; any file or folder you drag to the desktop shows up in your Desktop folder in Finder. We'll discuss the mechanics of adding and deleting files and folders in Chapter 6, "Managing Applications and Files."

Another type of icon that can display on the desktop is an alias. An alias is not a file or a folder, but merely a pointer to the actual file or folder. To create an alias, open the Finder and select any file or folder in the right pane. Click File in the menu bar and then click Make Alias. The alias displays in the right pane just below the original file or folder, as shown in Figure 4.4. To move the alias to the desktop, just drag it out of the Finder and drop it on an empty spot.

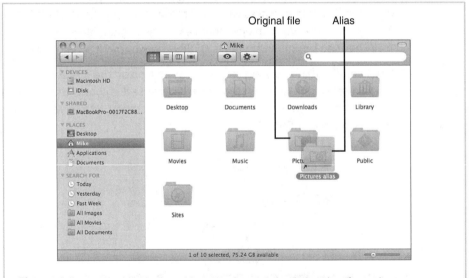

Figure 4.4 *Notice the visual cue (the curved arrow) that helps identify an alias.*

To delete an icon on the desktop, drag it to the Trash icon on the Dock. Release the icon when you see the word *Trash* above the icon. If you have interface sound effects turned on in the sound preferences and you have your volume turned up, you should hear the sound of the trash hitting the can.

Deleting an icon for a file or folder actually deletes the item, but deleting an icon for an alias does not delete the original file or folder—a good reason to use aliases on the desktop instead of actual files.

If you are a brand-new user, you really don't have enough icons on your desktop to perform some of the tasks in the next activities. I suggest you create four or five aliases and drag them to the desktop so you can try the steps in the next two topics.

Arranging Icons

You can arrange the icons on your desktop by dragging them to any location. Once you have positioned the icons where you want them, you can line them up with each other vertically and horizontally by using the Clean Up command on the desktop's shortcut menu (see Figure 4.5). This command aligns the icons with an invisible grid.

To change the grid spacing, Ctrl-click or right-click the desktop to open the shortcut menu and click Show View Options. Move the Grid Spacing slider to the left to make the grid tighter or to the right to make the grid larger.

If you don't want to arrange the icons yourself, you can let Mac OS X do it for you with the Arrange By command, available on the desktop's shortcut menu shown in Figure 4.5. The Arrange By command alignes icons with the invisible grid, sorted by name, date modified, date created, size, kind, or label. After arranging the icons with this command, you can still move the icons freely around the desktop.

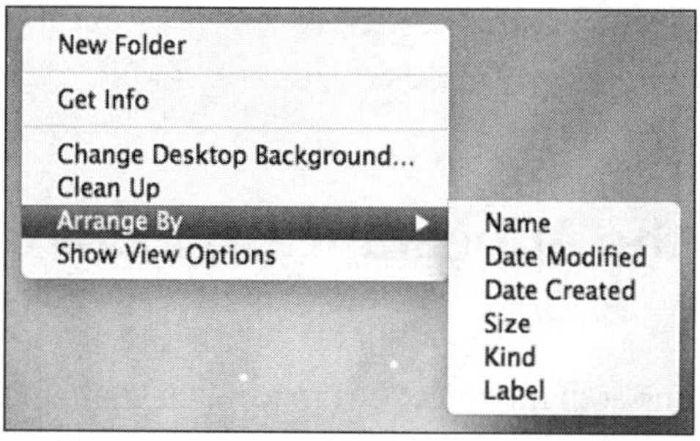

Figure 4.5 *To display the desktop shortcut menu, Ctrl-click or right-click a blank spot on the desktop.*

Curiously, however, the Arrange By command also appears in the Desktop options window, displayed by selecting Show View Options from the desktop's shortcut menu. Once positioned by this Arrange By command, the icons cannot be dragged out of position. To make the icons free-moving again, return to the Desktop options window and select None from the Arrange By pop-up menu, as shown in Figure 4.6. Close the window.

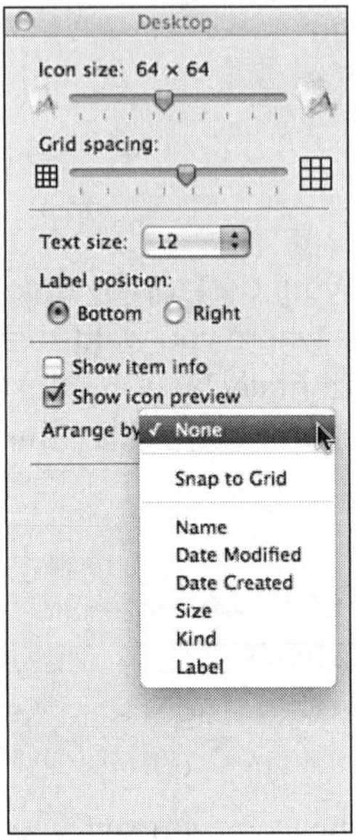

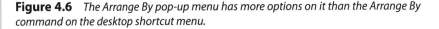

Figure 4.6   *The Arrange By pop-up menu has more options on it than the Arrange By command on the desktop shortcut menu.*

The Snap to Grid option helps you align icons when you are moving them yourself. When you drag an icon anywhere close to an invisible grid location and let it go, the icon snaps into place.

Customizing the Appearance of Icons on the Desktop

You can make a number of modifications to icons to change their appearance on the desktop. For example, you can change the size and the location of the label.

 **LET ME TRY IT**

Customizing Desktop Icons

All options for customizing icons on the desktop are located in the View Options window. As you make changes to the icon options, you can see the results on the desktop even before you close the window. To change the appearance of icons, follow these steps:

1. Ctrl-click or right-click the desktop to open the shortcut menu and click Show View Options. Figure 4.7 shows the Desktop options. (If you don't see the word *Desktop* at the top of the window on your screen, you need to close the Finder window.)

2. Make any changes in the window that you want to change the size, grid spacing, label position, and so on.

3. Close the window when finished.

Figure 4.7   *Notice how the settings affect the icons shown on the desktop.*

Customizing the Appearance of the Dock

Because the Dock is a key component in the operation of your Mac, it is important for you to customize it to your needs and preferences because you're going to be using it a lot. Like the new car on the showroom floor, it looks and runs just fine the way it is, but to get exactly what *you* want, you need to order a model with some additional options—maybe drop an option or two that the floor model has, select the wheels you like, maybe add the stealth-mode feature (Batmobile models only).

Positioning and Sizing the Dock

The Dock preferences window, shown in Figure 4.8, contains the options for setting the Dock's position and size. As you know, the Dock's default position is at the bottom of the screen, but you can change the position to the left or right side of the screen. Because the screen is wider than it is tall, leaving the Dock at the bottom of the screen gives you more space to use if you intend to load the Dock up with tons of icons. On the other hand, an application window could make better use of the space at the bottom of the screen if the Dock occupied a position on the side. For example, you could make a document window taller so you can see more of the document on the screen if the Dock were not in the way at the bottom.

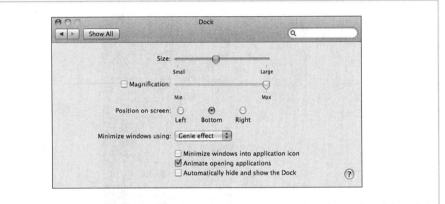

Figure 4.8   *To open this window, click the System Preferences icon in the Dock and then click Dock.*

Another approach to reclaiming space at the bottom of the screen is hiding the Dock in the Batcave with the Batmobile. This is not one of my favorite features, but you might like it. The Dock hides when not in use and reappears when you need it.

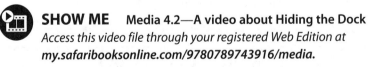

SHOW ME   **Media 4.2—A video about Hiding the Dock**
Access this video file through your registered Web Edition at my.safaribooksonline.com/9780789743916/media.

In the Dock preferences window, you can change the size of the Dock. Using a slider that goes from Small to Large, you can make the icons in the Dock smaller or larger, thus making the total size of the Dock smaller or larger, but, ultimately, the number of icons you have in the Dock determines how large the icons can get.

Try this shortcut for sizing the Dock: Point to the separator. The pointer changes to a two-headed arrow. Hold the Command key down as you drag the separator left or right.

If you have so many icons in the Dock that the icons are not very large, you can compensate for this with magnification. As you run the pointer over the icons in the Dock, the icons closest to the pointer are magnified.

To set the magnification, click Magnification in the Dock preferences window and then use the slider to set the size of the magnification. You can test the feature while the Dock preferences window is still open.

Animating the Dock

Notice the option in Figure 4.8 for Animate Opening Applications. If you select this option, application icons bounce up and down while the application is opening. Serious-minded users might think this option is just plain silly, but it does have a utilitarian side. If a program that is running in the background, possibly hidden under other windows, has a problem or needs input from you, its icon bounces up and down to get your attention.

Working with Stacks

Three icons on the right side of the Dock separator are special icons called *stacks*. These icons can have two different appearances. They can look like a folder, as the Applications stack and the Documents stack do, or they can look like a stack, as the Downloads stack does (see Figure 4.9). When the icon looks like a stack, it displays a preview icon for each item in the folder, but the icons are stacked on top of each other like a deck of cards, so only the top icon shows. If the items in the folder change, a new icon may come to the top of the stack and the icon for the stack would change to the preview of the new item.

Figure 4.9   *The Applications stack and the Documents stack have the appearance of a folder, whereas the Downloads stack has the appearance of a stack.*

I personally prefer all the stack icons to look like folders. To select the icon appearance you want to use, Ctrl-click or right-click the icon to display the menu shown in Figure 4.10. Then click either Folder or Stack, as you prefer.

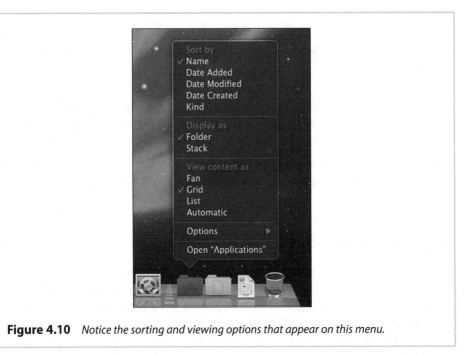

Figure 4.10   *Notice the sorting and viewing options that appear on this menu.*

Notice the four options under View Content As. If you select Fan, the content spreads out in an arc. If the folder contains too many items to display in the arc, the item at the top of the arc is a link that opens the folder in the Finder window. If you select Grid, all the items in the folder display in a pop-up window. The last icon in the pop-up window is a link that opens the folder in the Finder window. If you select List, the items display as a list. And finally, if you select Automatic, which is the default option, Mac OS X decides whether to show a fan or a grid, based on the number of files in the folder.

Working with Icons in the Dock

I'm sure the selection of icons in the Dock has been scientifically determined by extensive research on the icons that are the most popular with Mac users, but I like to think of the default configuration of the Dock like my husband thinks of the speed limit—it's just a suggestion.

Fortunately, Mac OS X sees it my way. Within certain limits, you can modify the icons that appear on the Dock and locate them to suit your needs.

Deleting Icons in the Dock

Deleting icons that you don't think you'll use is the first change you should make to the Dock. Then you'll know how much space you have for the icons you want to add.

To delete an icon in the Dock, drag the icon off the Dock. It's that simple. You'll see a little puff of smoke and hear a "poof" as the icon goes to meet its maker.

It's so easy to delete an icon from the Dock that sooner or later you're going to delete one by accident. You might not even notice which icon you deleted, but you'll hear that little "poof" and see the puff of smoke, and you'll know what you've done. Oh, no! Is there an undo? No. Have you deleted something that is going to cause untold pain and misery? No. Can you find out which one you deleted? No. Eventually, though, you'll figure it out. You'll start to click the iCal icon, and it won't be there. Then all you have to do is add it back to the Dock.

Adding Application Icons

As you know, all icons on the left side of the Dock represent applications. The key word in that last sentence is *represent*. The icons in the Dock are not the applications themselves; they are just links to them. That's why you do no great harm if you accidentally delete one.

To add an application icon to the Dock (like the one you accidentally deleted), find the application file and drag its icon to the Dock. So how do you find an application file? Use one of these two methods:

- In the Finder menu bar, click Go, Applications.

- Click the Finder icon in the Dock to open the Finder window and then click the Applications folder in the sidebar.

If you leave the Application stack on the Dock, you can use it to display the application icon you want to drag to the Dock.

When you drag an icon to the Dock, be careful to drag it between two icons and don't let go until the icons that are in the way move aside. If the icon you are trying to drag to the Dock just won't go in it, it could be that you are trying to put the wrong kind of icon on the wrong side of the separator. It's impossible to add any type of icon to the left side of the Dock except an application icon. It's also impossible to add an application icon to the right side of the Dock.

Adding Folder and File Icons

You can add a folder to the right side of the Dock separator by dragging the folder to the desired location. The best way to find the folder you want to add may be to open the Finder, although you could have a folder on the desktop that you just drag to the Dock. Remember that dragging a folder to the Dock creates a stack.

After dragging the folder to the Dock, you may want to customize the icon as described earlier in this chapter.

In addition to folders, you can drag icons for your frequently used files to the right side of the Dock. Clicking the icon for a file opens the file.

Moving Icons

After you get all the icons you want on the Dock, you can move them around by dragging them so that they are in some sequence that is logical to you. Note that you cannot move the Finder icon or the Trash icon, and, of course, you cannot drag icons across the separator.

Customizing the Finder

In this chapter, I'm not going to cover all the Finder preferences because most of them relate more to the topic of manipulating files and folders, which I discuss in Chapter 6. In this chapter, we will look at just a few simple customizations for the Finder.

Customizing the Finder Toolbar

By default, the Finder toolbar has eight buttons plus the Spotlight field. You can add, delete, and rearrange the buttons in the toolbar to suit yourself.

 **LET ME TRY IT**

Modifying the Toolbar

To me the most valuable modification you can make to the toolbar is to add three more buttons—specifically the Delete button, the New Folder button, and the Burn button. Although you can also remove buttons from the toolbar, I think you'll find you need all the buttons that are there by default. Follow these steps to modify the toolbar:

1. Click the Finder icon in the Dock to open the Finder window.

2. Click View in the menu bar and click Customize Toolbar. The dialog box shown in Figure 4.11 opens.

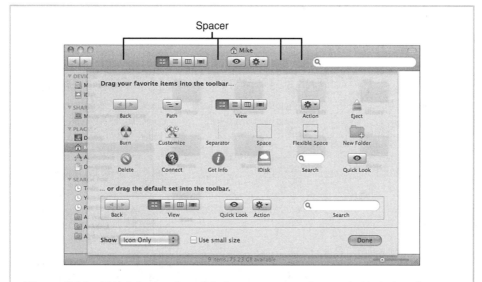

Spacer

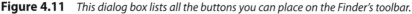

Figure 4.11   *This dialog box lists all the buttons you can place on the Finder's toolbar.*

3. I recommend you drag the spacers (the blank boxes) off the toolbar first. Then drag any new items you want to add into the toolbar.

4. Drag a Space or Separator into the toolbar anywhere you want to separate buttons.

5. In the Show pop-up menu, I recommend you select Icon and Text.

6. If you need to start over at any time, drag the default set into the toolbar.

7. When you are finished, click Done.

Customizing the Menu Bar

If you are designing a graphic masterpiece on your desktop, there is yet another modification that you can make for purely aesthetic reasons. You can change the appearance of the menu bar. The default setting for the menu bar makes it translucent. To remove the translucent setting and make the menu bar solid, open the System Preferences window and click Desktop & Screen Saver. Then click Desktop, if necessary. Deselect Translucent Menu Bar, if you want, and close the window.

A more substantive type of modification to the menu bar is the addition or deletion of Menu Extras on the right side of the menu bar. Table 4.1 describes some of the useful menulets you can add to the menu bar and tells you how to add them.

Table 4.1 How to Add Useful Menulets

Menulet	Description	How to Add
AirPort	Lets you turn your wireless card on or off	Open System Preferences and click Network. Select AirPort in the left pane. Select Show AirPort Status in Menu Bar.
Battery (laptops only)	Shows you how much power is still available in your laptop battery	Open System Preferences and click Energy Saver. Click the Battery tab. Select Show Battery Status in the Menu Bar.
Bluetooth	Connects to Bluetooth devices	Open System Preferences and click Bluetooth. Select Show Bluetooth Status in Menu Bar.
Clock	Displays the time (and date, if specified)	Open System Preferences and click Date & Time. Click the Clock tab. Select Show Date and Time in Menu Bar.
iChat	Displays a menu with options for Status (Offline, Available, Surfing the Web, and so on), Current iTunes, and Show Buddy List.	Open iChat. Click iChat in the menu bar and select Preferences. Click the General tab if necessary. Select Show Status in Menu Bar.
TimeMachine	Displays the status of a backup in progress	Open System Preferences and click TimeMachine. Select Show Time Machine Status in the Menu Bar.
Volume	Allows you to turn the volume up or down using a slider	Open System Preferences and click Sound. Click the Sound Effects tab. Select Show Volume in Menu Bar.

One other very useful menulet you can add to the Menu Extras is the Eject button. The steps to add this to the menu bar are a little more complicated.

 SHOW ME   **Media 4.3—A video abou Adding the Eject Button to Menu Extras**
Access this video file through your registered Web Edition at
my.safaribooksonline.com/9780789743916/media.

Of course, to remove a menulet from the menu bar, you can repeat your steps and uncheck the option to show the menulet. A quicker way is to press the Command key while you drag the icon off the menu bar.

Setting Date & Time Preferences

Mac OS X provides date and time preferences to reflect your culture and the area of the world where you live. For example, you can set a date preference to use the Japanese calendar or select a date/time format that Canadians use. Mac OS X determines what defaults to set for your date and time preferences based on information you supply when you initialize your computer, described in Chapter 1, "Setting Up Snow Leopard."

Setting the Mac's Date, Time, and Time Zone

It is important to have the correct date, time, and time zone set on your computer because the computer uses this information to time stamp files and email. By default, if you live in the U.S., your computer keeps the correct time, even the switch to and from daylight savings time, by continually communicating with time.apple.com.

 **LET ME TRY IT**

Setting the Date, Time, and Time Zone Preferences

If some rare circumstance causes your date and time to be incorrect, you can set the date and time manually. To set the date, time, and time zone, follow these steps:

1. Click the System Preferences icon in the Dock and then click Date & Time.

2. If necessary, click Date & Time.

3. Click the padlock, type your password, and click OK to open the padlock, as shown in Figure 4.12.

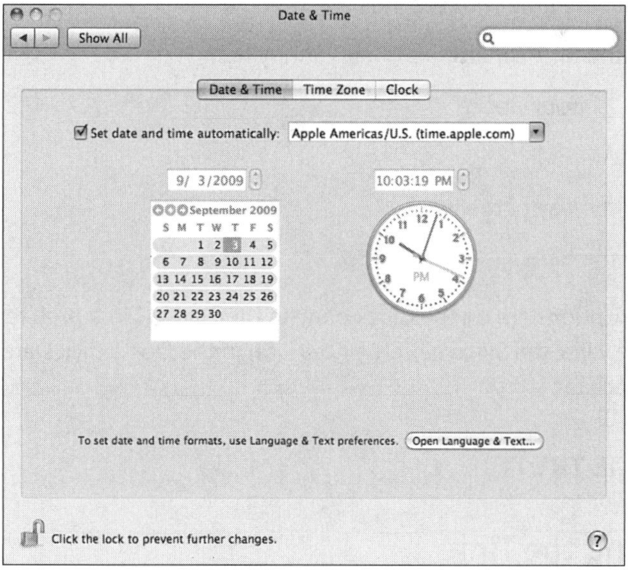

Figure 4.12 *Notice that the Date & Time pane has a link to the Language & Text preferences, where you can set date and time formats in the Format pane.*

4. Deselect Set Date and Time Automatically.

5. Type the correct date or click the correct date in the calendar.

6. Type the correct time or drag the hands of the clock to the correct time.

7. Click Save.

8. Click the Time Zone tab to display the pane.

9. Click the map where your city is located. A red dot in the time zone marks the closest city to you.

10. Select your city or the closest city to your location from the Closest City pop-up menu.

11. Close the Date & Time window.

Customizing the Clock

By default, Mac OS X displays the time on the right side of the menu bar. If you like an uncluttered menu bar, or you just don't like watching the clock, you can hide the time. If you like seeing the time in the menu bar, you can customize it to the nth degree. You can do any of the following:

- Display the clock as digital or analog.
- Display the time with seconds.
- Flash the time separators. (That's annoying!)
- Use a 24-hour clock.
- Show AM/PM.
- Show the day of the week.
- Show the date.

All of these options are on the Clock pane in the Date & Time preferences window. To get there, click the System Preferences icon in the Dock, click Date & Time, and click the Clock tab.

 **LET ME TRY IT**

Announcing the Time

If you are the type who lets the time get away from you, even if it is displayed on the screen, you might try letting the computer nag you by announcing the time every half hour or so. Here's how to set that up:

1. Open the Clock pane of the Date & Time preferences window, as described previously.

2. Click Announce the Time.

3. Select a frequency from the pop-up menu.

4. Click Customize Voice to display the options shown in Figure 4.13.

5. Select a voice from the pop-up menu and then click Play to see if you like it. You can adjust the rate and volume while the voice is playing.

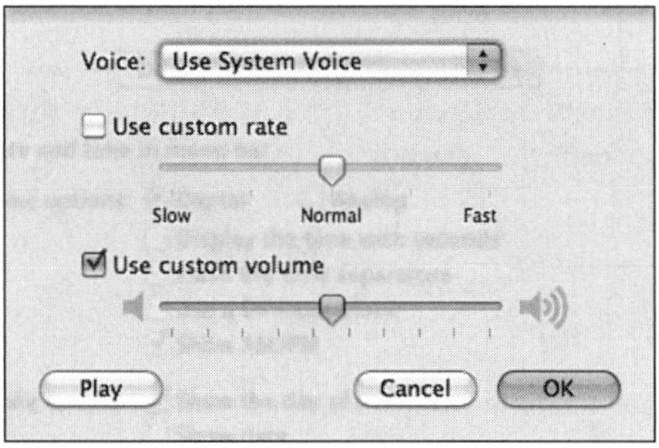

Figure 4.13   *The default voice is the system voice.*

This may take a while because you'll have to try all the male voices and then all the female voices. Then you'll have to click Show More Voices and try all the novelty voices, such as Deranged and Hysterical. To save you some time, I'll tell you that my favorites are Alex and Victoria.

6. When you are finished, click OK and then close the window.

Setting the Date and Time Formats

To select formats for dates and times, click the System Preferences icon in the Dock and click Language & Text. Click the Formats tab, if necessary, to display the pane shown in Figure 4.14.

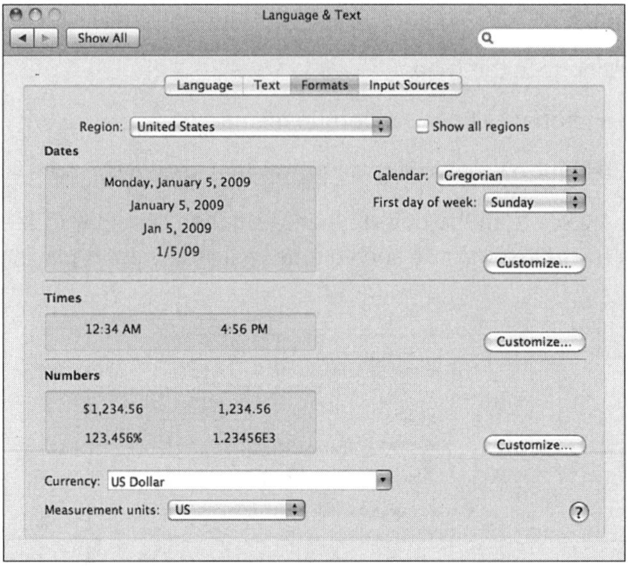

Figure 4.14   *U. S. date and time formats display because United States is selected for Region.*

To change the formats to that of another region in the world, select a region from the Region pop-up menu. To change the calendar in use, select a calendar from the Calendar pop-up menu. To customize a date format or a time format, click the associated Customize button. You can drag the elements of the date or time to rearrange them, drag the default elements out of the format, and drag new elements into the format.

One place where changes you make in date and time formats show up is in the Finder. Additionally, any programs that can complete a date or time for you as you type will use the formats you have selected for the date and time.

Using a Screen Saver

The original purpose of screen savers was to prevent the burning of an image on the screen during periods of inactivity. This is no longer an issue for Macs, and it hasn't been for quite a few years; but screen savers live on—they have just become part of the computer culture.

Essentially, screen savers are harmless and entertaining, but they fall under criticism by some because they use more energy than simply putting the computer in sleep mode. This is true, but I have calculated that if all Mac users worldwide stopped using screen savers for a year, we would save only enough electricity for me to go from here to the mall in a Chevy Volt. Unfortunately, we would not save enough energy for me to get back home, so I would have to stay at the mall all day (shopping) while the Volt recharges its battery. In other words, if you want to use a screen saver, go ahead. If you still feel guilty, turn off your printer when you're not using it.

 **LET ME TRY IT**

Turning On the Screen Saver

Mac has some cool screen savers. You can preview as many screen savers as you want before you select one. Follow these steps to select and use a screen saver:

1. Click the System Preferences icon in the Dock and click Desktop & Screen Saver.

2. Click the Screen Saver tab, if necessary, to display the pane shown in Figure 4.15.

3. Select a screen saver in the Screen Savers list and watch the preview. (Screen savers in the Pictures category have additional options.)

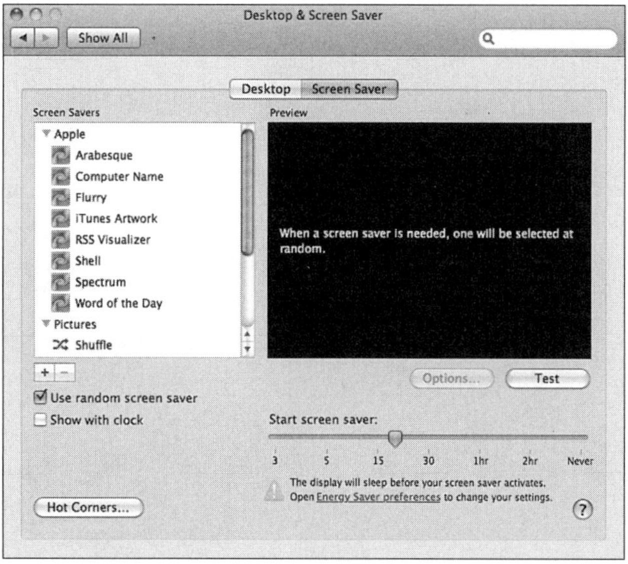

Figure 4.15   *You can view the screen saver in the Preview box or click Test to see it full screen.*

4. Click Show with Clock if you want to display the time. (The time doesn't show up in the preview, so click Test to see it on the screen. Press any key or move the mouse to return to the window.)

5. Select a starting point for the screen saver on the Start Screen Saver slider.

6. Close the window.

My favorite screen saver is the mosaic effect with the iPhoto library. It's truly amazing, but I can't use this one because I would never get any work done. To use this screensaver, you must have at least 100 photographs.

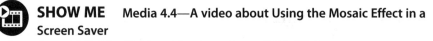

SHOW ME   Media 4.4—A video about Using the Mosaic Effect in a Screen Saver

Access this video file through your registered Web Edition at
my.safaribooksonline.com/9780789743916/media.

If I could assign homework, I would make this chapter
required reading so you would know in advance all
the sources you can turn to for help with a Mac.

5

Making Use of Support Resources

If you are new to Snow Leopard, you are going to have many questions along the way, but you have lots of resources for getting help, not the least of which is all the information I have uploaded to the Que Publishing website for you (http://www.quepublishing.com). Unfortunately, where and how to get help is like so many other things to a new user—it's not all that obvious. This chapter may be the most extensive coverage of the topic that you will see in any book, and I have placed it prominently at the beginning of the book so that you can be well informed early on about how to get the help you need as soon as you need it. If you take the time to learn to use the different Help resources, you'll be a more informed and self-sufficient user. You'll also remember something better, if you've sweated over it a little to learn it.

Using Help on the Mac

Mac OS X provides two kinds of help for you: the Help menu in an application's menu bar and the Help button found in system and application preferences windows. The Help menu is easy to find; it's always the last menu on the menu bar. If help is available in a preference window, you access it with the Help button, shown in Figure 5.1.

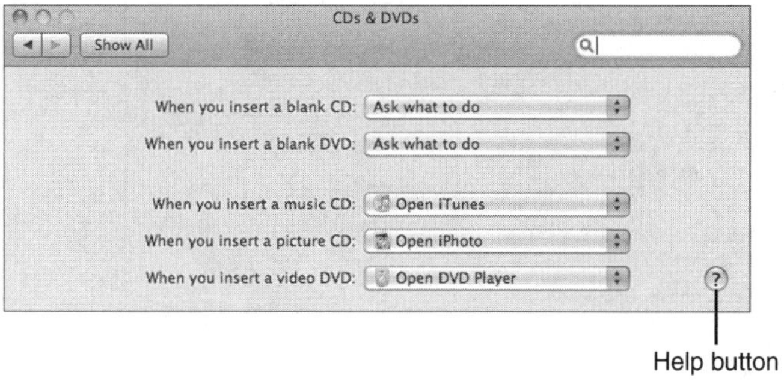

Help button

Figure 5.1 *The Help button is usually located in the bottom-right corner of the window.*

Figure 5.2 shows the menu for Help in the Finder application. As you can see, you have two choices—you can either type something in the Spotlight text box or click the name of the help file, which in this case is "Mac Help."

Figure 5.2   *Mac Help is the name of the Help file in the Finder.*

The name of the Help menu option changes to reflect the application you are in.

Navigating the Help Files

If you just want to learn something about an application, you can click Help and then click the name of the help file to go to the introductory page and start following the links that interest you. Figure 5.3 shows the introductory page for Finder Help in the Help window.

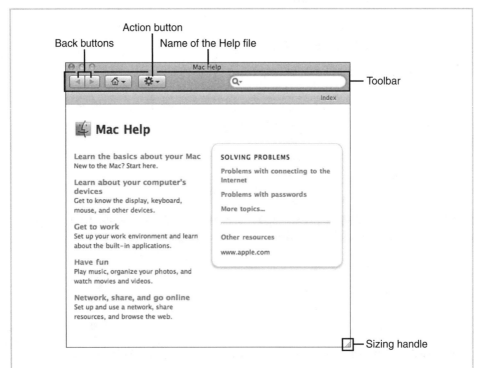

Figure 5.3   *The Help window has a title bar, a toolbar, Close, Minimize, and Zoom buttons, and a sizing handle.*

If you have a specific question, it is more efficient to type search text in the Spotlight. Figure 5.4 shows the Finder's Help menu with the results of a search for the words *get info*.

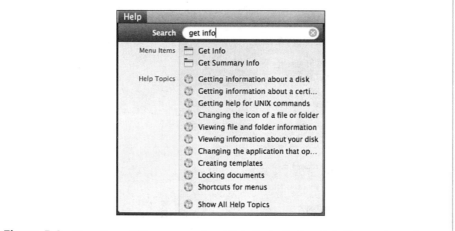

Figure 5.4 *Menu Items (if there are any) and Help Topics that contain the search word or phrase display on the Help menu.*

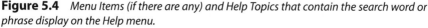

To clear the current search, click the X button on the right side of the Spotlight.

Notice that Spotlight displays two categories of results: Menu Items and Help Topics. Items listed under Menu Items are commands that are located somewhere on the current application's menus. Items listed under Help Topics are links to specific Help articles. Sometimes it takes a few seconds for the links to Help articles to appear in the menu, so if you see only Menu Items, be patient. Help Topics will display shortly. Not all possible topics display, however. If you don't see anything that looks helpful, click Show All Help Topics, the last item in the list, to open the window shown in Figure 5.5. A list of all topics, including topics that are on Apple's website (if any), display in the Help window.

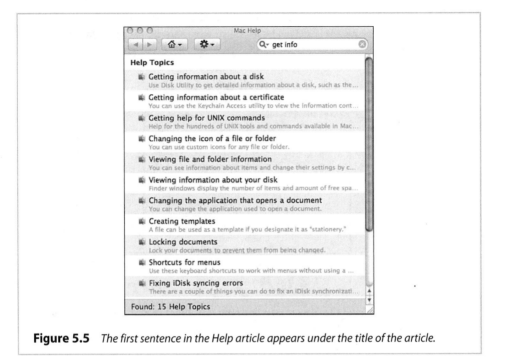

Figure 5.5 *The first sentence in the Help article appears under the title of the article.*

If you point to a Menu Item, the menu that contains the command opens and a floating blue arrow calls your attention to the command, as shown in Figure 5.6. At this point, you can click the command to execute it. If you click an item listed under Help Topics, the Help menu closes and the article opens in the Mac Help window. If you click an item listed under Support Articles, Help accesses the Apple website to display the article if you are connected to the Internet.

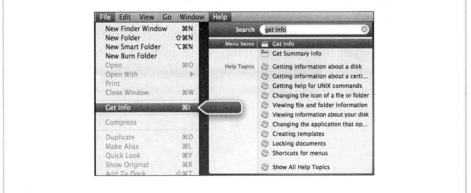

Figure 5.6 *Help opens the menu that contains the command.*

To go to a different item under Help Topics, just click Help in the menu bar to display it again and click the new item. All your search results remain in the Help menu as long as the current application is still open.

In a lengthy Help article, you can quickly search for a word or phrase without having to read the entire article. This helps you find out whether or not the article has the information you need.

 SHOW ME   Media 5.1—A video about Searching for Text in a Help Article

Access this video file through your registered Web Edition at
my.safaribooksonline.com/9780789743916/media.

Any blue text that you see in a Help article is a link to another Help article. At the bottom of most Help articles is a list of links to related topics. As you begin to follow links in the Help file, you can use the Back and Forward buttons in the toolbar (refer to Figure 5.3) to navigate back and forward again to articles you have already viewed. You also can go to the first page of the Help file any time by clicking the Home link just under the toolbar on the left.

Sizing the Help Window

If you are using Help to solve a problem in an application you are working in, you'll want to see the application window and the Help window at the same time. The Help window insists on being the top window, and there's nothing you can do to change that, so the best thing to do is to make the Help window tall and narrow so that you can see as much of the application window as possible. To resize the Help window, drag the bottom right corner.

Using the Index

The Index link, located on the same bar as the Home link, takes you to a page like the one shown in Figure 5.7. Use the letters across the top of the index to navigate. For example, to look up *password*, click the *P* at the top of the window. Then, to go to the specific Help article, click the index entry that looks most promising. If the one you select doesn't answer your question, click the Back button in the toolbar to go back to the P section of the index and try again.

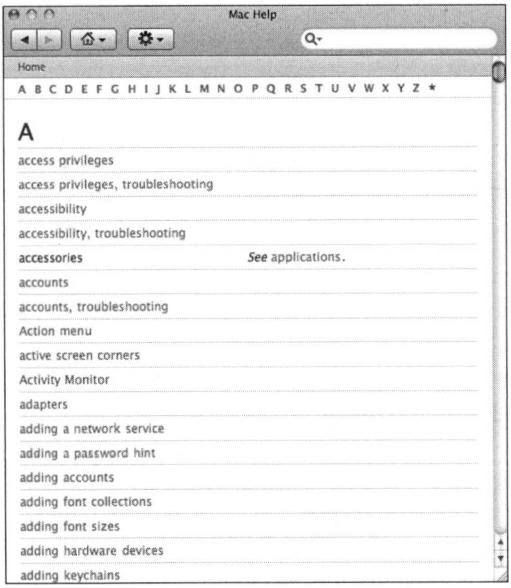

Figure 5.7   *Blue index entries are links to Help articles. Gray entries are cross-references.*

Using Apple's Online Support

The Help menus on the Mac are quite adequate, but not exhaustive. For more advanced questions and technical problems, you can use the Mac web browser, Safari, to go to the support section of Apple's website to access Apple's rich sources of information.

The amount of information at Apple.com, as my two-year-old grandson would say, is "humongous!" If you have trouble finding things, just scroll to the bottom of any page on the website and click the Site Map link. You can find things very easily on this page (see Figure 5.8).

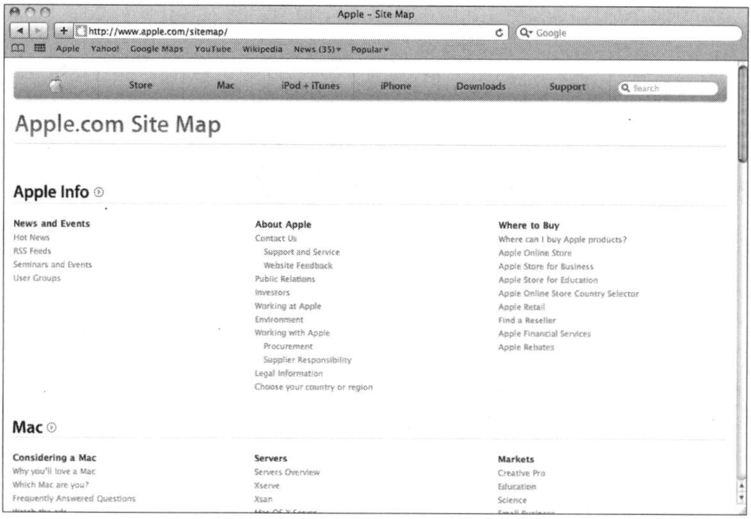

Figure 5.8   *The Site Map provides a concise, logical list of places you might want to go to on the Apple site.*

Going to the Apple Support Page

If you are using a new Mac and you've already been through the Safari Welcome, all you have to do to get to the Apple website is start Safari. By default, Safari goes to the Apple website as the Home page. To get to the support page, click the Support link. (The web address of the support page is http://www.apple.com/support.)

A general way get online help is to go to the support page that is dedicated to the individual product. On the main Apple support page, look for a pane titled *Browse Support*, as shown in Figure 5.9. Display the pop-up menu for All Products, scroll to the product you want, and click it. From this page, you can follow links to Downloads, Manuals, Tech Specs, and Tutorials.

> The pop-up product menu lists Snow Leopard as "Mac OS X v10.6 Snow Leopard."

Click here to reveal a link to Advanced Search.

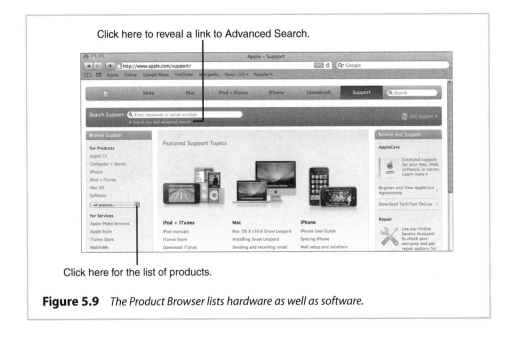

Click here for the list of products.

Figure 5.9   *The Product Browser lists hardware as well as software.*

Searching

On every support page, whether it's the main support page or a product's support page, you will find a Spotlight search box. You can type a word or phrase that contains key words in your question or problem and press Return to see a list of links to various forms of information. Some of the links go to Help articles, some go to excerpts from user manuals, some go to articles from the Knowledge Base, some go to discussion threads from forums, and so on.

If you initiate your search from the main support page instead of a product support page, when the results display, you may see a plus icon and the words "improve your search by selecting a product" under the Spotlight search box. This happens if your search is too broad. When you select the product, the search is performed again and this time the results returned are limited to the product you specified.

Each link included in the results displays a short excerpt from the information that helps you decide whether the information will be useful to you. To read the entire item, click the link. When you are finished, click Safari's Back button to return to the list of links.

Refining Search Techniques

Let's say that you want some information on emailing photos, so you type the search phrase *email photographs*. This particular phrase would return a tremendous number of links, most of which would not be helpful because Spotlight searches for all information that contains the word *email* and for all information that contains the word *photographs*. It also looks for synonyms such as *mail* and *pictures*.

Apple doesn't tell you how many links it has returned from the search.

You could improve your search by putting quotation marks around the phrase. This tells Spotlight to search for information that contains the two words (and synonyms) that appear together in the order you typed them. This is not the same as finding the *exact* phrase. If you use the search phrase *"email photographs"* in the Spotlight, the results can include *email selected photographs, email compressed photographs, mail that contains pictures*, and so on.

You also could improve your search by using the search phrase *email AND photographs*. "AND" is a Boolean operator that tells Spotlight to search for information that contains both words. Spotlight is not case sensitive; that is, you don't have to capitalize the words in a search, such as *Apple*, but you do have to type Boolean operators in uppercase.

 TELL ME MORE   Media 5.2—A discussion about Boolean Operators
Access this audio recording through your registered Web Edition at
my.safaribooksonline.com/9780789743916/media.

To get even better results, you could type the phrase *email AND photographs NOT iphone NOT ipod*. "NOT," another Boolean operator, tells Spotlight to ignore all information that contains the words *iphone* and *ipod* in this example. If you use the Boolean operator "OR" (as in, *email OR photographs*) Spotlight searches for all information that contains the word *email* and all information that contains the word *photograph*. If you remember, that's what Spotlight searches for if you simply type *email photographs*. So the OR operator, though not typed, is always assumed.

Using Advanced Search

Another way to refine a search is to use Advanced Search. To access this feature, click the link below the Search Support Spotlight box (refer to Figure 5.9) to reveal the Advanced Search link, as shown in Figure 5.10. Then click the Advanced Search link to display the search fields shown in Figure 5.11.

Figure 5.10   *Apple explains the search techniques it uses.*

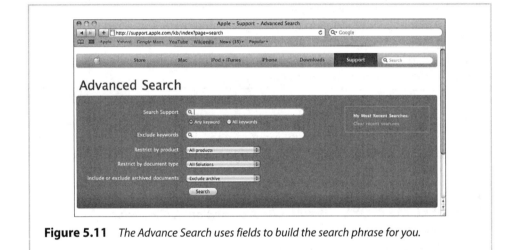

Figure 5.11   *The Advance Search uses fields to build the search phrase for you.*

Searching the Web for Help

Sometimes, instead of searching the Apple online support files, it's just easier to click in the Google Spotlight in Safari, type your question in plain English, and search the entire Web. To prove my point, I conducted a little experiment. I went to Apple's product support page for Mail and searched for *How can I make photograph attachments smaller*. (No question mark needed.) This is a common question that new users have. I could not find the answer in the first two pages of results. After checking 20 links, I stopped looking. Then, in the Google Spotlight in Safari, I typed *How can I make photograph attachments smaller in Mac mail*. Google returned about 99,000 results, but I only checked three links, and I found the answer half way down the first page.

To find many helpful Mac resources on the Web, try typing the search phrase *mac help forum* in the Google Spotlight.

Getting Help from Apple Discussion Forums

Apple hosts online discussion forums on a wide range of its products, including hardware and software. These forums are not questions posted by users that Apple's support engineers answer; they are discussions among Apple users who have varying levels of expertise.

In a discussion forum, you can perform a keyword search of the discussions, post a question of your own, or answer someone else's question. To get started in a discussion forum, launch Safari and go to http://www.discussions.apple.com.

You don't have to be a member of a forum to search and read postings freely, but if you want to reply to a post or post your own question, you must set up a user account and profile. To set up your account, you supply your Apple ID, type your Apple ID password, and give some information about yourself and your Mac computer(s). Your Apple ID then becomes your login to the forum. See Chapter 1, "Setting Up Snow Leopard" for information about Apple IDs.

Before you post a question in a forum, do a thorough search to see if your question has already been asked and answered.

Talking to an Apple Expert

If you have the AppleCare Protection Plan, you can call the Apple technical support number and speak to an Apple expert regarding any hardware or software question you have for a period of three years at no charge. If you didn't purchase the protection plan, you have 90 days of free telephone support from the date of your purchase. Telephone support is available seven days a week from the hours of 6:00 a.m. to 6:00 p.m. Pacific Time. After your warranty or AppleCare Protection Plan expires, there is a per-incident charge for using telephone support. At the time of this writing, the charge was $49.

Before placing the call, look up your operating system version number and your serial number. (See Chapter 1 for help with this if you need it.) The Apple Expert uses the serial number to access Apple's record for you and verify that you are a Mac owner.

Usually, when you call support, you have to hold for several minutes before an expert is available, so I like to make an appointment online for the expert to call me. Depending on the time of day and the current volume of calls, you may be able to schedule the callback immediately, or you may have to schedule it for a later time.

 SHOW ME   Media 5.3—A video about Scheduling a Callback from an Apple Expert
Access this video file through your registered Web Edition at
my.safaribooksonline.com/9780789743916/media.

Getting Help One to One

For $99, One to One might be the best money you spend on the Mac. If I were a new user on a budget, and I had to choose between buying One to One or the AppleCare Protection Plan, I would buy One to One.

If you could have a year of face-to-face support with One to One, that would surely be enough time to get all your questions and problems answered. Your hardware would be under warranty during that first year, too. After a year, you probably would be knowledgeable enough to find answers to any problems you had then by going online. For hardware problems, there is never a charge to get a diagnosis from the Genius Bar, and the cost of many repairs will be less than the cost of the AppleCare Protection Plan.

As a One to One member you are entitled to the following:

- Setup of your new Mac
- Transfer of your old files to your new Mac
- Installation of all new Apple software
- Exclusive One to One group workshops
- One-hour personal training sessions with an Apple trainer
- Three-hour sessions with an Apple trainer to help you with your own personal projects
- A personalized One to One web page where you can access hundreds of tutorials

One to One service is available only at the time of purchase of a new Mac, so if you missed it, it's too late to get it. Sorry.

Visiting the Genius Bar

The Genius Bar, located in the Apple Store, services Macs, iPods, Apple TVs, and iPhones. Although the purpose of the Genius Bar is generally analyzing and repairing your hardware, if your problem is a misbehaving application, the Genius who is waiting on you can fix that problem too. On Apple's website it says, "When you have questions or need hands-on technical support for your Mac…you can get friendly, expert advice at the Genius Bar in any Apple Retail Store." The Genius Bar also helps you with hardware issues that are not necessarily problems that need repair. For example, if you buy a new Mac and you need to transfer old files from a PC to the Mac, you can take your Mac and your PC into the Genius Bar and they will transfer the files for you.

You can't just drop in at your local Apple Store and walk up to the Genius Bar or even wait in line at the Genius Bar. You have to make an appointment online. Of course, you can drop in to your local Apple Store and make an appointment online right there. You might even luck out and get an appointment right away, but don't count on it.

 SHOW ME Media 5.4—A video about Making an Appointment at the Genius Bar
Access this video file through your registered Web Edition at
my.safaribooksonline.com/9780789743916/media.

When you arrive at the Apple Store with your computer and any related hardware that you think is part of the problem, you should look for the concierge (the person in the orange T-shirt). The concierge will tell you where to wait and point out the onscreen waiting list so you know where you are in the queue. If there's space at the counter, you can have a seat and wait for your name to be called.

When it's time for your appointment, your Genius will call your name. During your appointment, you can talk to the Genius about your problem and demonstrate what is happening. The Genius will assess the problem and fix it if possible. If a repair is needed, the Genius will check your equipment in and the repair technicians at the store will make the repair as quickly as possible. When your computer is repaired, you just pick it up at the store.

Before going to the Apple Store for your appointment, back up your data. Apple is not responsible for lost data.

Getting Free Training

Sometimes you need more help than just having a question answered—you actually need some training. Apple offers online training that you can take at your convenience as well as in-store workshops with a trainer.

Using Online Training

On its website, Apple offers many video and text tutorials on its applications and hardware. To access these tutorials, go to http://www.apple.com/findouthow/mac. Click the title of a video to watch it online, or click the title of a text tutorial to read it online. After you view a video or a text tutorial, a check mark appears in front of its title so you know you have already watched it or read it.

Taking a Free Workshop

Apple offers many free in-store workshops on its applications and hardware. Some are demonstrations by a presenter, but others are hands-on. To see a list of the workshops scheduled at a store near you, find the nearest store at http://www.apple.com/buy and go to the store's web page. There you will find a list of workshops scheduled. Click the Reserve link next to the title of the workshop you would like to attend. Fill out the information form and you're on your way. You'll be notified immediately if space is available. If it is, Apple sends you a confirmation email. I took one of these workshops just to see what they are like. They are very informal, and you can ask lots of questions. After the presentation I attended, one of the attendees was able to get some one-on-one time with the presenter to ask questions pertaining to a project he was working on. So even if a workshop looks like it might be too elementary for you, it may afford you an opportunity for personalized help.

This chapter explains how to install and work with applications as well as how to find, copy, move, and delete files and folders.

6

Managing Applications and Files

Applications are the heart and soul of any computer. In this chapter, I concentrate on how to handle application windows on the desktop and how to handle the files that applications create. Think of this as an overview that will apply to all the applications I discuss individually in subsequent chapters.

Handling Open Applications

By default, when you launch an application, it opens in a window and its icon displays on the Dock with a glowing blue bubble under it. An application window never takes up the entire screen. Apple designed them this way to facilitate having multiple windows open at the same time. When you have multiple windows open, you need to know how to navigate between them, resize them, move them, and so on.

When you open an application that doesn't have its own icon on the Dock, a temporary icon for the application shows up on the left side of the Dock. The icon remains in the Dock until you close the application.

Resizing and Moving Windows

If you need to make a window larger or smaller, point to the sizing handle in the bottom-right corner and drag the window to the desired size. Another way to resize a window is to use the green Zoom button on the left side of a window's title bar. The Zoom button alternates between a larger and smaller size window. It works like this: You open a window and it opens to a particular size. You use the sizing handle to make the window larger. You click the Zoom button and the window goes back to the smaller size. You click the Zoom button again and the window goes back to the larger size. The opposite also works. You can make the window smaller than it was when it first opened and use the Zoom button to alternate between those two sizes.

To move a window to another location on the screen, point to the title bar and drag it. You actually can drag part of the window off the screen at the left or right edge or at the bottom of the screen. This can come in handy when you need as much space on the screen as you can get.

Minimizing Windows

When you want to remove an application window from the screen temporarily, you can minimize it by clicking the yellow Minimize button in the upper-left corner of the window. By default, minimizing a window sends a preview of the window down to an icon in the right side of the Dock.

> If you have folders on the right side of the Dock that use the stack icon, it is difficult to differentiate a stack from a minimized window. That's why I like to use folder icons for stacks. See Chapter 4, "Tailoring the Desktop to Your Liking."

An alternative to minimizing the window to the right side of the Dock is minimizing to the application icon on the left side of the Dock. To make this the default, click the System Preferences icon and click Dock. Click Minimize Windows into Application Icon. There are pros and cons to both methods.

 TELL ME MORE   Media 6.1—A discussion about Contrasting Two Methods for Minimizing Windows
Access this audio recording through your registered Web Edition at
my.safaribooksonline.com/9780789743916/media.

If you have multiple windows open within an application, click and hold the mouse button on the application's icon in the Dock to see all the windows as thumbnails. (This is actually one of the features of Exposé, which is discussed in more detail later in this chapter.)

Closing Windows

Another way to manage open windows is to close the ones you aren't currently using with the red Close button in the title bar. In most cases, closing an application's window does not close the application. It simply hides the window in the application's icon on the Dock. If you click the application's icon, the window opens again.

Be careful with this procedure. If the application uses document windows, closing the document window actually closes the file you are working on, even though it leaves the application open. For example, if you are editing a document in TextEdit, and you click the Close button, that file will close, but TextEdit remains open and creates a new, unsaved document. If you close that window, the window hides in the TextEdit icon on the Dock.

Don't worry. You can't lose your work by closing a document window by mistake. The application always asks if you want to save the document before it closes it.

Switching Between Windows on the Desktop

Instead of minimizing windows, if it is more conducive to what you are doing, then you can leave all your windows open on the desktop. For instance, you might have two windows side by side, with three other windows underneath. Of course, only one window at a time can be active.

To make switching to other windows easier, try to size and position the windows so that at least part of each window is visible. To make a different window active, click any visible part of the window. If there is no visible part of the window to click, then click the application's icon in the Dock to bring the window forward.

Using Expose

Expose is a handy feature to use when multiple windows are open. It makes it easy to find windows when your desktop is filled with overlapping and hidden windows. Using a single keystroke, either the default or one you assign, you can view all windows at once, view all windows of the current application as small thumbnails, or hide all windows to view the desktop. Table 6.1 lists the default keystrokes for each of these tasks.

Table 6.1 Expose Keystrokes

Task	Default Keystroke to Invoke/Cancel
View all open windows at once.	F9
View all windows of the current application as small thumbnails.	F10
Hide all windows to view the desktop.	F11

Figure 6.1 shows the result of pressing F9. When all the windows are displayed, you can go to the one you want by clicking it, or you can go back to the normal display by pressing F9 again.

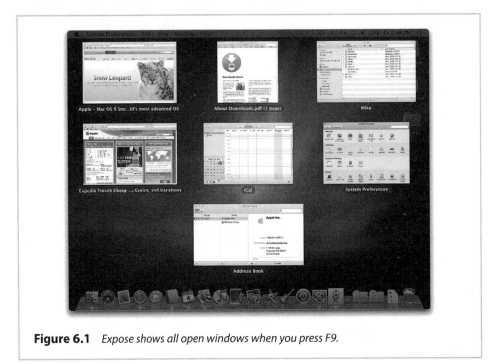

Figure 6.1 *Expose shows all open windows when you press F9.*

Using Spaces

The Spaces feature lets you organize windows into groups that you can display in four possible "spaces." Each space is like having a separate monitor attached to your computer. You can use Spaces to divide your work into different areas. For example, in one space you could trade stocks and use your spreadsheet application to track your trades; in another space you could use iPhoto and PhotoShop. By using different spaces, you also keep your desktop from getting cluttered. I recommend that you get used to working with multiple windows on one desktop before you try using Spaces.

SHOW ME Media 6.2—A video about Using Spaces
Access this video file through your registered Web Edition at
my.safaribooksonline.com/9780789743916/media.

Forcing an Application to Quit

It doesn't happen too often, but sometimes an application quits responding—that's computer-speak for *freezes up*. When this happens, the SBBOD (Spinning Beach Ball of Death) appears and keeps spinning indefinitely. It means that you have to force the application to quit.

Historically, Windows PC users were so used to programs freezing up, that they hardly thought anything of it. All PC users know the "three-fingered salute": Ctrl-Alt-Del. This keystroke used to reboot a PC immediately. Now it opens a dialog box that allows you to reboot or close a frozen program. For a Mac, the keystroke Cmd-Opt-Esc opens the Force Quit Applications window, as shown in Figure 6.2.

Figure 6.2 *When no applications are unresponsive, the Force Quit button becomes Relaunch.*

 **LET ME TRY IT**

Force Quitting a Frozen Application

If you have to force an application to quit, you may lose unsaved data! Some applications automatically back up your file while you are working, so you might not lose everything—just what you have done between the automatic save and the time the application freezes. To close an unresponsive application, follow these steps:

1. Press Cmd-Opt-Esc.

2. Select the unresponsive application in the window and click Force Quit. A dialog box opens asking, "Do you want to force *<application name>* to quit?"

3. Click Force Quit. A dialog box opens and you can either send a Report to Apple or just ignore the incident.

4. Click either button. If you click Report, a report will be sent to Apple, but you will never receive any feedback. The report simply serves to help Apple improve its applications.

5. Close the Force Quit window.

> Instead of using the shortcut keys (Cmd-Opt-Esc), you can click the Apple menu and click Force Quit. The trick is that you can't click the Apple menu while you are in the frozen program. You have to click into another application (such as Finder) and then click the Apple menu. It's really much easier to memorize Cmd-Opt-Esc. Alternatively, you can right-click the application icon in the Dock and click Force Quit.

Installing Applications

Naturally, I can't cover the exact steps for installing every application that exists for the Mac, but I can give you an overview that covers most of them.

Installing an application is usually a matter of dragging the new application icon to the Applications folder. The application that you want to install may have an installation or setup assistant that guides you through the process, but the end result is usually the same—copying one file into the Applications folder.

> The Applications folder is always the suggested folder for installing applications, but you can install applications anywhere in your Home folder, and they will run perfectly well. By installing an application in your Home folder, however, you make it inaccessible to others who log on to your computer. There is no reason to install an application anywhere but in the Applications folder, unless you are *trying* to deny other users access to the program.

Exploring the File Structure

Essential to working with applications is opening, creating, and saving files. Essential to opening, creating, and saving files is knowing where to put them or where to find them. This is why it is important to understand the file structure of your hard disk.

By default, the root of the hard drive has only five folders: Applications, Developer, Library, System, and Users. If you are not familiar with the term *root* as it applies to a drive, think of it as the primary level. A folder also has a root. Again, it is the primary level of the folder. Figure 6.3 shows part of the structure of the hard disk.

The Developer folder is in the root of the hard drive. The Developer folder has two folders in its root—Applications and Extras. The Extras folder has one folder in its root, and so on.

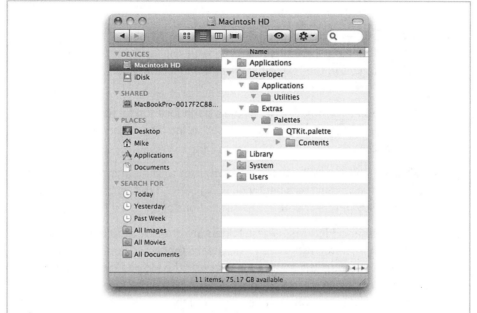

Figure 6.3 *Clicking the triangle beside the folder name reveals the folders in the root.*

As a user, you won't really be tromping around in the folders in the root of the hard drive. In fact, if you are a beginner, you should definitely not trespass in these folders unless you are guided by an Apple expert.

Two exceptions to the "no trespassing" rule exist, and Mac OS X gives you access to the two exceptions via Places in the sidebar. One exception is your Home folder, which is in the root of the Users folder, and the other exception is the Applications folder. By putting the Home folder on the sidebar, Mac OS X gives you access to it without making you open the Users folder where you could do some damage. The Applications folder contains all the default software on the Mac. You can open this folder and double-click anything in it to launch the application. If you recall, the Applications folder is also available to you on the Dock.

The Users folder contains the Home folders of all users who have user accounts set up on the Mac.

You will be using your Home folder constantly because it holds everything you do on the computer. It contains the following folders:

- **Desktop**—This folder holds all the files and folders found on your Desktop, the background of the screen.

- **Documents**—Apple designed this folder to be the default folder for storing most of your files. Therefore, when you issue the command to save a file you are creating (as in the TextEdit application), the default location suggested for the file is the Documents folder.

- **Downloads**—This folder is set as the default location for any files you download from the Internet. The default is set on the General pane in the Safari preferences window.

- **Library**—This is a folder that the system uses to store information about preferences that you set. As a beginner, you just need to stay out of this folder unless following the step-by-step instructions of a trusted Apple Expert.

- **Movies, Music, Pictures**—These folders are the default folders for iMovie, iTunes, and iPhoto, respectively. This means that when you save a file in the iMovie application, the application suggests the Movies folder as the location where the new file should be stored. You don't have to take the suggestion, of course, but in the long run, you may find that it has its benefits. For example, if you store photos in folders all over the place instead of in the Pictures folder, those pictures won't be readily available for use as a desktop background.

- **Public**—This folder can contain any files you want to share with people on your network or with other user accounts on your Mac. Anything you put in this folder can be accessed without a password, can be viewed or copied, but cannot be changed or deleted.

- **Sites**—Built into Mac OS X is the ability to make your Mac a web server. That's right. Your little Mac, sitting at home on your desk, can be the computer that makes your website available to the world. The Sites folder is the folder used to store the web pages you create for your website.

Every user on your Mac has the same set of folders in his Home folder. This is how Mac OS X keeps each user's work and preferences separate. Because the Applications folder is in the root of the hard disk, all users have access to it and can, therefore, run all programs unless restricted by Parental Controls.

Adapting the Finder to Your Use

Once you understand the file structure of your Mac, it's easier to understand what you see in the Finder. For example, knowing the file structure reveals that what you see in the right pane of the Finder is a hierarchical listing of the folders on the hard disk, whereas what you see in the Finder sidebar is *not* a hierarchical listing. It is, rather, a list of items provided for your convenience.

Customizing the Sidebar

The items you see in the sidebar are only a starting point—you have a great deal of control over what appears there. You can select from a list of default items for each category to determine whether you want them to be included in the sidebar. To select the default items you want to display, click Finder in the menu bar and then click Preferences. Click the Sidebar tab, if necessary. Check items you want to display and uncheck items you want to hide; then close the window.

Each item listed in the sidebar is not the *real* item, but an alias for the item. Normally aliases have a curved arrow added to their icons, but those in the sidebar do not.

In addition to showing or hiding the default items in the sidebar, you can add or delete your own files or folders at will. You also can change the order of items within the categories by simply dragging the items to new locations.

To add a file or folder to the sidebar, select the file or folder in the right pane of the Finder and drag it into the Places category in the sidebar, dropping it where you want it.

I recommend that you do *not* clutter the sidebar with files. For quick access, a better place to put a file (or an alias to a file) is on the desktop or on the right side of the Dock.

To delete an item from the sidebar, simply drag it off the bar. If you delete an item by mistake (say, your Home folder), don't panic. You haven't lost all your files. Remember the items in the sidebar are only aliases. If you delete a default item by mistake, just open the Sidebar tab of the Finder preferences window and put a check in the box for the item you deleted. If you delete an item that you placed on the sidebar yourself, simply find it in the Finder and drag it back again.

Setting the Default View

In Chapter 2, "Getting Comfortable with Snow Leopard," I explain the four views: Icon, List, Columns, and Cover Flow. The Finder remembers the last view you use, and that's the view it uses the next time you open it. You do have the option, however, of specifying a default view that the Finder always opens in, as well as a default view that a particular folder always opens in.

 **LET ME TRY IT**

Setting the Default Finder View

You may want to open the Finder in the same view every time if you use the Finder for the same thing most of the time. For example, if you typically use the Finder to locate files, you might want the Finder to open in the Columns view. Follow these steps to set the default view of the Finder:

1. Click the Finder icon in the Dock.

2. Click the view button in the toolbar for the view you want to make the default.

3. Click View in the menu bar and click Show View Options. The window shown in Figure 6.4 opens.

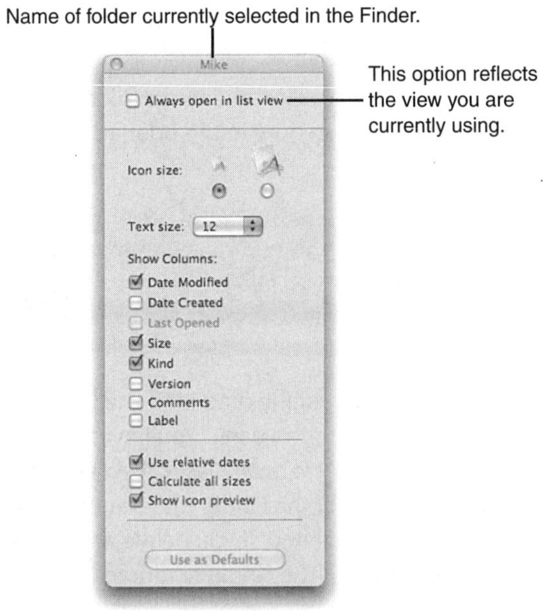

Name of folder currently selected in the Finder.

This option reflects the view you are currently using.

○   Mike

☐ Always open in list view

Icon size:

Text size: 12

Show Columns:
☑ Date Modified
☐ Date Created
☐ Last Opened
☑ Size
☑ Kind
☐ Version
☐ Comments
☐ Label

☑ Use relative dates
☐ Calculate all sizes
☑ Show icon preview

Use as Defaults

Figure 6.4 *Each type of view has different options specific to the view.*

4. Click Always Open in *<Name of View>* View.

At this point, you have set the view for only the selected folder.

5. Click Use as Defaults to make the view the default view for all folders.

6. Close the window.

Once you have set the default view, you can then set the view of individual folders if you want. For example, if you have the default view set on List, you might want to set the default view for the Pictures folder to Cover Flow. To set a default view for an individual folder, select the folder in the Finder and select the view. Open the View Options window (step 3 above), click Always Open in *<Name of View>* View, and close the window.

Each view has many options for customizing, but the subject is too lengthy to cover here. It's well worth knowing, though, so I have created a screencast that explains this feature, and I reveal a secret button you can use too.

 SHOW ME   Media 6.3—A video about Customizing Views in the Finder
Access this video file through your registered Web Edition at
my.safaribooksonline.com/9780789743916/media.

Creating Different Types of Folders

With the Finder, you can create three different types of folders: a regular folder (one that holds files as well as other folders), a Smart Folder (one that gathers files that meet specific search criteria and continually updates itself), and a Burn Folder (a folder that holds files you want to burn to a CD or DVD). In this chapter, I discuss creating regular folders and Smart Folders. See Chapter 18, "Making Your Own DVDs," for information on creating a Burn Folder.

Creating New Folders

If you look at the Finder's sidebar, you see a list of regular folders under the Places category. These include the Desktop folder, your home folder, Documents, Applications, Movies, Music, and Pictures.

When you think about it, Apple has provided all the major folders you need. Your only task is to create subfolders. Creating the folder is the simple part; figuring out which folders to create is more difficult. Before you begin creating all the folders you need, think about how you want to organize your work. In the Documents folder you store files such as word processing documents, spreadsheets, presentations, and PDFs. Rather than creating folders for the *type* of files you will be storing, it is usually better to create folders to store files (of any type) that relate to the same subject. Instead of creating folders named *Spreadsheets* and *Text*, for example, you might create folders named *Budget*, *Correspondence*, and *Miscellaneous*.

I highly recommend creating a folder called *Miscellaneous* (or *Misc*, if you prefer) in the Documents folder. When you save a file with a subject matter that doesn't relate to any of your existing folders, you can put it in the Miscellaneous folder instead of saving it in the root of the Documents folder. This keeps the Documents folder free of clutter, making it easier for you to find things at a glance. As the Miscellaneous folder gets more files in it, you will begin to see new groupings of subject matter emerge. Then you can create new folders and move the files into them.

I also recommend creating a folder named *Delete*. I store files in this folder that I know I am going to delete fairly soon.

The Movies folder is home to files created by iMovie. As you work with iMovie, it creates its own subfolders in the Movies folder; you don't need to create any other subfolders for the iMovie folders. If you store movies in the Movies folder that come from other sources, you may want to create some subfolders for these. I recommend using subject-content names for these subfolders, such as *My Dog*, *Family*, *Vacations*, and so on.

Now let's look at the Music folder. In this folder, it makes sense to have some folders that store files by application. In fact, when you start iTunes and GarageBand for the first time, Mac OS X creates subfolders for each of these applications. I don't recommend that you create subfolders in the iTunes folder. Any organization you want to bring to iTunes music you can affect within the application itself. In the GarageBand folder, you might want to create subfolders named for content, such as *Country*, *Jazz*, and so on, or for collections you are putting together for a CD.

The Pictures folder holds folders that iPhoto and PhotoBooth create. You can create your own subfolders for this folder and store photos in them, but there is little reason to do so when iPhoto manages your photos so much better.

 **LET ME TRY IT**

Creating a New Folder

After you have figured out a logical structure to contain all your files, you can start creating the folders you need. It's a good idea to create these folders and start storing your files in them before your files proliferate. To create a new folder, follow these steps:

1. Open the Finder and change the view to Columns.

> You can create a new folder in any view, but the Columns view is the most efficient because it displays the hierarchy so well.

2. Click the folder that should hold the new folder.

3. Click File in the menu bar and then click New Folder. A new folder appears in the column to the right with the name *untitled folder*. The name is selected and waiting for you to type a new name.

4. Type the name you want to give the folder and press Return. The folder moves to a new place in the list based on how the list is sorted.

> By default, folders and files are listed in alphabetical order by name, but they could be sorted by other criteria, such as Modified Date.

Creating Smart Folders

Did you know you've been staring Smart Folders in the face all along? All the items under Search For in the Finder sidebar are Smart Folders (Today, Yesterday, Past Week, All Images, and so on). This type of folder has a search criteria attached to it that it performs each time you open it. It can contain items from many different locations.

 SHOW ME Media 6.4—A video about Creating a Smart Folder
Access this video file through your registered Web Edition at
my.safaribooksonline.com/9780789743916/media.

Working with Files

To find, preview, rename, open, copy, move, or delete a file, the Finder is your one-stop-shopping location. Finder performs these functions on files and folders alike. In fact, to the computer, a folder is nothing more than a file. So in this section, when I talk about what you can do with a file, it also includes folders.

Finding Files

One way to find a file is to look for it with your own eyes—the "eyeball method." Let's say you know you created a file called *Budget.txt*, and you remember you saved it in the Documents subfolder named *Personal*. You can click the Documents folder in the Finder sidebar, click the triangle beside Personal in the right pane (if you are in the List view), and then just look for the file.

If you can't remember the name of the file, but you know you created it last month, you could sort the files in the folder by date and look for it that way. (In the List view, to sort by date, click the Date Modified column title.)

> To sort in any view, click the View menu and click Arrange By. Then click the criteria you want to sort by, such as Name or Date Modified.

Using Color Labels

Applying a colored label to a file is a good way to make the file stand out in a crowd when you are using the eyeball method. To apply a color label, select the file, click the Action button in the Finder's toolbar, and click the color you want.

If you apply different color labels to several files, you may benefit from sorting the files by color in the List view, but first, you have to display the Label column in the view. Click View in the menu bar and then click Show View Options. Click Label and then close the window. Once you add the column to the view, you can click the column heading to sort on that column.

Using Spotlight in the Finder

The eyeball method is fine to use if you really know where your files are, but what if you have no idea? Then it's time to use the Spotlight to search for the files. The Spotlight is the icon that looks like a magnifying glass, located on the right side of the Finder's toolbar. To find a file, type part of the name of the file if you know it, or type any words you know are in the file. Files that match your search criteria start appearing in the pane below while you type.

You can stack the deck a little to help Spotlight find files for you by adding Spotlight comments to a file's information. For example, as you create different files that relate to the same thing, you can add the same Spotlight comment to each so that you can search for that comment later.

SHOW ME Media 6.5—A video about Adding Spotlight Comments to Files
Access this video file through your registered Web Edition at
my.safaribooksonline.com/9780789743916/media.

Using Spotlight in the Menu Bar

The Spotlight button on the far right side of the menu bar is similar to the Spotlight in the Finder, but it is much more powerful. It reaches into the deepest crevices of the computer and finds everything that matches your search criteria. It lists the top 20 results in 14 different categories, including applications, System Preferences, documents, folders, mail messages, contacts, PDF files, web pages in your history, and so on. Figure 6.5 shows the search results for the word *Roman*.

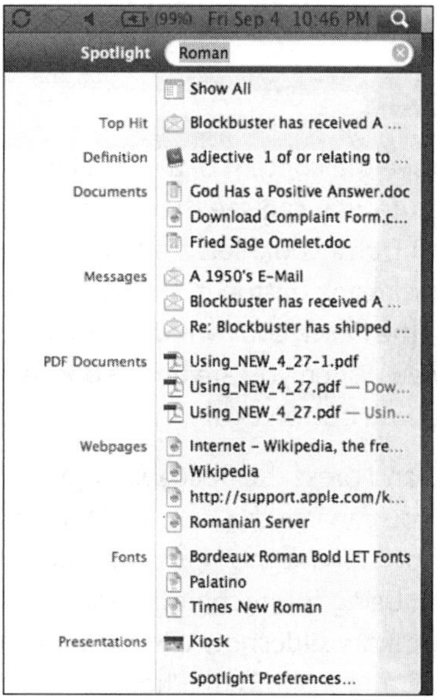

Figure 6.5 *Spotlight lists the result it thinks you are really looking for as the Top Hit.*

To see all the results, click Show All at the top, and a Finder window opens with all the results displayed. You can sort the items by Name, Kind, or Last Opened by clicking the corresponding column heading.

Using the power of the Spotlight, you can perform many otherwise lengthy procedures very quickly. For example, to find the address of a business associate who is listed in your Address Book application, just type the name of the street if you know it, or type the person's name in the Spotlight search box. Spotlight lists the Address Card entry, and you can click the entry to open it. To look up a word in the dictionary, type the word in the Spotlight search box and just point to the definition in the list to read it in a pop-up box.

There is so much to tell you about Spotlight that I could devote a complete chapter to it, but, unfortunately, we don't have the space available in this book. So I encourage you to find out as much as you can about Spotlight. To get started, watch the screencast I created for you.

 SHOW ME   Media 6.6—A video about Using Other Features of Spotlight
Access this video file through your registered Web Edition at
my.safaribooksonline.com/9780789743916/media.

Using Quick Look

Sometimes you have to see the content of a file to know if it's the one you want. With the Quick Look feature, you can see the content without actually opening the file. To preview a file with Quick Look, select the file in the folder and press the Spacebar or click the Quick Look button in the Finder toolbar (the button that looks like an eye). When the Quick Look window opens, click the Full Screen button to see a full screen preview. When you are finished viewing, press the Spacebar again or click the Quick Look button again.

If you select several files and press the Spacebar, the Quick Look preview window shows the first file, and you can use the Next and Previous buttons to navigate through all the files, or you can use the Play button to cycle through the files automatically (see Figure 6.6). Using this technique, you can select a group of photographs and create a temporary slideshow with Quick Look. Additionally, you can use the Camera button to add a photo to iPhoto or use the Index Sheet button to see all the files on a grid.

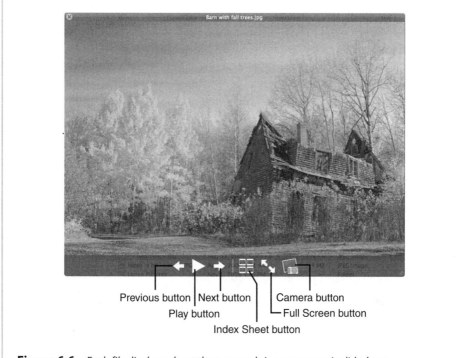

Previous button | Next button   Camera button
        Play button   └ Full Screen button
            Index Sheet button

Figure 6.6   *Each file displays about three seconds in an automatic slideshow.*

If you take a Quick Look at a folder, you just see a larger image of a folder icon, but you also see information that no other view gives you—the size of the folder. This information is critical, for example, if you need to know if the content will fit on a CD or DVD.

Opening and Closing Files

When you are working in an application (let's say TextEdit), you can open a file you have created with that application by using the menu command File, Open. The Finder opens, and you can navigate to the file and then double-click it to open it. If you don't have the application open yet, you can open the Finder, find the file, and double-click it to open it. This obviously opens the application at the same time.

Once a file is open in an application, if you make changes to it, you should save the file using the commands the application provides. If you make no changes to the file, you can simply close it again, using the commands the program provides.

Renaming Files and Folders

On many occasions, you may need to change the name of a file. Maybe you misspelled it, you need a more descriptive name, you need a shorter name, and so on. To rename a file, select it in the Finder and press Return. Then type the new name and press Return. Remember that a folder is simply a file, so the same steps apply to changing the name of a folder.

> **Caution**: Now that you know how to change a folder name, don't get the bright idea that you should change your Home folder name from harryhenderson to Harry, for example. It is a very grave mistake to rename your Home folder. Recovering from this error is not easy. Data could be and most likely will be lost. Just don't even go there.

In addition to the Home folder, you should not rename the following items:

- The system folders found on the hard drive
- Application files
- File extensions (the three letters after the period in the filename)

Renaming an application most likely will render it incapable of launching. Renaming it again with the correct name might fix the problem, but you may have to reinstall the application.

Opening Multiple Finder Windows

By default, the Finder keeps only one window open. This is a good setting because if Finder opened a new window every time you open a different folder, you'd soon have your desktop cluttered with Finder windows. There are times, however, when it is much more convenient to have two Finder windows open at the same time. This facilitates copying from one folder to another or moving a file to a new location.

To open a new Finder window when you need it, click File in the menu bar and then click New Finder Window.

> By default, the Finder always opens with your Home folder selected. If you want to specify another folder, click Finder in the menu bar and click Preferences. Next, select the folder you want from the pop-up menu for New Finder Windows Open and then close the window.

Copying Files

You probably know all the reasons you might want to copy a file, so let's get down to basics. No two files can have the same name if they reside in the same folder. If you copy and paste a file in the same folder, Mac OS X automatically appends "copy" to the end of the new filename (just before the extension). If you do it again, Mac OS X appends "copy 2" to the new filename, and so on. If you copy a file from one folder and paste it into a different folder, the copy retains the same name as the original.

 **LET ME TRY IT**

Copying Files Using Shortcut Keys

I like to use a keyboard shortcut to copy and paste files. This method has the added benefit of allowing you to copy the files once, but paste them multiple times. Here's what to do if you want to use shortcut keys to copy files:

1. Open the Finder and select the file (or multiple files) you want to copy.

2. Press Cmd-C to copy. This one is easy to remember because *C* stands for *copy*.

3. In the Finder, select the new location for the file.

4. Press Cmd-V to paste. I have always remembered this keystroke by thinking of the V as a pointed shovel that is going to plant the file in the new location.

5. Repeat steps 3 and 4 if you want to copy the same files to multiple locations.

If you have trouble remembering the keystrokes, you can always use the menu commands instead. They are Edit, Copy and Edit, Paste.

 SHOW ME Media 6.7—A video about Copying Files by Dragging
Access this video file through your registered Web Edition at
my.safaribooksonline.com/9780789743916/media.

 **LET ME TRY IT**

Copying Files by Dragging

Another way to copy files is by dragging, and here's where opening a new Finder window comes in handy. This is the way I like to proceed if I'm using the dragging method:

1. Open two Finder windows.

2. Set the view in one window to List and the other to Icon. The List view is easier to use to make your selections, and the Icon view gives you a bigger target for dropping the files.

3. In the List view window, select the file (or files) you want to copy.

4. Begin dragging the selection and then press the Opt key. A green circle with a plus in it displays to indicate that this is a copying procedure.

Step 4 is a little cumbersome on a trackpad, which is why I prefer the keyboard shortcut.

5. Drop the selection in the right pane of the Icon view window.

Moving Files

If you mistakenly put a file in the wrong folder, then, of course, you will want to move it, but that probably doesn't happen too often. The files I move more than any others are the files I download from the Internet. Remember that these files automatically go into the Downloads folder. For example, each month when I download my American Express bill, it goes into the Downloads folder, and then I move it to my Amex folder located in the Documents folder.

 SHOW ME   Media 6.8—A video about Moving Files by Dragging
Access this video file through your registered Web Edition at
my.safaribooksonline.com/9780789743916/media.

 **LET ME TRY IT**

Moving Files by Dragging

The steps for moving a file, or a group of files, are almost identical to the steps for copying files by dragging. Follow this procedure to move files:

1. Open two Finder windows.

2. Set the view in one window to List and the other to Icon. As I said before, the List view is easier to use to make your selections, and the Icon view gives you a bigger target for dropping the files.

3. In the List view window, select the file (or files) you want to copy.

4. Begin dragging the selection and then press the Cmd key. You get no visual cue for the Cmd key like you do when you press the Opt key to copy a file.

5. Drop the selection in the right pane of the Icon view window.

If it's difficult for you to remember that the Option key goes with the Copy command and the Command key goes with the Move command, just think of the federal employee who has been *co-opted* (Copy – Opt key) by the KGB and is *copying* secret documents. Or think of the fact that you are *commanding* (Cmd key) the files to *move*!

If you should happen to drag files from one place to another without pressing either the Opt key or the Cmd key, the files may be copied, or they may be moved, depending on the source and destination. If you drag *from* a location and *to* a location on the *same* disk, Mac OS X moves the files. If you drag *from* one disk *to* another disk, Mac OS X copies the files. It is easy to observe this if you have some file icons on your desktop as well as an icon for an external disk. When you drag a file icon to the disc icon, the green circle with the plus shows up, indicating that you are copying.

Moving Files to the Trash (Deleting)

The quickest and easiest way to move a file to the Trash is to select the file and press Cmd-Delete. Your other option is to drag the file to the Trash icon in the Dock. If you drag a file, be sure you see the word *Trash* before you drop the file. Otherwise, you will have successfully moved the file to the desktop instead of deleting it.

To see what's in the Trash, click the Trash icon. The Finder window opens displaying all the items in the Trash.

With the Finder window open to the Trash folder, you can perform the following tasks:

*   Put a previously deleted file back where it originally was by selecting the file, clicking File in the menu bar, and then clicking Put Back.

*   Empty the trash by clicking Finder in the menu bar and then clicking Empty Trash. (This command is always available even if the Trash window is not open.) When you empty the trash, the files are permanently deleted. You cannot retrieve them.

*   Open a file with Quick Look by selecting the file and pressing the Spacebar.

Getting Busy

7

This chapter focuses on the unique features of Safari that make web browsing more efficient and enjoyable.

Browsing the Web

The Internet has grown to such huge proportions that even its inventors could not come close to imagining its potential at its inception in 1969. All you need to tap into it is an Internet service provider (ISP). Mac supplies the modem and everything else you need for browsing the Web in its application called Safari.

I assume you already know a great deal about browsing the Web, so I don't want to waste time on the basics in this chapter. I'm not going to cover how to type a web address or what a hyperlink is. Instead, I want to tell you about some of the features in Safari that will turn you into more of a power user on the Web.

Opening Safari

The first time you open Safari, Mac OS X shows off its new Top Sites feature as discussed in Chapter 2, "Getting Comfortable with Snow Leopard." After that first time, the next time you open Safari, you go straight to the Apple website, and Top Sites are nowhere to be seen. What happened? As you have probably already guessed, you can trace Safari's behavior to its default preferences.

Setting Safari Preferences

To set Safari preferences, click Safari on the menu bar and then click Preferences. On the General pane of Safari's preference window, as shown in Figure 7.1, you can see that the New Window Opens With preference is Home Page. That's why you don't see Top Sites when you launch Safari. If you want to use Top Sites when you open Safari, change this preference to Top Sites. Top Sites *is* the default for New Tabs Open With, which means that if you use tabs for web browsing instead of windows, each new tab you open will open with Top Sites. I like Empty Page for this preference because I generally use a broadband wireless modem, and I don't like to wait for the Top Sites to load every single time I open a tab—not that they take that long, mind you. I'm just a nanosecond kind of girl.

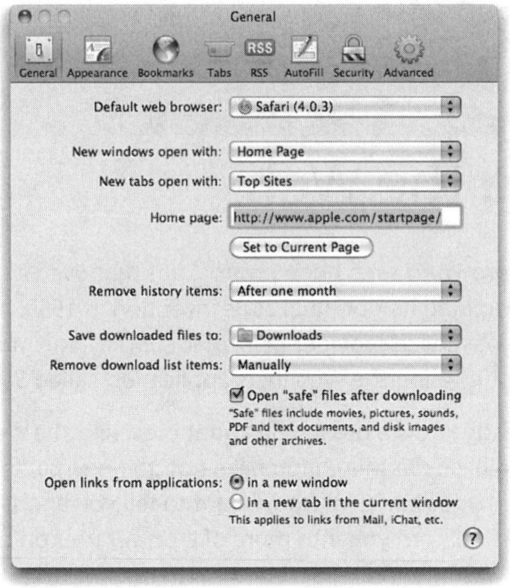

Figure 7.1   *Click Safari, Preferences, General to get to this pane.*

Now notice that the Home Page preference is set for the Apple website. Even if you don't set Safari to open to a home page, you should still change the Home Page preference to the address of a site that you frequent. Later in this chapter, I'm going to show you how to add a button to the toolbar that will take you immediately to the home page you specify here. If you know the address you want to use, you can type it in the text box now, or at some point, when you are on the website, you can come back to this window and click the Set to Current Page button.

One other important preference that Mac OS X turns on for you by default is the blocking of pop-up windows. This setting is located on the Safari menu.

I would describe all other preferences in Safari as "fine-tuned." You don't need to worry about them. If you're concerned about security, don't be. You can refer to Chapter 13, "Keeping Your Mac Safe, Updated, and Backed Up," if you are curious.

TELL ME MORE   **Media 7.1—A discussion about Setting Safari Preferences**
Access this audio recording through your registered Web Edition at
my.safaribooksonline.com/9780789743916/media.

Using Top Sites

Regardless of the preferences you have set for how a window or tab opens, you can toggle the use of Top Sites anytime with the Top Sites button in the Bookmarks bar. (It's the one with 12 little black rectangles on it.) When you have Top Sites turned on, you can go to one of the sites in the display by clicking its page. Notice that pointing to a site shows its web address at the bottom of the screen.

If new content has been added to a web page recently, its picture in Top Sites has a white star on a blue background in the upper-right corner of the page, as seen in Figure 7.2.

 SHOW ME   Media 7.2—A video about Customizing Top Sites
Access this video file through your registered Web Edition at
my.safaribooksonline.com/9780789743916/media.

 LET ME TRY IT

Customizing Top Sites

Remember that Snow Leopard provides you with default sites when you first start using Top Sites, but you can quickly make Top Sites exactly what you want. To customize Top Sites, follow these steps:

1. If necessary, click the Top Sites button to display Top Sites.

2. Click the Edit button at the bottom left of the screen.

3. Choose Small, Medium, or Large for the display.

4. Click the X button to eliminate a site.

5. Click the Pin button to keep a site from being replaced.

6. Rearrange the sites by dragging them to different locations.

7. When you are finished customizing, click the Done button.

Setting Parental Controls

If you have children of your own or supervise children, you undoubtedly have given them some guidelines you want them to follow concerning computer use.

Using the Parental Control feature, you can do the following:

- Allow unrestricted access to websites.

- Limit access to adult websites automatically and list additional websites you want to restrict.

- Restrict access to all sites except the ones you specify.

- Restrict the amount of time the computer is used (for any activities).

 SHOW ME   Media 7.3—A video about Setting Parental Controls for a User Account
Access this video file through your registered Web Edition at my.safaribooksonline.com/9780789743916/media.

 **LET ME TRY IT**

Setting Parental Controls for a User Account

If you have user accounts set up on your Mac for children, you can set parental controls to ensure your guidelines are being followed—at least on your computer. To set parental controls, follow these steps:

1. Click the System Preferences icon in the Dock and click Accounts.

2. Click the padlock icon to unlock it, type your password, and click OK.

3. Select the user account you want to restrict, click Enable Parental Controls, and then click Open Parental Controls.

4. Click each tab and set the options on each pane.

5. Click the padlock icon to lock it again and close the window.

Browsing in Tabs or Windows

By default, when you click a link to go to a new page, Safari opens that page in the current window. If you want to work in more than one window, you can click File in the menu bar and click New Window. Browsing in multiple windows allows you to compare websites side by side or open two windows to the same website so that you can follow different links.

If you want to work in one window with tabs for each new site you go to, you can click File in the menu bar and click New Tab each time you want to go to a new site. Working in a tabbed window is neat and efficient. You have only one window open, yet you know exactly what else is open because each tab displays a title identifying the site, as shown in Figure 7.2.

This star symbol indicates that new content has been added to the page.

Figure 7.2 *The more tabs you have open, the less you can see of the titles on the tabs.*

Cmd-T is an easy shortcut to remember for opening a new tab.

To close a Safari window, click the red Close button in the window. To close a tab, point to the tab to display the Close button and then click it.

Navigating the Web

When you boil things down, you have only two ways to get to a website. You can type a web address in the address bar, or you can click a link. If you type the address, you needn't type *http://www* in the web address. Just type the domain name, such as apple.com. If an address you don't want to do to already appears in the Address bar, triple-click to select it and type the new address. If you are clicking links to browse the Web, the links may be in a list of Google search results, in Top Sites, on the current page, in your Bookmarks, in your History, in a Contact or email message, or even in a document.

Anyone who has spent much time on the Internet at all knows how easy it is to start down one path and get off on a tangent that leads to another tangent, and so on. Safari provides a couple of methods to help you get back on course.

If you just want to retrace your steps within the current website, you can Cmd-click the title in the title bar to display a list of the pages you have viewed in the current site, as shown in Figure 7.3. To go back to one, just click it in the list. This works for windows and tabs within a window as well.

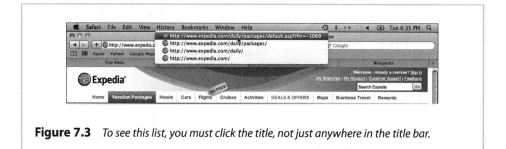

Figure 7.3 *To see this list, you must click the title, not just anywhere in the title bar.*

If you need to retrace your steps to other websites that you have visited in the current window or tab, you can go back one page at a time by clicking the Back button in the toolbar. An alternate method is to point to the Back button, hold down the mouse button to reveal a list of your last pages, and click one of those. The Back button's partner, the Forward button, reverses your direction again if you have been clicking the Back button. It also displays a list if you point to it and hold down the mouse button.

If you need a longer list of your clicking activities—everywhere you've been today, for example—you can open the History menu to access a complete list of links. In addition to the sites you've visited today, links to other dates also appear on the menu, as does the Show All History option.

Safari keeps web pages in your History list anywhere from one day to one year or until you remove them manually. You set this preference in the General pane of Safari's preferences window.

Working with Bookmarks

A bookmark is a link that you save so you can go back to a particular web page. Safari has a Bookmarks bar just below the toolbar that has bookmarks preloaded for you. You can add more bookmarks to this bar and remove any of the preloaded bookmarks you don't want.

Bookmarking a Web Page

When you go to a web page that you want to bookmark, click the Add Bookmark button (the button with the plus mark, to the left of the Address bar). Type a name for the bookmark and then click the pop-up button and select a location for the bookmark. Before you create any folders to organize your bookmarks, your choices for locations are Top Sites, the Bookmarks menu, and the Bookmarks bar, including the two default folders in the Bookmarks bar (News and Popular). After you pick a location, click Add.

Using a Bookmark

To go to a web page that you have bookmarked, you may use one of these four methods:

- If the bookmark is on the Bookmarks bar, click the bookmark. If you have too many bookmarks on the bar to display, you may have to click the double arrow at the right end of the Bookmarks bar to reveal the bookmark you want.

- If the bookmark is in a folder on the Bookmarks bar, click the pop-up button for the folder and then click the bookmark in the list.

- If the bookmark is on the Bookmarks menu, click Bookmarks and click the bookmark you want.

- If the bookmark is stored in a folder that you have created, click the Show All Bookmarks button in the Bookmarks bar to view the bookmarks list, as shown in Figure 7.4. Select the folder in the left pane and then double-click the bookmark in the right pane.

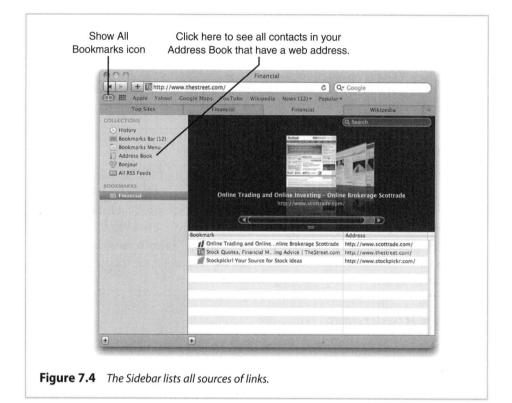

Figure 7.4 *The Sidebar lists all sources of links.*

Organizing Bookmarks

One logical way to organize bookmarks is to put them in folders. You might begin by saving your bookmarks in the News or Popular folders because they're the only ones available at first, but after a while, you'll need to create your own folders.

 SHOW ME   Media 7.4—A video about Creating a Bookmark Folder
Access this video file through your registered Web Edition at
my.safaribooksonline.com/9780789743916/media.

 LET ME TRY IT

Creating a Bookmark Folder

Think about the way you use the Internet and the sites you go to, and it will be very apparent to you what folders you need. For example, I have folders for Shopping, Investing, Novel Writing, Technical Writing, and so on. To create a new folder for bookmarks, follow these steps:

1. Click Bookmarks in the menu bar.

2. Click Add Bookmark Folder. The bookmarks list window opens, as shown previously in Figure 7.4. The new folder displays under the Bookmarks category in the left pane with its name (*untitled folder*) selected.

3. Type a name for the folder and press Return. The next time you want to add a bookmark, the name of your new folder will appear on the list of places where you can add the bookmark.

4. Close the bookmarks list window when you are finished.

You can move, copy, and delete bookmarks in the list window using the same techniques you use in the Finder to move, copy, and delete files.

Customizing the Bookmarks Bar

You can customize the Bookmarks bar in the following ways:

- To rearrange the order of bookmarks, drag the bookmark you want to move to the left or right.

- To move a bookmark currently on the bar to a folder on the bar, drag the bookmark and release it on top of the folder.

- To rename a bookmark, right-click the bookmark and click Edit Name. Type a new name and click OK.

- To delete a bookmark or a folder in the bar, right-click the bookmark or folder and click Delete.

Harnessing the Power of Bookmarks

Here's a power play that will put you right up there with the Mac gurus—opening all the sites that you visit daily with one command. Here's how you set it up: Create a new folder and add it to the Bookmarks bar. Add bookmarks to your favorite sites to the new folder. Then when you want to open all your favorites at once in different tabs, click the pop-up button beside the folder name in the Bookmarks bar and click Open Tabs. Each of your daily favorites opens in a tab, and you can start reading the first tab while the other sites are opening.

The Auto-Click feature is yet another way to automate the process of opening all the sites in a folder. After you set this preference, you can open all the sites in a folder with a single click.

SHOW ME   Media 7.5—A video about Setting the Auto-Click Preference in Safari

Access this video file through your registered Web Edition at my.safaribooksonline.com/9780789743916/media.

Downloading and Viewing Files

Many websites have files that you can download, including widgets, applications, music, movies, graphics, and so on. To download a file, simply click the link. The download window opens showing the progress of the download. When it is finished, the size of the download displays under the name of the downloaded file, and the file opens if it is a *safe* file (for example, movie, picture, sound, PDF, text file, disk image, and other archives).

While downloading a file, if you change your mind, first pause the download by clicking the **X** to the right of the filename and then click the **Clear** button. Remember that, by default, Mac OS X saves downloaded files in the Downloads folder.

Most files you can view on the Web are PDF files. When you click a PDF file on a web page, it opens in the Preview application where you can view the file or save it to your hard drive. While viewing the file, you can even copy text from it. With the new capabilities Snow Leopard has added, you now can copy text in a multicolumn PDF with ease.

SHOW ME   Media 7.6—A video about Copying Text in a PDF File

Access this video file through your registered Web Edition at my.safaribooksonline.com/9780789743916/media.

Saving Web Pages

If you don't have time to read a web page while you're online, save the page to your hard drive to read later by clicking File in the Safari menu bar and then clicking Save As. Type a different name for Export As, if desired. Select a location where you want to save it and then click Save. The default Web Archive Format saves everything on the web page (graphics, movies, and so on).

If you just want to save a graphic on a web page, drag the graphic to your desktop.

If you purchase items on the Web, you'll love the way Safari eliminates the need to print your confirmation or receipt by saving the page as a web receipt in its own special folder.

SHOW ME   Media 7.7—A video about Saving a Web Receipt

Access this video file through your registered Web Edition at
my.safaribooksonline.com/9780789743916/media.

Customizing Safari's Toolbar

Safari has quite a few buttons available to you that do not appear on the toolbar. I recommend that you add the Home button so you can go back quickly to the site you have specified as the home page on the General preferences pane. If you like to use tabs, you might also want to add the New Tab button.

To modify the toolbar, click View in Safari's menu bar and then click Customize Toolbar to open the dialog box shown in Figure 7.5. Drag the buttons you want onto the toolbar and click the Done button when finished.

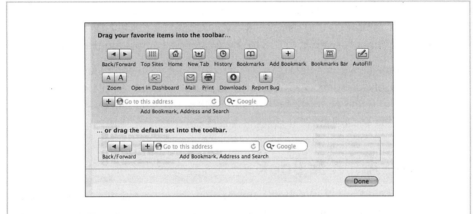

Figure 7.5   *As you add more buttons to the toolbar, the address box gets smaller to accommodate them.*

Quitting Safari

By this time, you know that you can quit an application by pressing Cmd-Q or by clicking the Quit Safari option from the Safari menu. If you have only one window open in Safari when you issue the Quit command, the application closes immediately.

If you browse Safari with multiple windows open or multiple tabs, you need to be sure that the Confirm Before Closing Multiple Tabs or Windows preference has not been deselected. (It's on the Tabs pane of the Safari preferences window.) With this option selected, a dialog box always displays first, asking you to confirm that you want to quit.

This chapter shows you how to use the Address Book and iCal applications to keep track of your contacts and your schedule.

8

Keeping Your Address Book and Schedule

The Address Book and the iCal applications are two programs that can play a key role in keeping you organized, not only on your Mac, but with practically all your other sources of contact and scheduling information. With its syncing capabilities, Address Book can coordinate its contacts with the contact information that you have on other computers and devices, such as your iPod and iPhone, and in Internet address books, such as Google Contacts and Yahoo! Address Book. iCal also syncs across computers and devices, and you can set up CalDAV, Exchange Server, Google, and Yahoo! accounts in iCal to share calendars across multiple platforms.

In this chapter, I cover the basic features and routines you need to know about these two applications: how to customize the Address Book template; how to add, edit, delete, and find contacts; how to add, edit, delete, and find events in iCal; and how to use the To Do list.

Using the Address Book

The Address Book application holds information about your contacts and dispenses it to other applications. For example, the Address Book supplies email addresses to the Mail application and birthdays to iCal. Additionally, you can print your contacts in a list, on envelopes, labels, or in the form of a pocket address book. The printout can include all contacts or just the ones you select, and you can specify the particular contact information you want to include.

To open the Address Book, click the Address Book icon in the Dock. As shown in Figure 8.1, you should have two address cards to start—one for Apple and one for yourself, both of which Mac OS X creates during the initialization process. With only two cards, you can't really tell, but the Address Book sorts contacts by first name by default. To change the sort order to Last Name, click Address Book in the menu bar and click Preferences. Change the Sort By option on the General pane.

To close the Address Book, press Cmd-Q or right-click the Address Book icon in the Dock and click Quit. Address Book remembers the contact you have selected when you quit and displays that contact when you launch the application again.

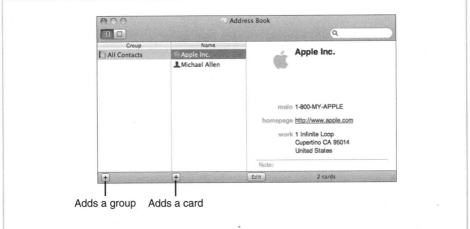

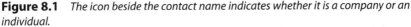

Adds a group   Adds a card

Figure 8.1 *The icon beside the contact name indicates whether it is a company or an individual.*

Customizing the Template

A template determines what fields appear on an address card by default, but you can add fields or delete fields in the template to suit your own needs. To create a useful address card, one that works for business as well as personal contacts, I suggest adding almost every field that is available to the template. Figure 8.2 shows the template with the fields I like to include. Not every card will use every field, of course, but empty fields don't show up on a card.

 SHOW ME   Media 8.1—A video about Editing the Address Card Template
Access this video file through your registered Web Edition at my.safaribooksonline.com/9780789743916/media.

 **LET ME TRY IT**

Editing the Address Card Template

When you make changes to the template, you can select the fields you want, but you have no control over where the fields appear on the card. Additionally, you can't format the appearance of the card in any way, such as by changing the fonts or colors. To make changes to the template, follow these steps:

1. Click Address Book in the menu bar and then click Preferences.

2. Click the Template tab, if necessary.

3. To add fields to the template, click the Add Field pop-up button and click the field you want to add. Fields that already appear on the template have a check mark beside them on the pop-up menu.

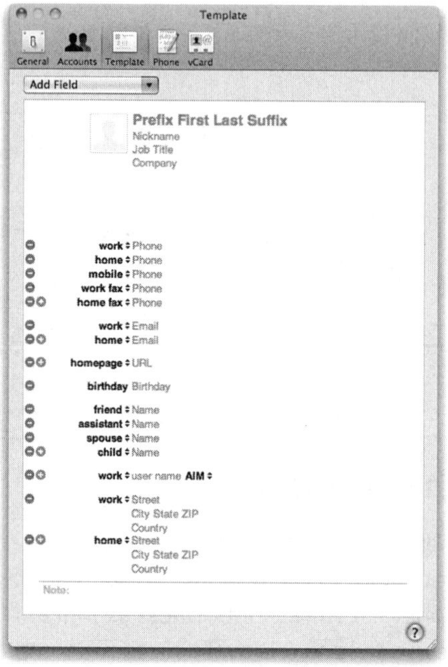

Figure 8.2 *Notice that I have added several more phone fields to the template.*

4. To add more fields of a particular type, such as a Phone field, click the Add button (the green circle with the plus in it) beside the field. (Field types that do not have the Add button do not allow additional fields. The Birthday field is an example of this.)

5. To remove a field, click the Remove button (red circle with a minus in it) beside the field. You can delete all fields except First, Last, and Company name.

6. Close the window when you are finished.

Creating Address Cards

Even though address cards can come into the Address Book from email or your iPhone, you probably are going to have to type some address cards manually.

SHOW ME Media 8.2—A video about Creating a New Address Card
Access this video file through your registered Web Edition at
my.safaribooksonline.com/9780789743916/media.

 **LET ME TRY IT**

Creating a New Address Card

You can use address cards as the repository for all the information you have about your friends, business contacts, and anyone you might need to contact. To create an address card, follow these steps:

1. Click the Add button at the bottom of the Name column.

2. Tab to each field and enter information, or skip a field if you have none to add.

3. If you want the contact to be listed (and therefore sorted) by company name instead of the individual's name, click the Company check box.

4. To add another field for the card you are creating (an additional field for a child's name, for example), click the Add button beside an existing field or click Card in the menu bar, click Add Field, and click the field you want to add. Adding a field to a particular card does not change the template or affect any other cards.

5. If you have a photograph of the contact or just a graphic you want to add, double-click the photo box beside the name to add the picture and then click Choose. Navigate to the file and double-click it. Use the slider to adjust the amount of the picture that shows and then click Set.

6. When finished creating the card, click the Edit button to save it and display it in final form. Notice that the fields you left blank do not appear on the card.

Finding, Editing, and Deleting an Address Card

To go quickly to a contact's card, type part of the contact's name or some information that you know is on the card in the Spotlight field. Cards that meet the criteria start displaying in the Name column as you type. The card at the top of the column is selected and displays in the right pane—ready for perusal or editing.

The first card you should edit is your own because other applications, such as iCal, iChat, and Mail use information from your card. To edit a card, select it in the Name column, click the Edit button, make the necessary changes, and then click the Edit button again to save the changes. If you have changes to make to other cards, you can stay in edit mode, go to other cards, make the changes, and then click the Edit button to save all changes made to all cards.

To delete a contact, click All Contacts in the Group column, select the contact in the Name column, and press the Delete key. When asked to confirm the deletion, click Delete. Oops! Deleted the wrong contact? Click Edit in the menu bar and click Undo Delete Contact.

Working with Groups

By default, the Address Book creates a group called All Contacts. All contacts that you add to your Address Book are in this group. To bring more organization to your Address Book, you can create additional groups, such as Family, Business, Soccer Team, and so on, and include cards of contacts that fit in the group. A single address card can belong to multiple groups.

The Mail application can email individual messages to all members in an Address Book group. It's called a distribution list in the Mail application.

To create a group, click the Add button at the bottom of the Group column, type a name for the group, and press Return. To populate the group, click All Contacts in the Group column so that all your possibilities display in the Name column. Drag the contacts from the Name column and drop them on the name of the group in the Group column. To speed things up, select multiple contacts in the Name column by Cmd-clicking them. Additionally, you can create a new card in a group by clicking the Add button in the Name column when the group is selected. Adding a contact to a group also adds the contact to the All Contacts list.

To see all the members of a group, click the name of the group in the Group column. Only members of the group display in the Name column, and all other contacts are hidden.

To delete a contact from a group, select the group in the Group column, select the name in the Name column, and press Delete. Click Delete to confirm, but don't think that just because you kicked your brother out of the Family group that you're rid of him. He's still in the list of All Contacts. If you change your mind about deleting a contact, click Edit in the menu bar and click Undo Delete Contact.

Using iCal

iCal is Mac's equivalent of the Day Timer® that everyone used to carry around before electronic PDAs and smart cell phones took their place. iCal keeps your schedule and your To Do list up to date and syncs them with your iPhone, iPod, and other calendars you may have on the Web, such as Google Calendar. Additionally, you can publish your calendar on MobileMe or a private web server.

TELL ME MORE   Media 8.3—A discussion about Publishing a
Calendar to the Web
Access this audio recording through your registered Web Edition at
my.safaribooksonline.com/9780789743916/media.

To open iCal, click the iCal icon in the Dock. The calendar page on the icon always
displays today's month and date, and the calendar, shown in Figure 8.3, always
opens to the current date. The iCal window can display two or three panes. At the
top of the pane on the left is the list of calendars you have. The area below the list
can display the mini-calendar, as shown in the figure, or invitations that you have
received. The pane in the middle is the main calendar viewing area, and the pane
on the right displays items in your To Do list.

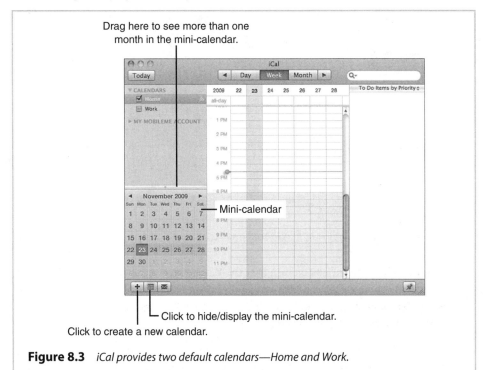

Figure 8.3   *iCal provides two default calendars—Home and Work.*

To close iCal, press Cmd-Q or use any of the other standard procedures for closing
an application. When you close iCal, it remembers the last view you used (Day,
Week, or Month) and displays that view the next time you open iCal.

Viewing, Navigating, and Printing the Calendar

The first time you open iCal, it opens in the Day view (seen in Figure 8.3). Additional views include Week and Month view, shown in Figure 8.4. The two default

calendars, Home and Work, are both checked, meaning that iCal displays events for both calendars in the main calendar viewing area.

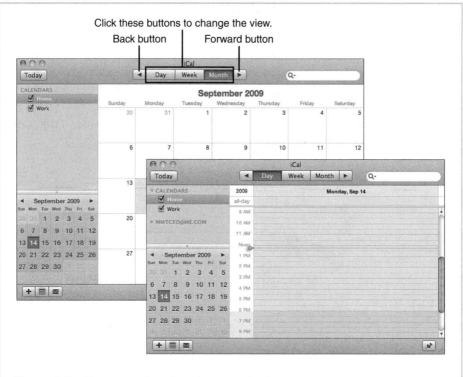

Figure 8.4 *The pane on the right is the main calendar view.*

The default iCal preferences dictate that the Week view has seven days, starting on Sunday, and the day starts at 8:00 a.m. and ends at 6:00 p.m. To change any of these preferences, click iCal in the menu bar and click Preferences. The preferences I mentioned appear on the General pane.

To navigate the calendar in the main calendar viewing pane, use the Back and Forward buttons at the top of the window to go back or forward one day, one week, or one month at a time. As an alternative, use the Back and Forward buttons in the mini-calendar to scroll the calendar and then click the date you want. The view in the main calendar changes to that date. To return to today's date, click the Today button in the upper-left corner.

To print a calendar, click File in the menu bar and click Print. Select all the options you want in the Print window shown in Figure 8.5. The view in the left pane reflects the options you select. Click Continue to open the Print dialog box. Select your printer and click Print.

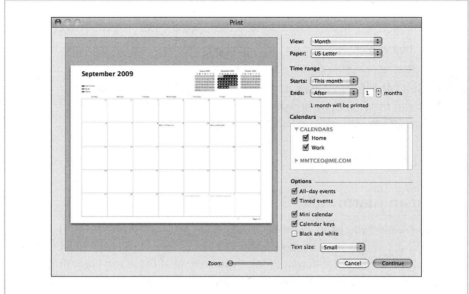

Figure 8.5   *The View option determines the layout of the printed calendar.*

If you want to print a blank monthly calendar, create a new calendar just for this purpose. Don't schedule any appointments on it, of course.

Adding Events to the Calendar

An event is an item you put on the calendar. It can be a meeting, an appointment, a reminder, a ball game, and so on. If you have an event that repeats on a regular basis, you can specify the recurrence interval, and iCal automatically adds the event to dates in the future.

 **LET ME TRY IT**

Creating an Event

Entering events in iCal is a great way to stay on schedule. To create an event, follow these steps:

1. In the left pane, click the name of the calendar that should contain the event.

2. Switch to Day or Week view.

3. Drag from the start time to the end time on the lined spaces.

4. Type a name for the event and press Return.

5. Double-click the event to add more information and click the Done button when you are finished.

 SHOW ME   Media 8.4—A video about Setting an Alarm
Access this video file through your registered Web Edition at
my.safaribooksonline.com/9780789743916/media.

 LET ME TRY IT

Setting an Alarm

iCal can remind you of an event by displaying a message onscreen—with or without sound, sending you an email, opening a file, or running a script. In fact, you can set multiple alarms for different times if you are one of those *very* forgetful people. For example, you could set a message alarm for the day before the event and one for two hours before the event. Additionally, you could send two email alarms to two different email addresses. To set an alarm, follow these steps:

1. Double-click the event and click the Alarm pop-up button.

2. Click the type of alarm you want.

3. Supply additional information as needed (such as which email address to use or which file to open).

4. Click the pop-up button beside the time and specify a time for when the alarm should go off.

5. Repeat steps 2 through 4 to set more alarms if you need them.

6. Click the Done button when finished.

Finding, Editing, and Deleting an Event

Once you have several calendars and events, you may need to use the Spotlight to help you find a particular event. Using the Spotlight in iCal has a few more steps to it than usual. Begin by checking all calendars that you want to search, click the Spotlight pop-up button, and select an item to limit the search. Then type text that appears in the item you want to find. The results appear in a pane at the bottom of the screen. Double-click the item to open it.

To make changes to an event, use an appropriate procedure from the following list:

- To change the start time, drag the event up or down. Note that the time changes in 15-minute increments.

- To change the end time, drag the bottom line of the event up or down.

- To change to a different date, switch to the Month view and drag the event to the new date or double-click the event and type the new date.

- To change the name of an event, double-click the event and click the Edit button. Type the new name and click the Done button.

- To delete an event, click the event and press the Delete key on the keyboard.

- To undo the deletion of an event, click Edit in the menu bar and click Undo Delete Event.

Creating a New Calendar

To create a new calendar, click the New Calendar button at the bottom of the left pane (refer to Figure 8.3). Type a name for the new calendar and press Return. One very useful type of calendar that iCal can create for you is a calendar of your contacts' birthdays.

 SHOW ME   Media 8.5—A video about Creating a Birthday Calendar
Access this video file through your registered Web Edition at
my.safaribooksonline.com/9780789743916/media.

Creating To Do Lists

iCal provides a convenient To Do feature for you in the third pane. It works in conjunction with your calendar so you can attach due dates and alarms to your To Do items. Click the To Do button (the button with a stickpin icon) to toggle the To Do pane on and off.

 SHOW ME   Media 8.6—A video about Creating a To Do Item
Access this video file through your registered Web Edition at
my.safaribooksonline.com/9780789743916/media.

LET ME TRY IT

Creating a To Do Item

Mail and iCal share the same To Do list. So when you create a To Do item in iCal, you can also see it in Mail, and vice versa. To create a To Do item, make sure the To Do pane is visible and then follow these steps:

1. Double-click in the pane to create a new To Do item.

2. Type a name for the item and press Return.

3. To make additional settings, double-click the To Do item.

4. To set a priority, click the pop-up button and click a priority.

5. To set a due date, click the Due Date box and type a date.

6. To set an alarm, click the Alarm pop-up button and select the type of alarm you want to set from the pop-up menu. If you select Email, Open File, or Run Script, supply the additional information that is needed. Repeat this step to set as many alarms as you want.

7. To attach the item to the appropriate calendar, click the Calendar pop-up button and then click the name of the calendar.

8. Click the URL box and type a web address if appropriate.

9. Click the Note box and type any text that you need to help you with this item.

10. When you are finished, click the Close button.

Use the pop-up menu at the top of the column to specify the sort order for your To Do list. Most people sort by priority so that the most important things are at the top of the list. When you accomplish a task, you can click the check box beside it. Nothing is quite so satisfying as a To Do list that is all checked off. At least, that's what I've been told.

9

This chapter covers the features of the two communication applications—Mail and iChat—including making presentations in video chats and screen sharing.

Emailing and Chatting Online

Mac OS X is bundled with two communication applications—Mail and iChat. Mail is for sending and receiving email, as I'm sure you guessed, and iChat is for sending and receiving instant messages. Both are best-of-breed, full-featured applications that provide you with everything you need and some handy extras as well.

Using Mac Mail

You probably have an email address already. Maybe it's a free email addresses from Google, Yahoo!, or Hotmail, or a MobileMe address that you bought from Apple. No matter what type of email you have, you can set it up in Mac's Mail application.

Getting Set Up

To open Mail, click the Mail icon in the Dock. The first time you open the Mail application, the dialog box shown in Figure 9.1 opens to assist you in setting up your mail account. Enter your email address and password and then click Continue. Mac OS X connects to your email server and checks the information you have supplied. (Mac OS X knows the server to connect with based on your email address.) If everything checks out, the Mail window opens, and you are ready to start emailing. Well, that was easy!

If you want to receive messages from an additional email address that you have, click File in the menu bar, click Add Account, and then repeat the procedure just described. Email messages for both addresses display together in the Inbox.

If your Mac has difficulty connecting or verifying your information, another dialog box opens requesting more information, such as the name of the mail server. You may have to get this information from your email provider.

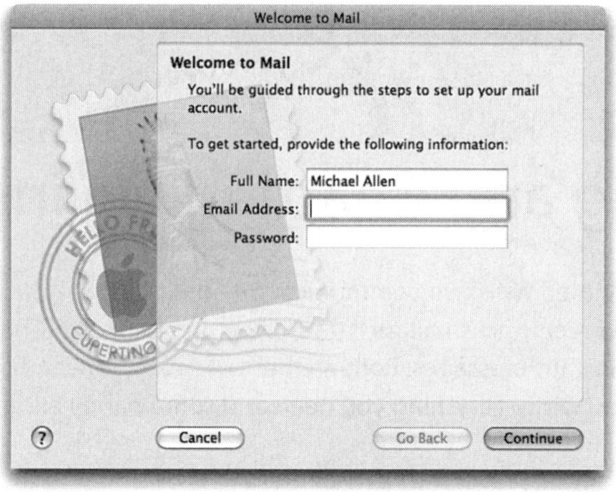

Figure 9.1   *Mac sets up your Mail account for you based on your email address.*

Exploring the Mail Window

The design of the Mail window, like so many other Mac applications, uses the familiar sidebar on the left with a viewing pane on the right, as shown in Figure 9.2. Mail's sidebar has the following categories of sources: Mailboxes, Reminders, RSS, and, in this example, Gmail. The name of this category is taken directly from the Description field in your account information. The sources under Gmail come directly from the Gmail account. Selecting a source from one of the categories in the left pane displays the items in that source in the Mail viewer window on the right. For example, selecting the Inbox in the Mailboxes categories displays all the email in the Inbox.

Other features of the Mail window should be familiar to you—the title bar, toolbar, sizing handle, and so on. Notice the lozenge-shaped button on the right side of the title bar. Can you remember where you've seen a button like this before? That's right—in the Finder. Clicking this button hides or displays the toolbar.

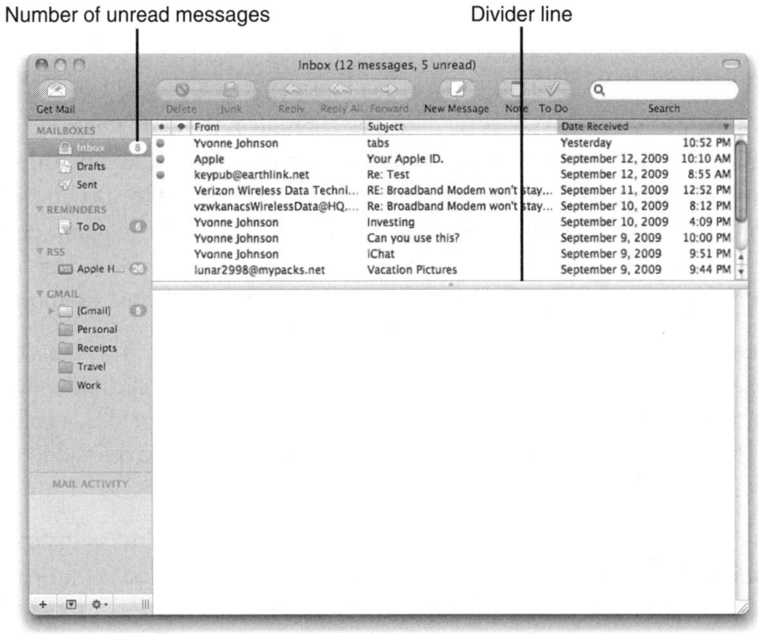

Number of unread messages   Divider line

Figure 9.2   *Unread email messages have a blue dot in the first column.*

Viewing and Reading Email

Before you can view or read your mail, you have to have some. By default, while you are online, Mail checks your mail server every five minutes. If new mail has arrived at the server, Mail pulls the messages down to your hard drive and puts them in your Inbox where you can view and read them any time (even when you're not online).

You can set the time interval for checking the server on the General pane of the Mail preferences window. Click Mail in the menu bar and click Preferences to open the window.

The Mail viewer has two panes—one at the top that displays all the messages, and one at the bottom that displays the content of the selected message. I recommend dragging the divider line down so that you can see more messages at the top and just a few lines of the content at the bottom—enough to give you a preview of what's in the email.

Columns in the upper pane display information about each email. The first column contains a blue dot if the message is unread. The second column shows Buddy Availability (for iChat). The next columns show you who sent the email, the subject line, and the received date.

By default, Mail sorts messages by date. The triangle in the Date Received column indicates that the sort is in ascending order, which for dates would be the most current date to the oldest date. Occasionally, you might want to sort on the From column or the Subject column. To sort on *any* column, click the column heading once. To reverse the sort order, click the column heading again. The direction the triangle is pointing tells you whether the sort is ascending or descending.

You can decide which columns you want to see in the viewer window and even arrange the order of the columns. To add or remove columns, click View in the menu bar and then click Columns. Click a column to select it, or click a column that has a check mark beside it to remove the column from view. To rearrange the columns, drag the column headings to the desired locations.

When I read my email, I like to open the message in its own window instead of try-ing to read it in the viewing pane. The advantage to this method is that you can have several messages open at the same time, and you can compare them or copy something out of one and into the other. To open a message in its own window, double-click any field of the message (From, Subject, Date, and so on). The new window shows the header information (From, Subject, Date, To, and so on) at the top and the body of the message under a thin dividing line. If the message is a reply, you generally see the original message in blue text below the new message. If you don't see the original message, there's nothing wrong with your application; the sender has the option not to include original text in a reply.

When you receive a message from someone who is not in your Address Book, you can add that person to your Address Book by right-clicking the sender's email address in the From field and clicking Add to Address Book. In a similar manner, using the Data Detector feature, you can add email addresses, phone numbers, or addresses within the body of an email message to the sender's existing card in the Address Book, or you can create a new card for the sender. Just point to the data, click the pop-up button that appears, and select Create New Contact or Add to Existing Contact.

Opening Attachments

Photos, documents, and other files that you send along with an email message are called *attachments*. If you receive a message with an attachment, the attachment information appears at the bottom of the header area, just above the dividing line, as shown in Figure 9.3.

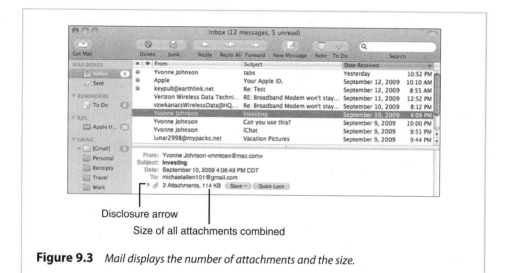

Disclosure arrow

Size of all attachments combined

Figure 9.3   *Mail displays the number of attachments and the size.*

To see the names of all attached files, click the disclosure arrow to the left of the paperclip icon. The attachments show as icons.

 **LET ME TRY IT**

Saving an Attachment in a Specific Location

To save all attachments to the Downloads folder at one time, click the Save button. If you want to decide where an attachment should be saved, follow these steps:

1. Click and hold the pop-up button on the Save button until you see the pop-up menu.

2. Click Save All for multiple files or click the name of the file. A dialog box opens, as shown in Figure 9.4. (If the Finder does not appear in the bottom portion of the dialog box, click the disclosure arrow to the right of the Save As box.)

Click this button to hide or display the Finder.

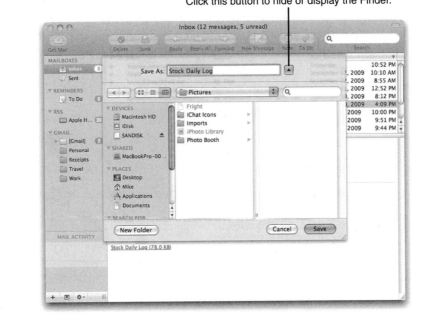

Figure 9.4 *Use the Finder to select the location where you want to save the attachment.*

3. Type a name for the file in the Save As box if you want to name it something else. (Note: If you are saving multiple files, you will not see a Save As box.)

4. In the Finder, navigate to the location where you want to save the file.

5. Click Save.

> For graphic files, you can click Add to iPhoto on the Save pop-up menu and import the files directly into iPhoto.

Sending New Messages and Replies

To send a new email message, click the New Message button located in the middle of the toolbar. The message form opens in its own window, as shown in Figure 9.5.

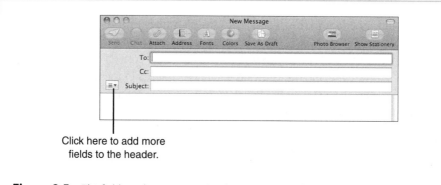

Click here to add more
fields to the header.

Figure 9.5 *The fields at the top comprise the message header. The body of the message is below the header.*

Your first task is to fill in the header information as follows:

- **To address field**—Fill in the To line with the first recipient's email address. As you start typing, the auto-complete feature kicks in. If the recipient's name and email address are in your Address Book, auto-complete pulls the information from there and completes the address for you, encapsulating the address in a blue bubble. Type additional recipients in the To field if necessary. All recipients of your message will be able to see all the addresses you include in this field and the Cc field.

Auto-complete allows you to type the person's name (exactly as it appears in the Address Book) instead of an email address that is too difficult to remember. For example, you can type **Brad Harris** in the To field instead of harris372.b.r@bestlittleinternetproviderintheworld.net.

Additionally, auto-complete pulls information from the Previous Recipients List that Mail keeps for you. This list contains the email addresses you have sent messages to in the past. Most addresses on the list do not have a name, so Mail can only complete those without names if you start typing the actual email address. To refer to the Previous Recipients List, click Window in the menu bar and then click Previous Recipients.

- **Cc address field**—Fill in the Cc line with addresses of recipients who should receive a copy of the message. Auto-complete works here too. All recipients of your message will be able to see all the addresses you include in this field and the To field. People in the Cc field may feel that they are not as important as the people in the To field or that they have no responsibility to take any action in regard to the subject of the email. They see a copied email as a simple FYI. You've been advised. Address accordingly.

- **Bcc address field**—The Bcc (blind carbon copy) field does not appear by default. To add it to the header, click the pop-up button to the left of the Subject line (see Figure 9.5) and then click Bcc Address Field. Fill in the Bcc line with addresses of recipients who should receive a copy of the email without the To and Cc recipients knowing it. Only recipients in the Bcc field will be able to see addresses in the Bcc field, but these recipients will be able to see everyone that you include in the To and Cc fields.

TELL ME MORE   Media 9.1—A discussion about Special Uses for the Bcc Field

Access this audio recording through your registered Web Edition at my.safaribooksonline.com/9780789743916/media.

- **Reply-To address field**—This field also does not appear by default. To add it to the header, click the pop-up button to the left of the Subject line (see Figure 9.5) and then click Reply-To Address Field. Type one of your other email addresses in this field if you do not want replies sent to the address that originates the message.

- Subject field—Type a word or phrase that relates to the content of the message.

> Instead of typing recipients in the To, Cc, or Bcc fields, you can drag them from the Address Book. Click Window in the menu bar and then click Address Panel to display it. To send email to a distribution list, drag a group from the Address Book.

After you fill in the appropriate header information, click in the large white space below the header to start typing the message. As you type, Mail checks your spelling, marking misspelled words with a dotted red underline. You can right-click a misspelled word to display a pop-up menu with suggestions for the word you meant to type. Click the correct word in the list to replace your mistake.

Mail gives you two different formats to use when you compose a message—plain text and rich text. Plain-text messages cannot use formatting, but rich-text messages can use bold, italic, numbered or bulleted lists, different fonts, different font sizes, colors, stationery, embedded graphics, and so on. Email purists, however, prefer plain text for several reasons:

- Any type of email service that the recipient might have can read it.

- It's a safe format for recipients who are PC users, unlike rich text, which can be used to mask security threats and malware, causing many system administrators to bounce incoming messages in rich text format. (This is not a problem for Mac users.)

- It's faster to send and uses less bandwidth.

- It opens faster for the recipient.

Although I almost always use plain-text emails, there are circumstances in which I use the rich-text format—if the recipient uses a Mac, or I need to make the message more readable by using bold text or formatted lists and I know the receiving mail server accepts rich text. If I need to use sophisticated formatting, I just create a document and attach it to the email. I hope you will follow my example and resist the urge to use ten different font colors and sizes, embedded pictures, and a colored background just to send the earth-shattering message, "Whassup?"

If you want to include some "light" formatting in a message, use these techniques:

- Click the Format menu and make sure that Rich Text is the selected format. I know it seems opposite, but Rich Text is the current format if the option on the menu is Make Plain Text.

- To add emphasis to some words in the text, use Cmd-B for bold and Cmd-I for italic. You can press the keys before and after you type the text to turn the emphasis on and then off, or you can select text that you have already typed and simply press the shortcut key to apply the emphasis.

- To use numbered or bulleted lists in your text, click Format in the menu bar and click Lists. Then click Insert Bulleted List or Insert Numbered List.

When you have finished typing the message, click the Send button. If you are online, the message goes out immediately. If you are offline, the message goes into the Outbox and waits until you are online again to be sent.

If you want to stop typing a message and finish it later, save the message as a draft by clicking the Save as Draft button in the toolbar. Then when you have time, click the Drafts folder in the sidebar, double-click the draft message, type the rest of the message, and click the Send button. (If you are a new user, you may not see a Drafts folder in the sidebar until you actually save a message as a draft.)

Opening Mail and sending a new message is not the only way to send an email. You can originate emails from other applications as well, including Address Book, iCal, iPhoto, Safari, TextEdit, and so on.

To reply to a message that you have received, click the message to select it in the upper pane or double-click it to open it in its own window. Click the Reply button to send a reply to the originator of the message, or click the Reply All button to send a reply to the originator and the original copied recipients. If you want to, add additional recipients. Type the message and click the Send button.

Sending Attachments

As explained earlier in this chapter, attachments are files that you send with an email. Technically, you can attach and send any file, but many email servers have a limit on the size of a file you can send and receive. Most email servers accept files under 5MB, but that's usually pressing the issue.

If you have a file that is over 5MB, you can compress it before you attach it; however, don't bother compressing JPG, GIF, PDF, MP3, AAC, WMV, WMA, or MOV files because the compressed file won't be any smaller than the original. To compress a file, select the file in Finder, click File on the menu bar, and click Compress.

To attach a text file to a new message or a new reply, click in the body of the message (maybe at the end of the message under your name) and click the Attach button. Locate the file in the Finder that you want to attach and double-click it. The file appears as an icon with the name and size displayed under it.

The easiest way to attach a photo that is stored in iPhoto is to use the iPhoto Browser. To display the browser, click the Photo Browser button on the right side of the toolbar. Scroll to the photo you want to attach and drag it into the body of the message. It comes in as a full size photo, but you can right-click the photo and click View as Icon. (Any graphic file, such as a PDF or GIF file, displays in full size.)

If you want to use the Attach button instead of using the iPhoto Browser, first click in the body of the message and then click Attach to open the Finder. Scroll the sidebar until you see the Media category. Click Photos in this category and then click iPhoto in the top pane on the right. As shown in Figure 9.6, Send Windows-Friendly Attachments should be selected by default. Scroll through the photos in the bottom pane and select the ones you want. To select adjacent photos, click the first one and Shift-click the last one. To select nonadjacent photos, Cmd-click each photo. Then click Choose File.

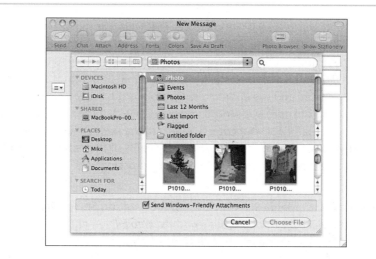

Figure 9.6 *Windows users may not be able to open your attachments if you don't send "friendly" ones.*

Filtering Spam

Spam is another one of those terms that needs no explanation. You know what it is whether it's fried and put on your plate or sent to your email address. Most mail servers have spam filters that they apply to incoming mail, and Mail has its own filters as well. So in all likelihood, you are doubly protected.

When you first start using Mail, you have to train it for a while to help it identify true junk mail. By default, it flags a message as junk if the sender is not in your Address Book, if you have not sent mail to the sender recently, or if the email is addressed to just your email address and not your full name. These messages appear in the Inbox with brown text so you can recognize them and confirm that they are actually junk mail. If Mail flags a message that is not spam, you should click the Not Junk button so that Mail knows not to mark it the next time.

After Mail seems to be getting it right most of the time, you can tell it to start putting the junk mail messages in the Junk mailbox so they are not mixed in with your regular mail in the Inbox. This instruction is on the Junk Mail pane of the Mail preferences window. (Click Mail in the menu bar and click Preferences to open the window.)

Finding Messages

Earlier in this chapter, I explained how to sort messages in ascending or descending order. That is one method you can use to find a particular email, but if you've read any other chapters in this book, you know that Spotlight is the go-to guy for finding anything. Here's how it works in Mail. First, click the mailbox you want to search (Inbox, Sent, Trash, and so on). Then type the search phrase in the Spotlight box. A bar opens under the toolbar with search attributes that you can use to modify the search. The information on the bar tells you that Spotlight is searching the mailbox you selected and the entire message. To narrow the search, click From, To, or Subject instead of Entire Message. If you want to widen the search, click All Mailboxes. Messages that meet your criteria appear in the pane below, and you can double-click a message to open it. To clear the results of the search and go back to the Inbox, delete the text in the Spotlight box by pressing Esc.

SHOW ME   Media 9.2—A video about Creating Smart Mailboxes
Access this video file through your registered Web Edition at
my.safaribooksonline.com/9780789743916/media.

Deleting Messages

Keeping up with email and deleting messages that you no longer need or want can be like bailing water on the Titanic with a teacup. I personally have hundreds of email messages in my Inbox this very minute and I haven't read 80 of them. I'm sure that at least half of those messages should be deleted. If you are diligent and delete messages right away instead of letting them pile up, all you have to do is click the Delete button in the toolbar after you read the message.

If you procrastinate like me, then you need a better method than deleting messages one by one. When I have time to go on a cleaning binge, I sort the Inbox by sender, and then I delete all the messages from my friend Betty Lou and my Aunt Eunice because neither one of them ever send me anything but the latest joke, the cutest animated picture of a dancing frog, or the world's stupidest home video. Then I delete all the automatic bill reminders, the newsletters that I haven't had time to read, and the expired notifications of weekly specials at Costco. To delete messages in bulk, click the first message in the group and Shift-click the last message to select the entire group. Then click the Delete button in the toolbar.

Organizing Your Messages

Because the Spotlight feature can find anything for you, you could just leave all your mail in the Inbox in one gigantically long list, but wouldn't you feel more in control if you could put your messages in folders like files? Well, actually you can. You don't really put them in folders; you put them in mailboxes, but for all intents and purposes, it's the same thing. To create a mailbox, click Mailbox in the menu bar and then click New Mailbox. Name it and click OK. Then drag messages from the Inbox to the new mailbox.

Working with Reminders

Mail includes two reminder features to help you stay on track—Notes and To Do items. In Chapter 8, "Keeping Your Address Book and Schedule," I discuss creating To Do items in iCal. You can access those same To Do items in Mail and even create new ones, which in turn show up in iCal. Creating To Do items in Mail is quite different from the way you create them in iCal, and space constraints do not permit a complete explanation here. If you want to take a dry run with the feature, however, open an email message, select some text such as "call no later than Thursday," and click the To Do button in the toolbar to make that text the title of the To Do item. Point to the item and click the Close button. Click To Do in the sidebar to see the item in the list.

 SHOW ME   Media 9.3—A video about Creating To Do Items in Mail
Access this video file through your registered Web Edition at
my.safaribooksonline.com/9780789743916/media.

The Note feature is a more versatile reminder than the To Do item, in my humble opinion. It not only acts as a note, but you can turn it into an email and even send it with attachments. The notes you create show up in the Note window, but they also show up in your Inbox, affording you top-of-mind awareness. To create a note, click the Note button in the toolbar. Type the note, click the Attach button and attach files if you want to, and then click the Done button. To edit or send a note as an email, open it in the Inbox, make any changes that you want, and click Done or click Send. If you click Send, address the email as you normally would and click the Send button.

Quitting Mail

When you quit Mail using any of the standard methods (clicking Mail, Quit Mail; pressing Cmd-Q; and so on), Mail closes all open windows. If you have email messages open in their own windows, it closes those. If you have started new messages or replies, it saves them in the Drafts folder and closes them. When you start Mail again, the same windows open.

Using iChat

Instant messaging has come a long way baby—from typed messages with "emoticons" to full-scale audio and video—and Mac's iChat application provides it all. All you need is an instant messaging account, and you are ready to chat with your friends.

Opening iChat the First Time

Before you open iChat for the first time, be prepared. You need to have an IM (instant message) account. If you don't have one, and you don't have time to set one up, don't even bother to open iChat. When you have the time to set up an account, then open iChat and let it guide you through the process. Naturally, you must be online to complete this process.

The first time you open iChat, a Welcome screen opens and gives you an overview of what you can do with iChat, your "personal video-conferencing system." Click Continue to move on. In the next dialog box, you must supply your IM account type, the name associated with your account, and your password. If you don't have an IM account, click Help and search for "Setting Up iChat." Read the help article, decide which account to set up, set up your account, return to the Account Setup window, fill in the information, and click the Continue button. Then click the Done button to start using iChat. Your Buddy List window opens, as shown in Figure 9.7.

Figure 9.7   *The title of the Buddy List window indicates the type of IM account you have open.*

Once you have set up one Buddy List, you can set up additional lists for other chat networks. For example, if you set up a Buddy List using a .Mac account, you are using the AIM network, and you can chat with MobileMe members, other people with .Mac accounts, and people with AOL accounts, but you cannot talk to people who use Google Talk. Google Talkers use the Jabber network. If you want to be able to chat with Google Talkers, just sign up for a free Gmail account and then use that address to create a Jabber account in iChat. This will create a second Buddy List for you.

To set up a new account, click iChat in the menu bar and click Preferences. Click the Accounts tab, if necessary, and click the Add button at the bottom of the Accounts list. Select the account type, type your name and password, and click Done.

Working with the Buddy List

The Buddy List contains the IM account names of other people you might like to chat with online. If you have an account with AIM as well as Jabber, you can display either or both Buddy Lists at once. Select the ones you want to display from the iChat Window menu.

If you are on a network, you also can display the Bonjour List to chat with other Macs on your network.

To add a name to the Buddy List, click the Add button in the bottom-left corner of the Buddy List (it has a plus on it) and then click Add Buddy. If you know the person is in your Address Book, click the button to the right of the Last Name field to reveal your Address Book. Click the name you want to add and select the group for the buddy (Buddies, Family, Co-Workers). If the person is not in your Address Book, enter the buddy's account name, select a group for the buddy, and enter the person's first and last names. When you are finished, click the Add button.

If the person you just added is not currently online, the name appears in the Offline category in your Buddy List. If the person *does* happen to be online, the name appears in its related category with an available status. (To see names in a category, click the disclosure triangle to the left of the category.)

If the buddy you want to add has a Google Talk or Jabber account, he receives an authorization notice that he can accept or decline. If he accepts, you're added to his list, and he's added to yours. If he declines, you aren't added to his list, but you still will be able to chat with him.

Showing Your Status

When you launch iChat, your status, shown in the Buddy List window, is automatically set to "Available." You can change your status at any time by clicking the pop-up button and selecting a status from the menu shown in Figure 9.8. The option you choose from the menu tells your AIM buddies what you're doing (even what iTunes song you are listening to, if they really care) because they see your status on their Buddy Lists. (Buddies on other networks don't see quite the same status descriptions, but they know whether you are online or idle.)

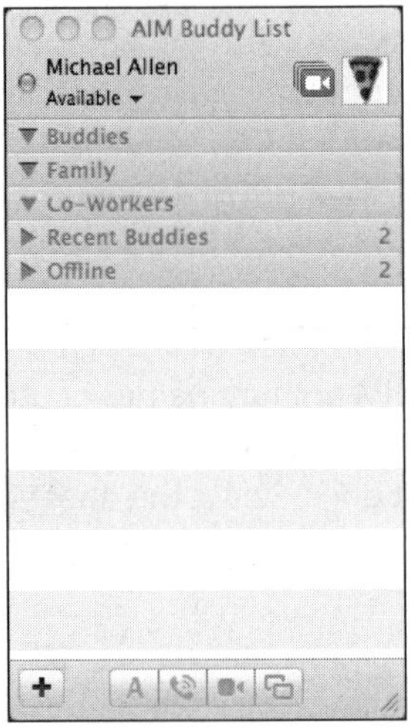

Figure 9.8 *Green dots denote Available statuses and red dots denote Away statuses.*

By default, when the computer is inactive, iChat automatically changes your status to "Away." When you are active on the computer again, a message asks if you want to change your status back to Available. You can click Change, and iChat changes your status back to Available (or whatever you had selected from the menu), or you can click Don't Change if you just don't want to be bothered for a while. When it's convenient for you to chat, you can change your status manually by selecting a status from the pop-up menu.

If you select Offline for your status, iChat disconnects itself from your Internet connection, but it doesn't disconnect you from the Internet. When you change your status to anything else, iChat reconnects again. If you want iChat to remain connected but give the appearance that you are offline, select the Invisible status.

SHOW ME   Media 9.4—A video about Creating a Status Description
Access this video file through your registered Web Edition at
my.safaribooksonline.com/9780789743916/media.

 **LET ME TRY IT**

Creating or Deleting a Status Description

If none of the default status options fit, you can delete the ones you don't want and create your own status description, such as "Available for Emergencies Only" or "Gone Shopping." Follow these steps to create your own status description:

1. Click the status pop-up button and click Edit Status Menu.

2. Click the Add button under the Available or Away column.

3. Type the text for the status, such as "Day Trading," and press Return.

4. Repeat steps 2 and 3 to create as many new descriptions as you want.

5. To delete a description, select the description in the Available or Away column and click the corresponding Remove button.

6. Click the OK button when you are finished.

Chatting with Text

To start a text conversation with a buddy, double-click the buddy's name in the Buddy List, and send an invitation by typing something like "Hey, Judy." Soon you will see a response on your screen from Judy if she types something and presses Return. When she responds, you know you are connected, and you can start typing messages back and forth to each other. While you are chatting, both of you can see your own text on the screen and the responses of the other person.

To start a chat with someone who is not in your Buddy List, click File, New Chat with Person. Type the IM account name and click OK.

An identifying icon or photo appears beside your comments and Judy's comments. If Judy has added a photograph of herself or a graphic to her *own* IM account, you see that photo or graphic. If you have added your own graphic or photo of Judy to her name in *your* Buddy List and have checked Always Use This Picture, then you see your picture for her. If neither one of you have added a graphic of any kind, then iChat shows a generic icon—a blue globe for .Mac and MobileMe accounts, a running man for AIM accounts, and a light bulb for Google Talk and other types of Jabber accounts.

If Judy sends *you* a text chat invitation, you see a window pop up on your screen with her buddy name in the title bar, the graphic that represents her, and the text she typed. To respond, type something in the box at the bottom of the window and click Accept or press Return.

While connected on iChat, you can send a file to your buddy by dragging the file's icon from the Finder into the box where you normally type.

Sending a Text Message

You need to call your friend because you have an emergency. You ditched your landline phone a year ago, and you can't find where in the heck you put your cell phone. Your friend doesn't get email on his phone, so what can you do? Send him a text message via iChat!

SHOW ME **Media 9.5—A video about Sending a Text Message in iChat**
Access this video file through your registered Web Edition at
my.safaribooksonline.com/9780789743916/media.

Chatting with Audio

Sending your mom who lives in another state an invitation to an audio chat is equivalent to making a free long-distance call! Of course, the catch is that you both have to have a microphone. You're using a Mac, so we know you have a microphone. Now you just need to make sure your mom has one. If she does, a telephone icon should appear beside her name in the Buddy List.

To start an audio chat, click the telephone icon next to the buddy's name or right-click the buddy's name and click Invite to Audio Chat. The buddy must accept your invitation and then you can start talking. You can talk to each other just as you would on the phone; that is, you can hear and speak at the same time. Depending on the speed of your connections, there may be a slight delay, however. When you are finished talking, close the audio window.

A meter showing your sound level displays while you are chatting. This lets you know that your microphone is working.

Chatting with Video

Video chats require both parties to have a broadband connection. To start a video chat, click the camera icon next to the buddy's name. A preview window opens on your screen showing you "live and on camera." This is what your video buddy will see when he accepts, only in a larger window. A window showing your video buddy opens on your screen when he accepts the video invitation. Now you can talk to each other "face to face." The preview window you are in reduces to a small window inside of the larger window that displays your buddy. If you don't want to see your preview, click Video in the menu bar and click Hide Local Video. When you are finished, close the video chat window.

If *you* receive a video invitation, click the invitation and then click the Decline or the Accept button. If you accept, a large window showing the sender opens on your screen and your preview window showing you appears in the lower-right corner of the larger window.

Making Presentations with iChat Theater

Using iChat Theater, you can make presentations with iPhoto slideshows, iPhoto albums, or just about any type of file on your computer. You don't even need a video camera to use iChat Theater, but everyone on the chat must be using the same service (that is, MobileMe, AIM, Google Talk, or Jabber).

 SHOW ME   Media 9.6—A video about Presenting an iPhoto Slideshow
Access this video file through your registered Web Edition at
my.safaribooksonline.com/9780789743916/media.

 LET ME TRY IT

Presenting an iPhoto Slideshow

If you are already in a video chat, you can start presenting immediately, but you don't have to start the video chat first if you don't want to. You can take your time and get everything ready first. To use iChat Theater to present a slideshow, follow these steps:

1. Click File, Share iPhoto with iChat Theater.

2. Select the album you want to share and click Share. If you are not already on a video chat, a dialog box opens saying that iChat Theater is ready to begin, but you need to invite a buddy.

3. Double-click the buddy in your Buddy List.

4. iChat opens iPhoto on your screen, and you can use its navigation keys to move through the photos.

5. When you are finished, close the slideshow window.

6. When you are finished with the video chat, close the chat window.

To make a presentation with any other type of file, click File in the menu bar and click Share a File with iChat Theater. Select one or more items from the Finder and click Share. If you are not already on a video chat, a dialog box opens saying that iChat Theater is ready to begin, but you need to invite a buddy. Double-click the buddy in your Buddy List. When the buddy accepts, iChat opens Quick Look on your screen, and you can use its navigation keys to move through the file. When the presentation is finished, close the Quick Look window. End the video conference when you are ready by closing the video chat window.

Sharing Your Computer

One other feature that iChat provides is the ability to share another Mac user's screen and have full control of his computer. You connect with the user via iChat and then set up the screen sharing. When you are sharing the user's screen, his screen replaces your screen, and your screen reduces to a small window in the lower-right corner of your display. You can toggle between the two. This feature is good for troubleshooting a friend's problem or demonstrating how to do something on the Mac, but it only works for two computers that have OS X 10.5 (Leopard) or later.

 SHOW ME Media 9.7—A video about Sharing Your Screen with Another Mac User
Access this video file through your registered Web Edition at
my.safaribooksonline.com/9780789743916/media.

Quitting iChat

When you quit iChat, there is no need to close the Buddy List first. Just click iChat in the menu bar and then click Quit iChat or press Cmd-Q. The next time you open iChat, the Buddy List displays for you.

This chapter gives you enough information about using TextEdit that you may not need any other word processing program.

10

Using TextEdit

Chances are, if you've been using any kind of computer for any length of time, you are familiar with Microsoft Word. For years, it has been the universally accepted standard in word processing software. All other word processing programs must be compatible with it to survive, and Mac's word processing application, TextEdit, is no exception.

TextEdit is a cross between the old text-editing window that programmers used to use and a scaled-down version of a sophisticated word processing application. If you were thrown into TextEdit for the very first time with no instruction whatsoever, I'm confident you could create a satisfactory document. This happened to my husband recently, and he was able to. If my husband could do it, trust me, *anyone* can do it.

Working with Documents

People usually refer to the files that word processing programs create as "documents." A document has a page layout with margins and tabs. It can include tables, formatting, graphics, as well as numbered and bulleted lists.

When you create a document with TextEdit, it uses the New Document preferences shown in Figure 10.1 to determine the format of the new document. By default, TextEdit is set up to operate as the "old text-editing window that programmers used," which I mentioned previously. If you intend to use TextEdit for all your word processing needs, I recommend that you change the preferences so TextEdit behaves like its better half, the scaled-down, sophisticated word processing program.

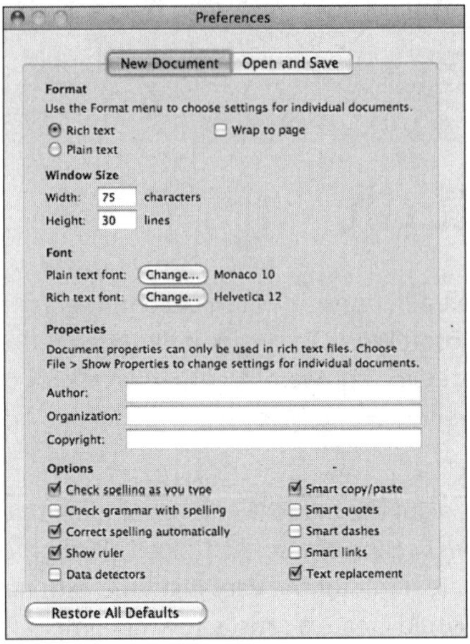

Figure 10.1   *TextEdit uses these preferences in all new documents.*

LET ME TRY IT

You just need to make one small change to the New Document preferences to make the "programmer window" behavior go away. Click TextEdit in the menu bar and click Preferences. On the New Document pane, click Wrap to Page and close the window. To see the change that has come over TextEdit, create a new document and notice the rectangle that now appears in the window. This is the typing area, and text wraps within the rectangle regardless of the size of the window. When TextEdit is in "programmer-window" mode, changing the width of the window causes the text to rewrap to fit the new width of the window. You really don't want that!

Creating a Document with TextEdit

Once you have TextEdit behaving like a real word processing program, you are ready to start creating your documents. To create a new document, follow these steps:

1. Click the Applications folder on the right side of the Dock, scroll to TextEdit, and click it. TextEdit creates a new document automatically.

If TextEdit is already open, you can create a new document by clicking File in the menu bar and clicking New. To open an existing document, click File in the menu bar and click Open. Select the document in the Finder and double-click it. If you want to work on a document that you have opened recently, click File, Open Recent. Click the document you want from the list of documents that displays.

2. Begin typing the document. You'll see the text cursor blinking at the left side of the window on the first line when you begin. This cursor always follows the last character you type. It marks the location where you can type new text.

3. When you have typed enough text that you'd be hard-pressed to type it again from memory if you lost it due to a power outage, click File in the menu bar, and click Save.

4. Type a name for the document and select a location where you want to store it. The default folder is Documents.

5. Select the format from the File Format pop-up menu. The default format is Rich Text Format. Almost all word processing programs can read this format, and it can include paragraph and font formatting, tables, graphics, and lists.

6. Click Save.

7. Continue typing and saving the document periodically until finished.

If you have failed to save your work as you go and the power goes out, TextEdit's got your back. It saves a backup of your document every 30 seconds. Normally, TextEdit deletes the backup when you save a document, but if TextEdit quits improperly, it keeps the backup document and opens it the next time you launch TextEdit.

8. After the last save, you can close the document by clicking the Close button.

9. To close TextEdit, click TextEdit, Quit TextEdit or press Cmd-Q.

You also can save a TextEdit document in PDF format by clicking File in the menu bar and clicking Save as PDF. This format can include paragraph and font formatting, tables, graphics, and lists. It is the standard format used for printable files on the Web.

Navigating and Editing Text

Seldom, if ever, do you type a complete document, then go back, and edit it. It's a mixed process. You type new text and edit as you go.

Navigating in a Document

In order to edit text, you have to position the text cursor in the right place. Certainly, you can use the mouse to position the mouse pointer, shaped like an I-beam, in the right place. However, because you are generally *typing* in a document, it just makes sense to learn the keystrokes that help you move around in a document as well. Table 10.1 lists some of the common keystrokes used to navigate in a document.

Table 10.1   Navigation Techniques

To Move To:	Press:
The beginning or end of a line	Cmd-Home or Cmd-End
The top or bottom of the document	Cmd-Up Arrow or Cmd-Down Arrow
The beginning or end of a word	Option-Left Arrow or Option-Right Arrow
The beginning of a word	Option-Left Arrow
Up or down one line	Up Arrow or Down Arrow

Editing Text

Editing text requires inserting text, deleting text, and copying, cutting, and pasting text. Table 10.2 lists some of the most common editing commands and shortcuts.

Table 10.2   Editing Techniques

To:	Do this:
Insert text.	Click the cursor where the new text should go and type the text.
Delete the character to the left of the text cursor.	Press Delete.
Delete the character to the right of the text cursor.	Press Fn-Delete.
Delete a complete word.	Double-click the word and press Delete.
Delete a complete line.	Triple-click the line and press Delete.
Delete a section of text.	Drag the cursor through the text and press Delete.
Copy text.	Drag the cursor through the text and click Edit, Copy or press Cmd-C.
Cut text.	Drag the cursor through the text and click Edit, Cut or press Cmd-X.
Paste text.	Click the cursor in the new location and click Edit, Paste or press Cmd-V.

If you make a revision in a document that you'd like to take back, press Cmd-Z. (The menu command is Edit, Undo.) You can undo changes in a document until the cows come home—all the way back to the way the document was when you first opened it. The opposite of Undo is Redo (Shift-Cmd-Z). The Redo command reverses an Undo action.

Correcting Spelling

As you type, you may notice that TextEdit corrects some of your typographical or spelling errors for you and underlines others with a dotted red line. This occurs because Correct Spelling Automatically and Check Spelling As You Type are the default settings in the New Document preferences. To correct a misspelling, right-click the word with the red underline and click the correct spelling in the list that appears at the top of the shortcut menu. If you want to correct all misspellings at once, just wait until you have finished typing the document, click Edit in the menu bar, and then click Spelling and Grammar, Show Spelling and Grammar. This opens TextEdit's full-blown spell checker.

Finding and Replacing Text

Sometimes you need to make global revisions in a document; that is, you need to change the same word or phrase that appears multiple times in the document. The Find command not only can find each occurrence for you, but can replace it for you as well.

 SHOW ME   Media 10.1—A video about Using the Find Command
Access this video file through your registered Web Edition at
my.safaribooksonline.com/9780789743916/media.

 **LET ME TRY IT**

Using the Find Command

The Find command can locate the text that you specify even if the text is in the middle of a word or just at the beginning of a word. To find a particular word or phrase and replace it with something else, follow these steps:

1. Click Edit in the menu bar and then click Find.

2. Type the word you want to find in the Find field. If you select Ignore Case, TextEdit finds all occurrences of the text regardless of the capitalization used in the document.

3. Type the word you want to replace it with in the Replace With field.

4. Specify in the pop-up menu whether the text in the Find field is contained in a word, starts a word, or is a complete word.

6. Click Replace All if you want to replace all occurrences of the text and close the window.

7. If you don't want to change all occurrences of the text, click Next to find the next occurrence that appears in the document after the point of the cursor. (If you didn't begin the search at the top of the document, then make sure you select Wrap Around so that the Find command will continue searching from the top of the document after it has reached the end.)

8. Click Replace to replace the currently selected text or click Replace & Find to replace the currently selected text and find the next text.

9. Close the window when finished.

Inserting Page Breaks

Eventually, you will fill up a page, and TextEdit will insert a page break automatically. If you want a page to stop before it fills up, you can insert a page break yourself by clicking Edit in the menu bar and clicking Insert, Page Break.

Setting Margins and Tabs

TextEdit sets margins for you on all sides (top, bottom, left, and right) at one inch. It is impossible to change the margin settings using formatting commands or printing commands in the application, but one-inch margins are probably adequate for 75% to 90% of the documents most home users create.

Figure 10.2 shows the ruler where margins and tabs are set. The first line indent and left indent icons are set at the same place initially, but the figure shows the left indent icon moved to the right so you can see both icons separately.

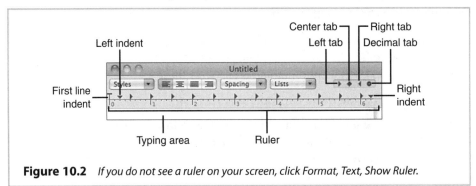

Figure 10.2   *If you do not see a ruler on your screen, click Format, Text, Show Ruler.*

Setting the Margins

"Wait a minute. There must be some mistake," you say. "You told us we couldn't change the margins. So why is this topic in here?" Simple. I said you couldn't change margins with any formatting or printing commands, and that's true, but there *is* a way to change margins. Very few people seem to know about this method, so maybe it's a little Mac OS X secret.

 **LET ME TRY IT**

Changing the Margins

The secret to changing the margins is to display some normally hidden codes and change them. To do this you have to create a document, close it, and then reopen it. It's a bit "clunky," but it works! To change the top, bottom, left, or right margin, follow these steps:

1. Create a new document. Save it and then close it.

2. Click File in the menu bar, click Open and select the document you just saved and closed.

3. Check the option Ignore Rich Text Commands.

4. Click Open.

5. Find the following text: \margl1440\margr1440. These are the Rich Text Commands for the left and right margins, respectively. The value 1440 equals one inch. So 720 would equal half an inch, 1960 would equal an inch and a half, and so on.

6. Change the value of 1440 to the value you want.

7. Add the commands for the top and bottom margins (\margt and \margb, respectively) including the values that you want. When you are finished revising the margins, the commands would look like this if you set half-inch margins all the way around:
   `\margl720\margr720\margt720\margb720`

8. Save the document and close it. Reopen it without the Rich Text commands this time and type the document.

Being able to set margins means that you can create mailing labels and many other documents that might have been too much trouble or impossible to create otherwise. Consider this your "Get Out of Jail Free" card.

Setting Tabs

By default, TextEdit places a left tab every half inch on the ruler. These tabs are always there for you while you are typing, and they come in quite handy. If you need to type text that uses different kinds of tabs, however, as shown in Figure 10.3, the left tabs just get in your way, and you need to delete them. To remove any type of tab that has been set on the ruler, drag the tab icon off the ruler. To set a tab, point to the type of tab that you want in the toolbar, drag it to the ruler, and then drop it in the precise location where you want it. (The measurement shows in a box above the tab as you are dragging it on the ruler.) To change the location of a tab, drag it to the desired location on the ruler.

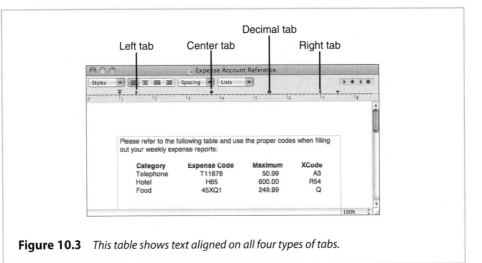

Figure 10.3   *This table shows text aligned on all four types of tabs.*

SHOW ME   Media 10.2—A video about Setting Tabs
Access this video file through your registered Web Edition at
my.safaribooksonline.com/9780789743916/media.

Formatting Text

The purpose of changing the appearance of text in a document is to make the document more readable and understandable. For example, if you want to let the reader know that a word or phrase is very important, you could make it bold or red. To differentiate headings from regular paragraph text, you could make the headings a different font and a larger size than the regular paragraph text.

Additionally, you can change some of the typesetting attributes of a font such as kerning, use of ligatures, and position of the baseline. Kerning adjusts the space between characters, and you might use this feature to lengthen or shorten a headline to fit a specific space. Ligatures are archaic, and I doubt you would ever need to use them. They are combinations of characters, such as *f* and *i*, and they are not even available in most fonts. Adjusting the position of the baseline allows you to create a superscript or a subscript. I don't have space in this book to explain the typesetting attributes in detail, but you can find them on the Format, Font menu.

Adding Emphasis

You can apply the following types of emphasis to text: bold, italic, underline, outline, and color. To add any of the first four, select the text and then click Format in the menu bar and click Font. Select the emphasis that you want to add. If you memorize the keyboard shortcuts, Cmd-B, Cmd-I, Cmd-U, you can use them as you type. For example, if you know you want to make a word bold, you press Cmd-B, type the word, and press Cmd-B again. In other words, turn the attribute on before typing the text and turn it off after you type the text.

If you want to use color in a document, display the Colors window by clicking Format in the menu bar and clicking Font, Show Colors. Click the type of color palette that you want to use by clicking an icon in the toolbar. As you can see in Figure 10.4, I selected the Crayons palette. To apply color to text, select the text and click the color in the palette you want to use. To apply the color as you type, position the cursor where you want colored text, click the color you want in the color palette, and start typing. Change the color back to black when you have finished typing the colored text.

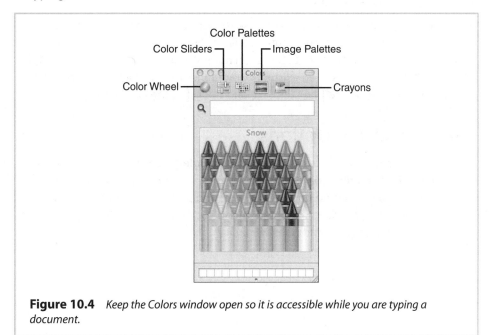

Figure 10.4   *Keep the Colors window open so it is accessible while you are typing a document.*

Selecting a Font Type and Size

Each new document you create in TextEdit uses the default font specified in the New Document preferences. In Figure 10.1, you can see that the default font for Rich Text Format documents is 12-point Helvetica. To change the font, open the Fonts window by clicking Format in the menu bar and then clicking Font, Show Fonts. In the Fonts window, you first select the font collection, and then you can select the family, the typeface, and the size. To use a different font, you can select text and apply font attributes or select the font attributes first and then type the text—similar to the two ways of applying color.

The Fonts window also has buttons to apply underlines, strikethroughs, font color, and page background color.

Formatting Paragraphs

If you start looking for a Paragraph command on the Format menu, you won't find it because TextEdit lists all paragraph-formatting options on the Text menu. They include paragraph alignment and spacing options. By default, a new paragraph always has the same alignment and spacing options as the one before it.

Setting Alignment

The paragraph alignment options include the following: Align left (left margin straight, right margin ragged), Center (all lines centered), Justify (left and right margins straight), and Align Right (left margin ragged, right margin straight). To apply any of these alignments to an existing paragraph, click anywhere in the paragraph, click Format in the menu bar, click Text, and then click the alignment you want.

Setting Spacing Options

Spacing options include line height multiple (single space, double space, and so on), line height, interline spacing, and paragraph spacing (space before and after paragraphs). To set spacing options in an existing paragraph, click in the paragraph you want to format, click Format in the menu bar, and then click Text, Spacing. Set all the options that apply and click OK.

TELL ME MORE   Media 10.3—A discussion about Using
Paragraph Spacing
Access this audio recording through your registered Web Edition at
my.safaribooksonline.com/9780789743916/media.

Exploring Other Formatting Features

TextEdit has several other powerful features that I just don't have space to cover,
but I want you to know about them so you can learn how to use them if you need
them. I have created videos of several of the items in Table 10.3, which lists other
things you can do in TextEdit and points you in the right direction to find them.

Table 10.3   Other Features

To:	Select:
Create a numbered or bulleted list.	Format, List
Create a table.	Format, Table
Apply styles.	Format, Text, Styles
Go back to the last saved copy before the current revisions were made.	File, Revert to Saved
Embed another file in the TextEdit document.	File, Attach File
Insert a live link to a URL.	Edit, Add Link
Automatically hyphenate words.	Format, Allow Hyphenation
Detect telephone numbers, addresses, and dates to send to other Mac applications.	Edit, Substitutions, Data Detectors
Transform capitalization.	Edit, Transformations
Speak selected text.	Edit, Speech
Insert symbols and other special characters.	Edit, Special Characters
Print the document title and date in the header and the page number in the footer.	File, Print, Print Header and Footer

 SHOW ME   Media 10.4a–d—Videos about Other Formatting
Features (Table 10.3)
Access video files about the topics Creating Numbered Lists,
Creating a Table, Creating Styles, and Inserting Special Characters
through your registered Web Edition at
my.safaribooksonline.com/9780789743916/media.

Printing

By default, TextEdit formats a page for printing on 8.5×11-inch paper in portrait orientation at 100% scale. If you want to change any of these settings, click File in the menu bar and click Page Setup. To print a document, click File in the menu bar and click Print. Select your printer and the other options that apply. Scroll through the pages in the preview on the left to be sure the document looks the way you want it to and then click Print.

If the Print dialog doesn't contain all the options you were expecting (such as the number of copies you want to print or the page range options), click the disclosure triangle beside the Printer pop-up menu at the top of the window.

This chapter covers viewing, organizing, editing, and sharing photos in iPhoto.

11

Managing and Editing Your Photos

In this chapter, I give you all the fundamentals of working with iPhoto: how to import photos and view them in various ways; how to annotate and flag photos to facilitate sorting and searching; how to organize photos by events, faces, places, and albums; and how to share your photos with others. Although iPhoto '09 is not really a part of Mac OS X Snow Leopard, it is one of the applications in the iLife suite that comes free on every new Mac. In my opinion, this book wouldn't be complete without discussing the iLife applications, and iPhoto is like the central diamond in the cluster of applications that make up iLife.

Setting Up iPhoto

To open iPhoto, click the iPhoto icon in the Dock. The first time you open iPhoto on your Mac, a Welcome screen displays with information about online tutorials and hands-on help. These kinds of screens are common, and most people just click the option that turns them off; but I recommend that you leave the check in the Show this Window When iPhoto Opens until you have time to click the link to go online and view some of the tutorials. They are excellent learning tools for beginners.

When you close the Welcome screen, you see two questions waiting for your answers. One question is, "Do you want to use iPhoto when you connect your digital camera?" Click Yes for this one, unless you want to use a different program. The other question is, "Would you like to see your photos on a map?" Even if you don't care, click Yes just for the fun of it.

When the iPhoto window displays, as shown in Figure 11.1, you see that it has the familiar Finder design with the sidebar on the left and a main viewing pane on the right. The default categories in the sidebar include Library and Recent. Additional categories, such as Albums, Slideshows, MobileMe Gallery, Facebook, and Keepsakes show up when you use the corresponding features in iPhoto. Items listed under the categories are called *sources*, and they are similar to a folder in the Finder.

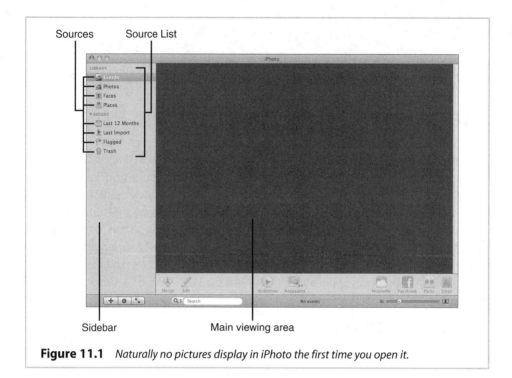

Figure labels: Sources, Source List, Sidebar, Main viewing area

Figure 11.1 *Naturally no pictures display in iPhoto the first time you open it.*

Importing Photos and Movies

You can import digital photos and movies into iPhoto directly from your camera, an external drive, a CD, or a DVD. Additionally, you can add photographs directly from an email message, PhotoBooth, or the Web without going through an importing process at all. So many possibilities; so little time!

 **LET ME TRY IT**

Importing Photos or Movies from a Camera

Follow these steps to import photos or movies from a digital camera:

1. Plug the USB cable into the camera and into your Mac.

2. Turn the camera on. iPhoto launches automatically if it isn't already running. All the photos or movies on the camera appear as thumbnails ready for your selection, as shown in Figure 11.2.

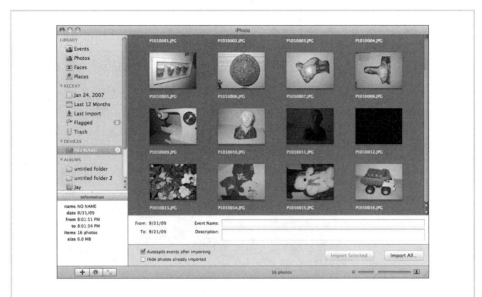

Figure 11.2 *Select the photos you want if you don't want to import them all.*

3. If you have already imported some of the items on your camera, select Hide Photos Already Imported so you won't accidentally select them.

4. If you don't want to import all the items, select the ones you want by Cmd-clicking or Shift-clicking the thumbnails.

5. Type a name for Event Name if you want to. If you leave this blank, iPhoto names the event *untitled event*.

6. Decide whether you want all the photos and movies to go into one event or if you want them split into separate events. If you don't want photos and movies taken on the same date grouped together in their own event, deselect Autosplit Events after Importing.

7. Click Import Selected or Import All.

8. At the end of the import process, iPhoto asks if you want to delete the photos on the camera or keep them. Answer this final question, turn off the camera, eject it in the Finder or drag its icon to the Trash, and then unplug it. The photos you imported show as thumbnails in the viewing area and the selected source in the sidebar is Last Import, as shown in Figure 11.3.

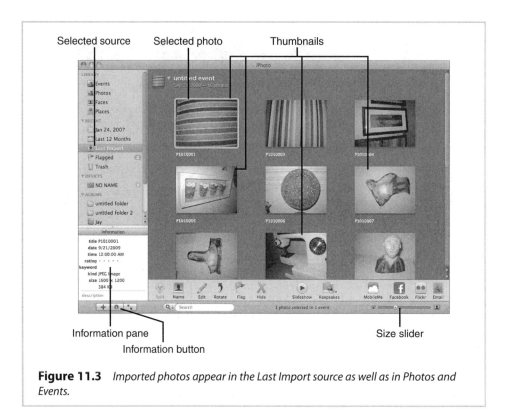

Selected source   Selected photo   Thumbnails

Information pane   Size slider
Information button

Figure 11.3   *Imported photos appear in the Last Import source as well as in Photos and Events.*

You also can add photos to iPhoto from the following:

- **Disc or external drive**—In iPhoto, click File in the menu bar and click Import to Library. Using the Finder, locate graphic files that you want to import, select them, and click Import. Alternatively, you can simply drag graphic files from the Finder into iPhoto.

- **PhotoBooth**—In PhotoBooth, select the photos and click the iPhoto button.

- **Email message**—Open the message, click and hold the pop-up button on the Save button to display the pop-up menu, and click Add to iPhoto.

- **The Web**—Right-click the picture and click Add Image to iPhoto Library.

When downloading photos from the Web, remember that most are copyright protected; so use them for your own enjoyment, not for commercial purposes. If you need a photo for commercial use, you can purchase great quality photos for very little money from sites such as iStock.com, DreamsTime.com, and BigStock-Photo.com.

Viewing Photos

To view a photo, you first have to select a source from the sidebar. In the Library category, your choices are Events, Photos, Faces, and Places. It probably makes more sense to a new user to compare the way you look at photographs in iPhoto with the way you look at real photographs. Think of your real photos sorted in envelopes with labels such as "First Birthday," "Christmas-08," "Mediterranean Cruise," and so on. In iPhoto, the labeled envelops are equivalent to Events in the sidebar. If you make duplicate prints of your favorite people and put them in envelopes with labels such as "Aunt Margaret," "John Thomas," and "Mom," this is equivalent to the Faces source in the sidebar. Likewise, if you make duplicate prints of your favorite places and put them in envelopes labeled "Santa Fe," "London," and "Grand Canyon," this is equivalent to the Places source in the sidebar.

Now think about taking all the photos out of their labeled envelopes and lining them up, still keeping them in groups so they can go back in the envelopes. This is equivalent to the Photos source in the sidebar with Event Titles turned on. Turn off the Event Titles, and you have the equivalent of all your photos mixed together in one big pile. Although this might seem like the most unorganized way to view your photos, it does have a purpose, which I explain later in this chapter when I get to the subject of sorting on keywords.

All the photos that you have in iPhoto are in Events as well as in Photos. Events and Photos are simply two different ways of looking at the same photos, while Faces and Places are ways of looking at virtual copies of the original photos. Deleting a photo in Faces or Places only deletes the virtual copy, not the real file.

 **LET ME TRY IT**

Viewing Photos in the Events Source

An event is similar to a folder in the Finder. Just as a folder contains files, an event contains photographs. All photos that you add to the iPhoto library are imported into Events. After the photos are imported, you can move them to other events or split the event into multiple events. I tell you how to do that later in this chapter.

To view photos in an event, follow these steps:

1. Click Events in the sidebar. All the events display as thumbnails in the right pane in date order. Each event thumbnail usually represents a group of photos, but only one photo appears in the thumbnail. It is called the *key photo*.

2. To see the other photos in the event within the frame of the thumbnail, skim the cursor across the thumbnail. Skimming the cursor means moving the cursor without clicking or dragging.

> To change the key photo that represents an event, skim the photos until the photo you want is visible. Right-click the photo and click Make Key Photo.

3. Double-click an event's thumbnail in the right pane to open it. All photos in the event display as thumbnails in the right pane.

4. Double-click a photo's thumbnail to view it in a larger size and then use the right- and left-arrow keys on the keyboard to scroll through the other photos in the event at this larger viewing size.

5. When you are finished, click the photo you are viewing. All photos in the selected event display again as thumbnails.

6. To close the event, click All Events (see Figure 11.4).

Figure 11.4   *Click All Events to return to the thumbnails of all events.*

 **LET ME TRY IT**

Viewing Photos in the Photos Source

The Photos source in the sidebar shows every photo in your iPhoto library as a single photo. To view photographs in the Photos source, follow these steps:

1. Click Photos in the sidebar. The photographs display as thumbnails in the right pane. The first time you view Photos, the thumbnails are divided by event titles, and the events appear in date order, from the oldest date to the most recent date. Even the photos within the events display in date order.

2. If you don't want the photos to be divided by event titles, click View in the menu bar and then click Event Titles.

3. Double-click a photo's thumbnail to view it in a larger size. Use the right- and left-arrow keys on the keyboard to scroll through the other photos at this larger viewing size.

4. When you are finished, click the current photo to return to viewing the thumbnails.

Increasing the Photo Size on Screen

Regardless of what source you are viewing, you can make the photograph you are viewing larger in either of the following ways:

- To make thumbnails larger or smaller, drag the slider (see Figure 11.5) to the right or left. Alternatively, you can press 1 to jump to the largest size and press 0 to jump to the smallest size.

- To see a photo in full screen, click the Full Screen button (see Figure 11.5). Point to the bottom of the screen to reveal the toolbar (as shown in Figure 11.5), and click the Previous or Next button to continue viewing photos in full-screen mode. Click the Exit Full Screen button when finished.

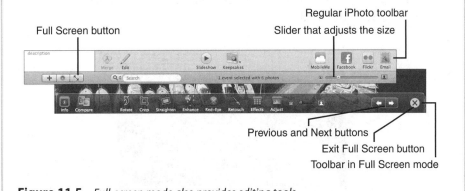

Figure 11.5 *Full-screen mode also provides editing tools.*

Viewing Photos in a Simple Slideshow

One very entertaining way to view a group of pictures is to create a slideshow, complete with music and transitions. I'm not talking about doing a lot of work, here. You can use iPhoto's defaults and just create a slideshow on the fly. Once you exit the slideshow, though, it's gone. In Chapter 15, "Being Creative with Photos," I show you how to create a slideshow with your own preferences and how to save it so you can view it again and again.

SHOW ME   Media 11.1—A video about Selecting and Viewing Photos in a Slideshow

Access this video file through your registered Web Edition at my.safaribooksonline.com/9780789743916/media.

 **LET ME TRY IT**

Selecting and Viewing Photos in a Slideshow

Why view your photos in Events or Photos when you can view them as slideshows complete with music and special themes? And, of course, the photos display in full-screen size, which adds even greater impact. To view selected photos in a slideshow, follow these steps:

1. Select the photos you want to include in the slideshow. You could select an event, an album, various photos that you Cmd-click in the Photo's source, and so on.

2. Click the Slideshow button. The first photo displays in full-screen mode with a dialog box superimposed. This dialog box, shown in Figure 11.6, has three panes—Themes, Music, and Settings, but in this chapter, we're only interested in Themes.

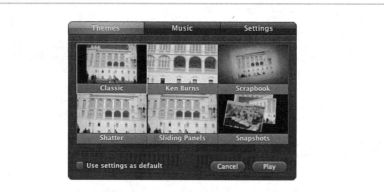

Figure 11.6   *Each theme has its own default music and settings.*

3. Point to each theme to see how the slideshow would look with that theme. When you have reviewed them, click the one you want to use.

4. Click the Play button and enjoy. Music plays while each slide displays for five seconds. When the slideshow is finished, it repeats.

5. Move the pointer across the bottom of the screen to display the controls. You can click Pause to stop the show or click the Previous or Next button to see a different slide. When you are finished, click the Close button (or press the Esc key).

Viewing, Changing, and Adding Photo Information

When you import a photo into iPhoto, it comes with Exchangeable Image File (EXIF) information that is stored with the file. This information includes the width and height of the photo in pixels, the date and time the photo was taken (assuming the correct date and time was set in the camera), the file name and size, the date the photo was modified and imported, and information about the camera used to take the photo.

After a photo is added to your iPhoto library, you can add more information that iPhoto will store with the file. This information includes title, keywords, ratings, and description.

Viewing Information for Photos

iPhoto provides three locations for viewing photo information: the information panel (shown in Figure 11.3), the "back" of a photo, and the Extended Photo Info window. The information panel and the back of a photo accommodate editing some of the information that it displays, whereas the Extended Photo Info window does not.

 **LET ME TRY IT**

Viewing Photo Information

The following information displays in the information panel: title, date, time, rating, keyword, kind of file, dimensions, file size, and description. To view the information, follow these steps:

1. Select a source from the source list in the sidebar.

2. Select the photo.

3. Click the information button at the bottom of the sidebar (see Figure 11.3) to open the information panel if it isn't already open.

Additionally, you can flip a photo over and read information on the back by clicking the information button in the bottom-right corner of the photo thumbnail as shown in Figure 11.7. "What button in the corner?" you ask? It doesn't appear until you point to the corner. The information on the back of a photo includes title, date and time, rating, photo place, and description.

Figure 11.7   *Clicking the information button on a photo flips the photo over.*

 **LET ME TRY IT**

Viewing All EXIF Information for a Photo

The EXIF information that iPhoto doesn't display in the information panel displays in its own window. The information that you can view about the camera can include the type of camera, the model, the software, as well as the shutter speed, aperture, and ISO film speed used to take the photo. To view the EXIF information window, follow these steps:

1. Select a source from the source list in the sidebar.

2. Select the photo.

3. Click Photos in the menu bar and then click Show Extended Photo Info. A window opens with the information.

4. Select another photo and the EXIF info for that photo displays in the window.

5. When finished viewing the data, click the close button in the window.

Changing Photo Information

When you import a photo, the title of the photo is the same as the file name, which is something like P10010.jpg or DSC01628.jpg. iPhoto allows you to change the title to something more descriptive, which is easier to remember and more useful for sorting.

Additionally, if you haven't set the date or time correctly on your camera, you will probably want to correct this information for the photographs, at least within a reasonable estimate if you don't really know the actual date. Remember that photos are sorted by date by default, and photos taken in the last year also appear in the Last 12 Months source.

 **LET ME TRY IT**

Changing the Photo Title, Date, or Time

Changing a photo's title, date, or time does not actually change the file name or the original date and time stored in the EXIF information. It simply changes what displays in the information panel or on the back of the photo, which is the data that iPhoto uses to sort the photos. To change photo information, follow these steps:

1. Select a source from the source list in the sidebar.

2. Select the photo.

3. Click the information button at the bottom of the sidebar to open the information panel if necessary.

4. Double-click the existing title, date, or time (triple-click the title if it's more than one word), type the new information, and press Return.

If you change dates in the information panel, the photo jumps to a new location. See "Sorting Photos" later in this chapter for a solution.

5. Click in the description field and type a description

Another way to change some of the photo information is to flip the photo over and make changes on the back. Note that the back of the photo doesn't show the time, and it doesn't allow you to change the date. If you want to change the titles of quite a few photos, it's much easier to do so on the back of the photos than in the information pane.

 **LET ME TRY IT**

Changing Photo Titles Using the "Assembly Line" Method

When you flip a photo over to change the title, you also flip the switch on a virtual "assembly line" that can run your photos through a title-changing process for you in short order. You could actually start with the first photo in the Photos source or the first photo in an event and keep going until you get to the last photo. Here's what you do:

1. Click Photos or click Events in the sidebar. If you click Events, double-click the event.

2. Click the information button in the lower-right corner of the first photo you want to rename to flip the photo over so that you can view the back side.

3. Select the text of the name, type a new name, and click the Next arrow in the lower-left corner to go to the next photo.

4. Repeat the process until you are finished and then click the Done button.

Using Keywords

One very helpful piece of information that you can add to a photo is a keyword—a word or phrase that describes the photo in some way that is meaningful to you. Adding keywords to photos makes it possible for you to search for all photos with a particular keyword or sort photos on keywords.

 **LET ME TRY IT**

Assigning a Default Keyword

iPhoto gives you a few keywords to get you started, but you can create your own keywords and delete any of the default keywords. The default iPhoto keywords are Birthday, Family, Favorite, Kids, Photo Booth, and Vacation. To assign a default keyword, follow these steps:

1. Select a source from the source list in the sidebar.

2. Select the photo.

3. Click Window in the menu bar and click Show Keywords to display the default list.

4. Select a photo and click the keyword you want to assign to it.

Notice also that one of the default keywords in the list is a check mark. Use this in any way that makes sense to you. For example, all checked photos need some research to pinpoint the correct dates, or all checked photos need to be cropped, and so on.

Another way to assign keywords is to display the keyword field below the photograph and type the keywords directly into the field. To display the field, click View in the menu bar and click Keywords. If you type a keyword that is not in the default keyword list, iPhoto automatically adds it to the list. You also can type multiple keywords in the field if you separate them with commas.

You can't assign keywords to events.

Assigning Ratings

iPhoto has a rating system you can apply to photos, ranging from one star to five stars. The rating, an arbitrary standard that you set, could refer to the quality of the photos or just how well you like a photograph. To assign a rating to a photograph, click the first, second, third, fourth, or fifth dot in the Rating field. (The information panel and the back of a photo both display the Rating field.)

 SHOW ME Media 11.2—A video about Assigning Ratings to Photos
Access this video file through your registered Web Edition at
my.safaribooksonline.com/9780789743916/media.

Viewing and Changing Information for Events

iPhoto also stores information about events. This information includes the name of the event, the range of dates of the photos included in the event, the number of photos in the event, the total file size for all photos in the event, the description, and the event place.

 **LET ME TRY IT**

Viewing Event Information

All event information displays in the information panel except the event place. To view event information, follow these steps:

1. Click Events in the sidebar.

2. Click the event.

3. Click the information button at the bottom of the sidebar to open the information panel if it isn't already open.

Additionally, you can flip an event over and read the information on the back by pointing to the bottom-right corner of an event thumbnail and clicking the information button when it becomes visible. The information on the back of an event includes the event name, date, number of photos, place, and description.

 **LET ME TRY IT**

Changing Event Information

The only event information you can change is the name, description, and place. By default, iPhoto names events with a date, but you can change the name to something more descriptive, such as "Christmas 2009," and you can add a description with further details, such as "Decorating the tree, opening presents, and Christmas dinner." To change an event's name or add a description, follow these steps:

1. Click Events in the sidebar.

2. Click the event in the right pane.

3. Click the information button at the bottom of the sidebar to open the information panel if necessary, or click the information button in the bottom-right corner to flip the event over.

4. Double-click the existing title, date, or time (triple-click the title if it's more than one word), type the new information, and press Return.

Adding Place information is a little more involved. See "Organizing by Place" later in this chapter.

Sorting Photos

You can sort your photos on four different criteria: date, keyword, title, and rating. The command to sort is on the View menu. If you are sorting in the Photos source, the command is View, Sort Photos. If you are sorting in the Events source, the command is View, Sort Events. In addition to the four criteria, you also can sort most sources manually, which just means that you can drag the photos into whatever order you want.

The commands to sort are relatively simple; it's all the if, ands, or buts that apply to *what* you are sorting that get confusing. Some sources, such as Faces and Slideshows, are not sortable at all. Table 11.1 explains exactly how you can sort various sources.

Table 11.1 Sorting Different Sources

Source	How You Can Sort
Events	By date or title in ascending or descending order and manually. Sorting events does not sort photos within the events.
Photos within an event	By date, keyword, title, or rating in ascending or descending order and manually.
Photos (with Event Titles on)	By date, keyword, title, or rating in ascending or descending order and manually. Sorts all photos within all events.
Photos (with Event Titles off)	By date, keyword, title, or rating in ascending or descending order and manually. Sorts all photos as one group.
Places	By date, keyword, title, or rating in ascending or descending order. No manual sort.
Any source in the Recent category except Flagged	By date, keyword, title, or rating in ascending or descending order. No manual sort.
Flagged	By date, keyword, title, or rating in ascending or descending order. No manual sort.
Trash	By date, keyword, title, or rating. No manual, ascending, or descending sort.
Photos in an album	By date, keyword, title, or rating in ascending or descending order and manually.

When you're working in the Photos source and changing the dates on photos, it's a little disconcerting when you change the date and the photo seems to disappear. What really happens is that the picture jumps into its correct place because the default sort is by date. To keep photos from jumping out of sight after changing the date, you can change the sort to Manually.

Sorting on keywords is my favorite way to display the Photos source. First, I hide the Event titles, which as mentioned earlier, is like dumping your photos into one big pile, but then I sort on keywords. To keep things simple, I usually assign only one keyword to a photo because if you assign multiple keywords, iPhoto sorts all the photos together that have only one keyword, and then all the photos together that have two keywords, and so on.

Exploring Methods to Organize Photos

iPhoto provides many ways to organize photos and mark them so they can appear in different groups. For example, in iPhoto you can include the picture of Suzy at her sweet sixteen party in a Birthday event, include the same photo with others that are tagged with the keyword *family*, include the photo with other photos that have a five-star rating, include it in the collection of photos showing her face, and include it in an album. To achieve the same thing with printed photos, you would have to make four extra prints of the photo.

Splitting, Merging, and Creating Events

The events that iPhoto creates for you automatically when you import photos are often not exactly what you need. Let's say, for example, that you have 30 photos on your camera—10 photos taken on Thanksgiving and 20 photos taken over a two-week period during your Maui vacation. If you import the photos as one event, you subsequently will have to split the event into two events—one for Thanksgiving and one for your vacation. If you allow iPhoto to autosplit the events when it imports the photos, you subsequently will have to merge all the events it creates for your vacation. Remember that iPhoto creates a separate event for each date.

 SHOW ME   Media 11.3—A video about Splitting and Merging Events
Access this video file through your registered Web Edition at
my.safaribooksonline.com/9780789743916/media.

 LET ME TRY IT

Splitting an Event

In the preceding example, if you imported all 30 photos in one event, you will need to follow these steps to split the event:

1. Click Events in the sidebar and then double-click the event thumbnail to see all the photographs.

2. Click the photograph that should be the first photo in the new event and click the Split button in the toolbar. Both events display on the screen at the same time.

3. Click the name of the new untitled event, type a name for the event, and press Return.

4. Repeat step 3 to create additional new events and name the new events.

5. If some photos are still in the wrong events, drag them to the correct events.

While you're organizing, why not select a key photo to represent the event? Right-click the photo and click Make Key Photo.

6. When you are finished splitting events and moving photos, click All Events at the top of the screen.

 **LET ME TRY IT**

Merging Events

Going back to our example, let's assume you allowed iPhoto to autosplit the photos into events when you imported them. Now you want to merge the events for different dates into one event for your vacation. To merge events, follow these steps:

1. Click Events in the sidebar.

2. Cmd-click or Shift-click the events you want to merge.

3. Click the Merge button in the toolbar. The events merge into the first event and use the name of that event.

If a dialog box asks you to confirm the merge, you can click Don't Ask Again and then click Merge.

You can create a new blank event and put photos in it later or create a new event with selected photos. To create a new blank event, click Events in the source list and click a blank space in the right pane so that no event is selected. Click Events in the menu bar and then click New Event. To create a new event for selected photos, click any source in the source list except Faces, select the photos you want to include (using Cmd-click or Shift-click), click Events in the menu bar, and click Create Event.

You can open an event and select multiple photos in that event to create a new one, but you cannot create a new event from an event that has only one photo in it.

Copying, Deleting, and Moving Photos

I generally like to make a copy of a photo if I'm going to edit it. That way, I have the original if I ever want to use it, and I have the version that I have edited, which I might use in a different way. To copy a photo, click the photo, click Photos in the menu bar, and click Duplicate. The new photo appears beside the original photo and uses the photo's name with the word *copy* appended.

It's tempting to keep every picture you take, but eventually you will run out of space. Deleting poor-quality, uninteresting, and almost-duplicate photos makes your photo library more manageable. To delete a photograph, select it and press the Delete key.

Once you have several events, you may find that you want to move a photo that's in one event into another event. Obviously, dragging comes to mind first, but how do you get both events open at the same time? Use the same technique you would use to select nonadjacent photos: Cmd-click each event you want to open at the same time and then double-click the last one. Once the events are open, drag photos anywhere. Click All Events when you are finished.

Organizing by People's Faces

Using iPhoto's face-recognition feature, you can organize photos of your friends and relatives by their faces. For each person that you identify, iPhoto creates a group (similar to an event) and places it on the Faces corkboard. You can add the person's real name and email address to the group, which is useful if you publish photos to your Facebook account. If the email of the photo that you publish matches a Facebook ID, Facebook alerts the person that you have published new photos.

 **LET ME TRY IT**

Getting Faces Set Up

All you have to do to get things started is identify a picture of each person, supply the person's name, and iPhoto will take over. It might identify a few pictures of

Joyce as her sister Jane, but you can help iPhoto become more accurate by correcting its mistakes. Follow these steps to identify the faces you want iPhoto to find and group for you:

1. Click Faces in the source list so that iPhoto will perform a scan of all your photos. If you see a note telling you how to get started, then iPhoto has completed the scan.

2. Click a source in the source list and then open any photo of the first person you want to identify. If the photo has more than one person in it, you can identify additional faces too.

3. Click the Name button in the toolbar and click Unnamed under the face in the photo. The text changes to *Type Name*.

4. Type a name for the person and press Return.

If iPhoto fails to frame a face in a photo, click the Add Missing Face button and drag the frame to the face, sizing it if necessary.

5. Repeat steps 3 and 4 for other faces in the current photograph or click the Next button to go to a new photograph that has faces you want to identify. After you have identified a person, iPhoto might not recognize the person in a subsequent photo. If you click Unnamed and begin to type the name, iPhoto displays a list of names that start with the same letters. You can select the name from this list and press Return.

As you are identifying people, so is iPhoto. Instead of displaying "Unnamed" under a face, it might say, "Is this Joyce?" If it is, you can click the check mark; if it isn't, click the X, type the name, and press Return.

6. When you have identified at least one photo of each person, you're finished. Click the Done button. Don't go through every photograph yourself; that's iPhoto's job.

 SHOW ME Media 11.4—A video about Viewing Faces and **Making Corrections**
Access this video file through your registered Web Edition at
my.safaribooksonline.com/9780789743916/media.

 **LET ME TRY IT**

Viewing Faces and Making Corrections

After you have identified several different faces, you can see how good a job iPhoto did and correct its mistakes. As you train iPhoto on each face, it will find photographs it missed the first time and hold them for your confirmation. To view all the faces in one group and make corrections, follow these steps:

1. Click Faces in the source list and then double-click a face to see how many photos iPhoto associated with it. The window is divided into two panes, as shown in Figure 11.8.

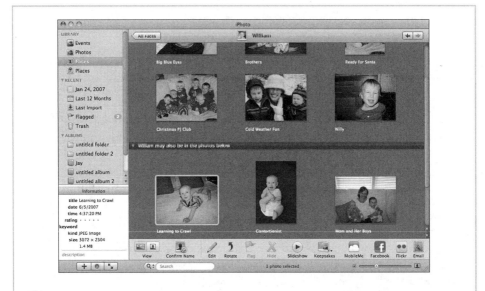

Figure 11.8 *Photos in the upper pane may need to be rejected.*

2. Check the faces in the upper pane. If one is incorrect, click once to reject the photo.

3. If no additional photos appear in the lower pane, skip to step 6.

4. If additional faces do appear in the lower pane, click the Confirm Name button to process the photos. Click each photo that is correctly identified one time. Click each photo that is not correct twice.

5. Click the Done button, and iPhoto may show you more pictures to confirm. You can repeat steps 3 and 4 until all photos are processed or skip to step 6 or 7 and come back later to finish processing.

6. Click the Next or Previous button in the upper-right corner to view another face and start over again.

7. When you are finished, click All Faces in the upper-left corner.

To be very thorough, you can run a final check of your photos. Click Photos in the source list and double-click the first photo. Click the Name button. Scroll through all the photos and see if there are any faces that are yet unnamed, using the techniques explained earlier to name them.

As you add new photos to the library, iPhoto continues to check Faces. You can see a circle icon spinning beside Faces in the source list when iPhoto is working.

Organizing by Place

Specifying the geographic location of a photo is one more way to organize your photos. You can enter a location, such as Nashville, TN, and iPhoto looks it up in its geographic database and then maps it.

 **LET ME TRY IT**

Adding Place Information to Photos

Some cameras, notably the iPhone camera, embed GPS information in photos, which associates them with a place automatically. If your camera doesn't embed GPS information, you can add the information yourself on the back of the photo. To add places to photos, first make sure you are online and then follow these steps:

1. Point to the bottom-right corner of a photo until you see the information button and then click it to flip the photo over.

2. Begin typing the location in the Photo Place box, such as "Manhattan," "Golden Gate Bridge," or "101 Main St., Louisville, KY." iPhoto suggests locations for you as you type if it can, and you can select the one that is correct if it's listed. Then, a Google map of the location shows in the lower pane with a stickpin in the exact location.

If you type a place that Google can't find on the map, a prompt asks you to locate it. Click the Spotlight to see a map. If it's not the right area, click Cancel. Type a nearby, well-known location and click the Spotlight again. This should give you the right map. Then you can drag the stickpin to the approximate location and click the Assign to Photo button.

3. While you're here, you might as well take the time to type a description. (It's just one more piece of information that you can search on later.)

4. Click the Next or Previous button to go directly to the back of the next or previous photo and repeat steps 2 and 3.

5. When you are finished, click the Done button.

To view your photographs by location, click Places in the source list. You can view a map with stickpins in the locations, as shown in Figure 11.9, or a list of locations, as shown in Figure 11.10. To toggle the view, click the appropriate View button in the toolbar.

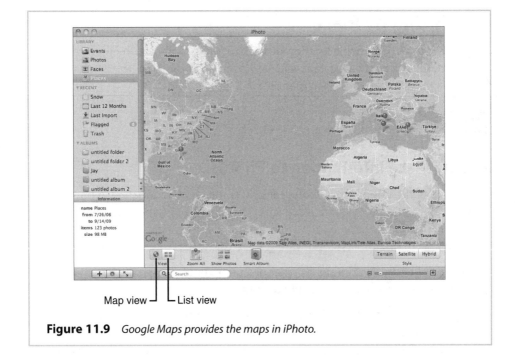

Figure 11.9   *Google Maps provides the maps in iPhoto.*

In map view, you can point to a pin and the name of the location displays. Click the arrow at the end of the location name to see the photos.

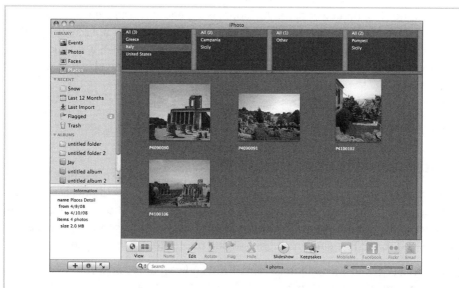

Figure 11.10   *Each column lists the number of places, not the number of photos.*

In List view, the first column lists the country, the second lists the state or province, the third lists the city, and the last column lists everything else—islands, ancient excavation sites, landmarks, and so on. Click any collection that is listed in any column to see the pictures in that location.

Flagging Photos

With all the ways that iPhoto gives you to categorize photos (keywords, faces, locations, descriptions, and so on), sometimes there is no category for what you want—particularly if what you want is just random. Maybe you are putting together a group of pictures that are representative of what you did last year. How do you categorize that? If I had this challenge, I would start by searching on the date and then review the photos, flagging the ones I want by clicking the Flag button in the toolbar.

Flagging a photo attaches a flag icon to the upper-left corner of the photo and adds a copy of the photo to the Flagged folder under the Recent category. Once you have flagged the photos, you can create an event, an album, a slideshow, and so on.

Collecting Pictures in Photo Albums

A photo album is a collection of photographs that you select from other locations and arrange in a particular order. An album is a great source to view as a slideshow, as explained earlier in this chapter. You also can use an album for a screen saver that displays the photos in the album as a slideshow, a collage, or a mosaic. See Chapter 4, "Tailoring the Desktop to Your Liking," for information about using a screen saver.

 **LET ME TRY IT**

Creating an Album

When you create and name an album, iPhoto lists it under the Albums category in the sidebar. Albums are useful, not only for organizing your photos for viewing, but for grouping pictures you want to burn to a CD, use on a website, upload to Facebook, and so on. To create an album and add photos to it, follow these steps.

1. Select photos to go in the album if you know what pictures you want to include, or skip to step 2.

2. Click the Add button at the bottom of the sidebar to open a dialog box. Album is always selected by default at the top.

3. Type a name for the album and notice that Use Selected Items in New Album is selected by default. This is exactly what you want if you selected photos in step 1.

4. Click the Create button. The new album you create displays as a source in the Albums category in the sidebar. If you did not select photos in step 1, continue to step 5.

5. To add photos to an empty album (or to one that already has photos included in it, for that matter), view the photos, select them, and drag them to the source list, dropping them on the album name. A green circle with a plus in it shows up right before you drop the photos in the album.

> You can drag entire events, individual photos, photos from other albums, and so on, and you can have the same photo in multiple albums.

6. Click the album in the source list to see the photos and then drag them into the order you want.

 **LET ME TRY IT**

Organizing Albums in Folders

If you create quite a few albums, you may want to create folders for them. For example, if you have an album for each vacation trip that you take, you may want to create a folder called "Vacations." To do this, follow these steps:

1. Click File in the menu bar and click New Folder. The folder shows in the source list under Albums.

2. Type a name for the folder and press Return.

3. Drag albums that you want to store there to the new folder.

Searching for Photos

It doesn't take long to have hundreds of photos in iPhoto, which can be just as bad as having them in a box somewhere if you don't take the time to add meaningful labels, keywords, locations, and so on, after you import them. If you take advantage of only a few of iPhoto's classification methods, you can make finding a photo much easier.

Mac's standard search feature, Spotlight, is located under the toolbar. (You can see it in Figure 11.10.) If you want to find a photo by name, description, face, or location, just type the criteria in the search text box. If you want to search by date, keyword, or rating, first select an option from the pop-up menu. As you type the text, photos that match the search text start to show in the Viewing pane.

Use searches as an efficient way to group photos for a particular purpose. For example, search for all one-star-rated photos for possible deletion. Search for all photos with the keyword *Vacation 09* to create an album, a slideshow, an event, and so on.

Editing Photos

iPhoto contains some powerful tools for editing and improving a photo. These tools are available on the toolbar in the Edit mode. Edits made to a photo are not only reflected in the photo in iPhoto, but everywhere the photo appears—in an album, a slideshow, or a document, for example.

Using the Edit Mode

Before editing a photo, you might want to make a copy and edit the copy instead of the original. In this way, you can have both versions of the photo and use them for different things. To edit a photo, follow these general steps:

1. Select a photo from any source and click the Edit button in the toolbar.

2. Click a tool in the toolbar and take the appropriate actions to make the edits with the particular tool you chose. (See specific instructions for various editing functions in this section.)

3. Repeat step 2 for all the other edits you want to make to a particular photo.

> Click Edit in the menu bar and then click Undo if you make a change that you want to reverse.

4. When you are finished, click the Next or Previous button to save the edits and go to the next or previous photo to edit it. If you don't want to edit any other photos, click the Done button.

Cropping a Photo

Cropping is a technique that trims the edges of photos. When you crop a photo, iPhoto doesn't make it smaller—it resizes the photo, thereby making the important part of the picture even larger. To crop a photo, follow these steps:

1. Select the photo from any source and click the Edit button.

2. Click the Crop button.

3. Click Constrain and select a proportional size from the pop-up menu. A frame that suggests the crop appears.

4. Drag the frame to position it and drag a corner to resize it.

5. Click the Apply button.

SHOW ME Media 11.5—A video about Using Automatic and Manual Red-Eye Removal

Access this video file through your registered Web Edition at my.safaribooksonline.com/9780789743916/media.

 **LET ME TRY IT**

Using Automatic and Manual Red-Eye Removal

Red-eye is a common problem in photographs that have been taken with a flash. The red-eye tool has two modes: automatic and manual. If you use the automatic method and it doesn't do a good enough job, you can switch to manual. Follow these steps to try the automatic mode first and then try the manual mode:

1. Select the photo from any source and click the Edit button.

2. Click the Red-eye button and then click Auto. If you are not satisfied, click Edit in the menu bar and click Undo.

3. Using the slider at the bottom of the window, zoom in on the photo and navigate to the portion where the red eyes are.

4. Using the Size slider, make the cursor about the same size as the pupils of the eyes.

5. Click the pupils to replace the red with a black circle.

6. Resize the photo and close the Navigation window.

7. Click Done when you are finished.

Refer to the following list to learn how to use other common editing techniques:

- **Rotating**—If you turn your camera sideways to take a photo, that picture might be imported into iPhoto "lying on its side." This is actually a function of the camera, but once the photo is imported, iPhoto can turn it back up the right way. To turn a photo, select it from any source and click the Rotate button as many times as necessary to rotate the picture to the correct position. To rotate in the opposite direction, hold the Option key down as you click the Rotate button.

- **Enhancing**—Enhancing a photo automatically adjusts any of a photo's many attributes that need tweaking, including exposure, contrast, color saturation, definition, highlights, and shadows. To enhance a photo, select it from any source, click the Edit button in the toolbar, and click the Enhance button.

TELL ME MORE   Media 11.6—A discussion about Enhancing Photo
Attributes
Access this audio recording through your registered Web Edition at
my.safaribooksonline.com/9780789743916/media.

- **Applying special effects**—Special effects include black and white, sepia, antique, blurred edges, and vignette. To apply a special effect to a photo, select the photo, click the Edit button, and click the Effects button. A palette of 12 choices opens. Click the effect you want.

- **Reverting to original**—Even after you have made changes to a photo and exited the Edit mode, you can revert to the original photo. Click the photo (in any view), click Photo in the menu bar, and click Revert to Original.

 SHOW ME   Media 11.7—A video about Retouching a Photo
Access this video file through your registered Web Edition at
my.safaribooksonline.com/9780789743916/media.

Sharing Photos with Others

In this section, I discuss some of the more common ways to share your photos with other people—emailing, burning a disc to give to someone, printing the photos on your own printer, and sharing photos online. In Chapter 15, "Being Creative with Photos," I discuss some of the more creative ways to share your photos, such as photo books, calendars, and greeting cards.

Emailing Photos

You can approach emailing photos from the Mail application or from the iPhoto application. If you send photos from iPhoto, you select the photos first and iPhoto creates the email for you. If you send them from Mail, you create the message first and then select the photos.

 **LET ME TRY IT**

Emailing Photos from iPhoto

Initiating the sending of photos from iPhoto has a slight advantage over initiating from Mail. In iPhoto, you are presented with the option of downsizing the photographs before you compose the mail. In Mail, the photo attaches at its original size. You can change the size, but you aren't prompted to do so.

To email photos from iPhoto, follow these steps:

1. Select the photos you want to send and click the Email button.

2. Select the Size and other options in the dialog box that opens and then click Compose Message. The Mail application opens with a new message. The photos are attached and the Subject line is filled in for you.

3. Address the message, type something in the body of the message if you want, and click Send.

If you don't have your email account set up on your Mac, then sending photos as attachments becomes a little more difficult. You can't use the Finder to select photos from iPhoto because once you navigate to the iPhoto Library, it's a dead end—you can't really get into the internal structure of the library where the files are stored. The easiest thing to do is export the photos you want to email by dragging the photos directly from iPhoto to the desktop. Then you can navigate to them with the Finder. After you attach the photos, you can drag them to the Trash.

Putting Photos on a Disc

In iPhoto, you can burn a disc to share with other iPhoto users, but if you want to burn a disc for a Windows user, you'll have to export your photos and then use the Burn command in the Finder. Burning an iPhoto disc is also a quick and easy way to back up your photos, and it has the benefit of maintaining your iPhoto structure on the disc.

 **LET ME TRY IT**

Creating an iPhoto Disc

Burning photos to a disk from iPhoto enables you to select the photos you want to put on the disc—something you can't do in the Finder. To burn a disc of an iPhoto Library, follow these steps

1. Insert a blank disc in the drive and select the photos you want to include on the disc. You can select them individually with Cmd-click, as well as select events, albums, and so on.

2. Click Share in the menu bar and then click Burn. Information about how many photos you are burning and the space they will use displays above the toolbar. You can select more photos at this time, and the information updates automatically so you know when you are getting close to filling the disc.

3. Change the name of the disc if you want or keep the default name that iPhoto supplies for you.

4. Click the Burn button located above the iWeb button in the toolbar.

5. A dialog box opens to confirm your action. Click Burn. When the disc is ready, iPhoto ejects it by default.

> If you are the recipient of an iPhoto disc, you can see the photos if you insert the disc in your disc drive. iPhoto opens automatically and selects the disc for you in the source list in the sidebar (under the Shares Category).

Printing Photos

With iPhoto, you can print your photos in many different ways. Of course, you can print individual photos that look like a standard photograph, but you also can print one to four photographs on a page and format them with a simple border, a mat, or a double mat, as well as add titles. If you want to print thumbnails to proof, you can print a contact sheet with as many as 130 photos on a single sheet.

If you're just printing individual photos at home, it's probably less expensive (by the time you pay for the photographic paper, the ink, and your mistakes) to print your photos at a lab or order them online. To print at a lab, take the photos on a disc that you have burned for use with Windows. To order prints online from Apple, select the photos, click File in the menu bar, and then click Order Prints. The sizes and prices are listed, and you can specify the number of prints of each that you want. If the resolution of a photo is too low to make a good quality print, a low-resolution alert symbol appears by the size.

 SHOW ME   Media 11.8—A video about Printing Customized Photos
Access this video file through your registered Web Edition at
my.safaribooksonline.com/9780789743916/media.

 **LET ME TRY IT**

Printing Customized Photos At Home

If you want to print photographs that are more creative than just single prints, you can use the customization features. Follow these steps to print photographs with customized settings:

1. Select the photos, click File in the menu bar, and click Print.

If you select an event, iPhoto assumes you want to print all the photos in the event.

2. Select a theme from the left pane.

3. Scroll the photos in the right pane by clicking the right or left arrow under the preview of the photo.

4. Click Customize.

5. Click the Layout button in the toolbar and select the layout you want. If you select a layout that has descriptive text, select the text in the box, type the text you want to use, and press Return.

6. Click the Background button to select colors, and click the Borders button to select the style of borders.

7. Click Print. Select the printer and set options as needed.

Look for a setting in the Print menu that governs the print resolution. The higher the resolution you use, the better quality the print. The trade-off is that the higher the resolution, the more ink it uses and the longer it takes to print. Note, however, that there is no degree of quality gained by printing a photo at a higher resolution than it was taken.

8. Click Print.

Sharing Photos Online

In iPhoto, sharing your photos in MobileMe, Facebook, or Flickr is just a click away. The toolbar contains buttons for all three. Of course, to upload photos to a MobileMe Photo Gallery, you must have a MobileMe account with Apple. Likewise, to upload photos to Facebook or Flickr, you must have existing accounts at these sites. Facebook and Flickr accounts are free; MobileMe isn't.

Assuming that you have the proper accounts set up, to publish to one of these locations, select the photos and click the appropriate button in the toolbar. Then fill in the dialog boxes that open and click Publish. After you publish the photos, an album displays in the sidebar under the associated category. In other words, if you publish photos to Facebook, an album appears under the Facebook category. After you publish the photos to any of these three locations (MobileMe, Facebook, or Flickr), you can add more photos by dragging photos to the album in the sidebar and clicking the Publish icon.

This chapter deals with many of the valuable "little" applications that can increase your efficiency and make your life on the computer so much easier, such as widgets, Preview, Dictionary, and more.

12

Using Widgets and Other Applications

Whereas other chapters concentrate on major Mac OS X Snow Leopard applications such as Safari, Mail, and TextEdit, this chapter concentrates on the applications that can assist you in small ways while you are working in the major applications. In this chapter, I explain how to select the widgets you want to use, how to download more widgets, and even how to create your own web widgets. Additionally, the chapter covers using Preview, looking up words in the dictionary, creating sticky notes, and using the calculator. Snow Leopard provides you with so many features to help you do whatever it is you do.

Using Widgets

Widgets are mini-applications that perform functions such as accessing Wikipeidia, accessing your address book, or telling the time in any part of the world. When you launch the Dashboard for the first time, several widgets open, but there are many more waiting in the wings for you to select them.

 TELL ME MORE Media 12.1—A discussion about Exploring Default Widgets
Access this audio recording through your registered Web Edition at
my.safaribooksonline.com/9780789743916/media.

Managing Widgets

The default widgets that appear on the Dashboard may be just the ones you want to use, but you might also want to select some additional widgets to use. If you don't need some of the default widgets that Snow Leopard selected for you, you can disable them and select different widgets. When you disable a widget, it closes on the Dashboard, but it's still available for use in the future.

Many widgets depend on the Internet for data, so keep that in mind when you select them. Additionally, some widgets need additional information from you in order to perform their functions. For example, you would need to supply a Zip code or geographic location for a weather widget.

 **LET ME TRIY IT**

Configuring the Dashboard

Configuring the Dashboard involves enabling and disabling widgets, arranging them on the Dashboard, and supplying additional information to widgets that require it. To configure your own selection and arrangement of widgets on the Dashboard, follow these steps:

1. Click the Dashboard icon in the Dock or press F4 to open the Dashboard.

2. Click the plus icon in the bottom-left corner of the screen to display a bar with the installed widgets (see Figure 12.1).

Scroll arrows

Figure 12.1 *The Widgets icon and the Manage Widgets button both open the same dialog box.*

3. Click the arrows at the right and left of the bar to scroll the widgets, and click each widget in the bar that you want to add to the Dashboard.

Just for fun, you could add the Translation widget to the Dashboard and translate the French caption for the first figure in Chapter 1.

4. Point to any part of a widget that you have added and drag it to the location you want it to occupy on the screen.

5. Point to the bottom-right corner of the widget to see if it has an information button. If it does, click it to flip the widget over to the back side. Complete additional information or make selections as required, and click Done.

6. Click the X in the upper-right corner of any widget that you want to disable.

7. When you are finished configuring the Dashboard, click the X just above the left side of the widget bar.

Downloading More Widgets

Tons of free widgets await your download on the Apple website. For the serious crowd, there are widgets that give you Mac tips and tricks, convert currency, and keep track of the hours you've worked. For the fun crowd, there are widgets that take you on a nonstop rollercoaster ride, count down to Christmas with the Grinch, and list upcoming gigs and events (called the *Gigometer*, of course). To access these widgets, click the Manage Widgets button (see Figure 12.1) and click the More Widgets button at the bottom of the dialog box. This button takes you directly to the page on Apple's website where you can download all the widgets your little heart desires. After the widget downloads to your computer, just click Install to install it in the Dashboard and then click Keep.

Creating Your Own Web Clip Widget

The purpose of about half a dozen of the default widgets is to deliver real-time information from the Web, such as weather, sports, and stock prices. If your interests lie elsewhere, you can go to a website that has the information you want and create your own widget by clipping a frame from the site. Then, instead of going to the website, you can check the data you want to see in the web clip widget on your Dashboard.

 SHOW ME   Media 12.2—A video about Clipping a Widget from the Web
Access this video file through your registered Web Edition at
my.safaribooksonline.com/9780789743916/media.

 **LET ME TRY IT**

Clipping a Widget from the Web

Some websites have features on them that are always located in the same place on the page. These are the sites that are good candidates for clipping a web widget. Follow these steps to create a web clip widget:

1. Open Safari and navigate to the page that has the content you want—the daily deal on eBay, for example.

2. Click the Web Clip button in the Safari toolbar.

This button does not appear on the toolbar by default. Refer to Chapter 7, "Browsing the Web," for instructions on how to add it.

3. Move the cursor close to the information that you want and the white rectangle snaps to fit the section. Click to anchor the rectangle.

4. Adjust the borders to fit, if necessary, and click Add. The widget shows up on your Dashboard.

After you create a widget, test it to see if it really works. For example, if you clipped a log-in area, in all probability, it won't work. If your web clip is working and you really like it, don't ever remove it from the Dashboard because you'll lose it. If you accidentally remove a clipped widget or one gets ruined because the web page design has changed, you can always create a new one.

Using Preview

The Preview application is a graphics-editing program that has joined forces with an Adobe Reader clone. Most Mac users don't utilize all the capabilities of Preview for several reasons:

- iPhoto duplicates some of its graphic capabilities (for example, cropping and adjusting exposure, brightness, and color).

- Users rarely need to edit or annotate PDF files.

- Users don't know what the full capabilities of the program are.

Normally, Preview opens automatically when you double-click certain types of files, but you can open the application *on purpose* from the Applications menu or from its icon in the Dock.

As a PDF reader, Preview is awesome. It lets you search PDF documents; select and copy text from them; highlight, underline, or strike through text; click hyperlinks and add your own links; draw arrows, circles and rectangles; add your own comments about the text and add text boxes to the text; format the text of your comments and text boxes; bookmark your place in the file; email the file; crop and rotate pages; and take a screen shot of the file.

The Annotation toolbar, which displays at the bottom of the window when you click the Annotate button, provides much of the functionality of Preview. Tools on the left side perform various actions in the file, and tools on the right perform formatting functions. Figure 12.2 shows the Preview window with a PDF file that has been annotated.

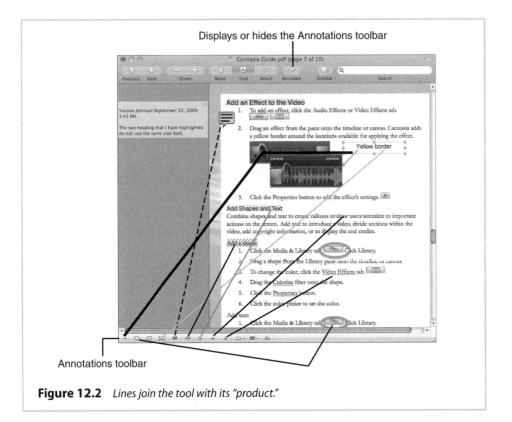

Figure 12.2 *Lines join the tool with its "product."*

As a graphic viewer, Preview can open practically any graphic format. In addition to viewing a graphic file in Preview, you can use annotation tools to draw arrows, circles, or rectangles and to add text boxes to the graphic. Think what you could do with that!

One other useful function that Preview can perform on a graphic is changing its dimensions and resolution. You might use this feature to reduce the size or resolution of a photo that is too large to email. (Reducing the dimensions and resolution automatically reduces the file size.) To change a photograph's size, double-click the file to open it in Preview. Click Tools in the menu bar and click Adjust Size. The dialog box shown in Figure 12.3 opens. Make desired changes in width, height, and resolution and click OK. Then save the file.

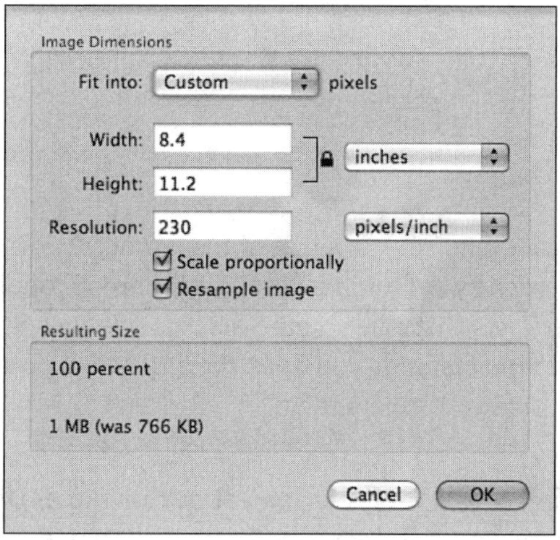

Figure 12.3   *To reduce file size, not dimensions, reduce the resolution and select Resample Image.*

Consulting the Dictionary

At my house, we use the Dictionary on my MacBook Pro all the time when we play *Scrabble*. It's much easier than using the two-ton, unabridged version, and it's much more up to date. We play so often that I've actually put the Dictionary in the Dock, but you can open it from Applications.

Another quick way to open Dictionary is to click the Spotlight and type Di. Then click Dictionary in the list of results.

The Dictionary application actually has three separate dictionaries and a thesaurus: the complete *New Oxford American Dictionary*, the Apple Dictionary, Wikipedia, and the complete *Oxford American Writers Thesaurus*. Of course, the Wikipedia dictionary is actually online, and Dictionary just searches it for you. When you type a word to look up, you can click the All button at the top or just click one of the sources. To read a definition of any word in the results list, double-click it.

To quit Dictionary, click Cmd-Q or right-click the icon in the Dock and click Quit. Dictionary remembers which source you have selected when you quit, and it selects the same source the next time you open it.

The Dictionary widget in the Dashboard uses the same dictionaries and thesaurus but does not include Wikipedia.

Posting Stickies

The Stickies application is the equivalent of the famous Post-It Note®. This application is not on the Dock by default, so to open it, open the Applications folder and click **Stickies**. Two notes that give you the quick lowdown on creating and formatting stickies appear the first time you open the application. After you read them, you can save the content or delete them.

 SHOW ME   Media 12.3—A video about Saving or Deleting a Note
Access this video file through your registered Web Edition at
my.safaribooksonline.com/9780789743916/media.

 LET ME TRY IT

Saving or Deleting a Note

When a sticky note is outdated or no longer needed, such as the two notes that appear the first time you use the Stickies application, you can delete them. Sometimes a note that you want to delete may contain information that you want to save. In this case, you should save the data in some format, such as a TextEdit file, before deleting the note. To save and delete notes, follow these steps.

1. Click the note to select it and click the Close button in the upper-left corner.

2. To save the contents of the note, click Save. Type a name for the file, specify Where, select a Format, and click Save.

3. To delete a selected note, click the Close button and click Don't Save.

The Dashboard has a Sticky widget also, but it is not as robust as the Stickies application.

To create a sticky note, click File in the menu bar and click New. You can type text, paste or drag it from another file, or import it. Additionally, you can paste or drag graphics, movies, or sounds, and you can add web links. By default, notes are yellow, but you can click Color in the menu bar and select from five other colors in the pop-up menu.

 SHOW ME   Media 12.4—A video about Saving Screen Captures on Sticky Notes

Access this video file through your registered Web Edition at my.safaribooksonline.com/9780789743916/media.

LET ME TRY IT

Positioning Stickies on the Screen

You can drag a sticky note to any location on the screen, and you can make it float on top of other windows that are open. Additionally, you can make a note translucent so that you can read what might be under the note. To position notes and change their appearance, follow these steps:

1. Point to the title bar at the top of the sticky note and drag the note anywhere on the screen.

2. If windows are covering your notes, click Window in the Stickies toolbar and click Bring All to Front.

3. To ensure that a sticky is always on top of other windows, click the note, click Note in the menu bar, and click Floating Window.

4. To make a note translucent so you can see what's underneath it, click the note, click Note in the menu bar, and click Translucent Window.

5. To apply the floating and translucent settings to all notes, click Note in the menu bar and then click Use as Default. Figure 12.4 shows several notes.

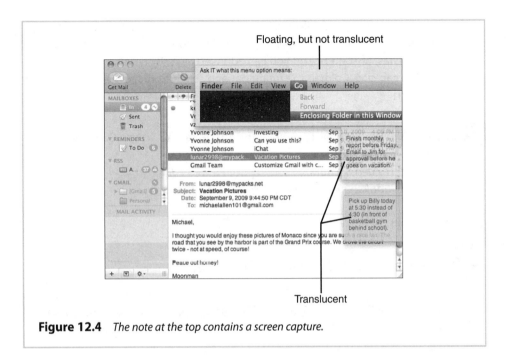

Figure 12.4 *The note at the top contains a screen capture.*

If you get too many notes on the screen, you can collapse them to one line by double-clicking the title bar. Expand them by double-clicking again.

6. Press Cmd-Q to quit Stickies. This closes all the notes, but the next time you open Stickies, the notes display again.

Using the Calculator

After watching HGTV all day, the lady of the house decides that the driveway would look great with big pink circles painted all over it. She uses a piece of chalk and a string that is 1.75-feet long to scribe circles at random on the driveway—10 of them. Now she needs to know how much paint to buy.

Enter the calculator. Not that little dinky (though very useful) calculator in the Dashboard—the *big* calculator with the tape and the scientific mode, as shown in Figure 12.5. (Open it from the Applications folder.)

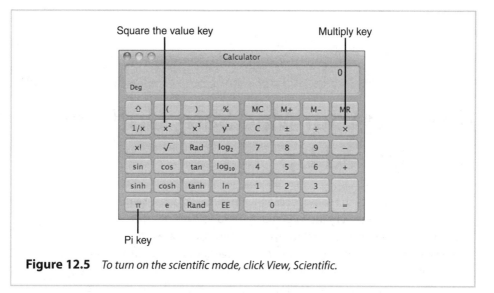

Square the value key   Multiply key

Pi key

Figure 12.5   *To turn on the scientific mode, click View, Scientific.*

She remembers the formula for the area of a circle from her high school geometry class (πr^2), but she doesn't remember the value of pi. No problem. Using the calculator she clicks π followed by ×, 1.75, and x2. Then she multiplies by 10 (the number of circles) and finally by 2 (number of coats of paint) to find out that the total area is 192 square feet. As a reminder, she saves the tape of her calculation by clicking File in the menu bar and clicking Save Tape As. Then she types a name and clicks Save and prints the file. The next day she goes to the paint store with her print out. She determines that she only needs a quart of paint (*Pink Petunia Perfection*), so she buys it and goes right to work on her masterpiece.

When her husband comes home from work and sees the driveway, he uses the calculator to calculate the amount of blacktop sealer it will take to resurface the driveway. He quits the calculator by clicking the Close button, and then he calls the cable company to drop HGTV from their entertainment package. Bada-bing, bada-boom!

This chapter discusses the security features of your Mac, keeping your applications up-to-date, and backing up your entire system.

13

Keeping Your Mac Safe, Updated, and Backed Up

One of the reasons so many people love the Mac is because the operating system is so secure. There's very little you have to do to facilitate this—in most cases, just accept the default security settings and keep your software updated. Apple provides a safety net, though. In the unlikely event that some catastrophe wipes out all your data, you can use Time Machine backups to restore your entire system. This chapter covers the security settings for surfing the Web and how to turn on the firewall, the Keychain application that keeps your passwords, installing application updates, and backing up and restoring with Time Machine.

Safely Surfing the Web

To date, there has never been a successful, broad-scale virus or spyware attack launched on Mac OS X. There seems to be no need for antivirus or spyware detectors, but such programs are available for the Mac. It's a matter of personal preference whether you use them. Most people don't.

Exploring Security Settings

Safari's default settings for surfing the Web securely are the best settings and you don't need to change them, but it won't hurt you to know what they are. To open the Security pane where these settings reside, click Safari in the menu bar, click Preferences, and click the Security tab, if necessary.

Following is an explanation of the Security preferences shown in Figure 13.1:

- **Fraudulent Sites**—Fraudulent sites often use various tricks to make their addresses appear to be the address of the site they are impersonating. Safari warns you when you land on one of these sites because it checks the site's certificate, which cannot be faked.

- **Web Content**—Plug-ins, Java, and JavaScript are all elements that websites may use to deliver content to you. If you disable any of these, a website may not function correctly. Most of the time you do not want to see pop-up windows, but occasionally a website may use a pop-up window for a legitimate reason. You can turn off the blocking while you are on that site by clicking Safari in the menu bar and clicking Block Pop-Up Windows to uncheck the option. When you leave the site, repeat the steps to start blocking again.

- **Accept Cookies**—A cookie is a small piece of text that a website stores on your computer so that it recognizes you when you go back to it. Rejecting cookies makes some websites unusable.

- **Database Storage Allowed Before Asking**—Some websites download files to your hard drive for you to use on their sites. If a site requires additional space, a message displays on your screen, which is your cue to open the Preferences window and increase the space.

- **Ask Before Sending a Non-Secure Form from a Secure Website**—This preference is essential! *Do not change it.* Even if you are on a secure site, a form may not be secure. If Safari warns you that a form is not secure and it contains sensitive information such as your credit card or social security number, do *not* send the form.

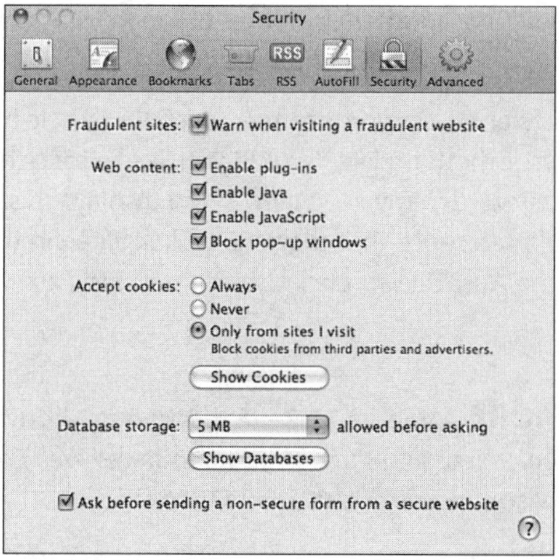

Figure 13.1 *Safari default preferences have the optimum settings.*

Using a Firewall

A firewall blocks unwanted incoming connections from other computers on a network or the Internet. It is on by default, and it allows connections by software and services that have a signed, trusted certificate. The Firewall preferences reside in the Firewall pane of the Security Preferences window. To access the preferences, click the System Preferences button in the Dock, click Security, and then click Firewall.

 TELL ME MORE   **Media 13.1—A discussion about Understanding Certificates**
Access this audio recording through your registered Web Edition at
my.safaribooksonline.com/9780789743916/media.

Working with the Keychain

The Keychain is an application that stores your user names and passwords. Using passwords is an integral part of using your Mac in a secure way. If you're one of those people who use the same login name and password for everything (not a good idea) because it's too difficult to remember a slew of different passwords, you'll love the Keychain feature. It remembers your login names and passwords and can even enter them for you automatically in some cases. Before you throw away your little black book of passwords, however, realize that the Keychain is on *your* hard drive. If you use another computer to log in to a password-protected site, you have to know your login name and password.

You add login names and passwords to the Keychain by selecting an option in a dialog box that says something like, "Would you like to save this password?" or "Remember this password in my keychain." Safari displays this type of dialog box if you set the AutoFill preference that triggers it. Click Safari in the menu bar and click Preferences. Click the AutoFill tab, click User Names and Passwords, and close the window.

 TELL ME MORE   Media 13.2—A discussion about Using the Keychain
Access this audio recording through your registered Web Edition at
my.safaribooksonline.com/9780789743916/media

Maintaining Your Mac Software

Mac OS X performs maintenance routines in the background between 3:15 a.m. and 5:30 a.m. in your local time zone if the computer is not in sleep mode. These routines remove system files that are no longer needed, purge log files, and delete temporary items. So periodically, you should leave your computer on overnight and turn off the sleep mode. Otherwise, you should learn to run these routines.

SHOW ME   Media 13.3—A video about Running Maintenance Routines
Access this video file through your registered Web Edition at
my.safaribooksonline.com/9780789743916/media.

Getting Software Updates

After the release of a major version of any Mac application, such as Snow Leopard 10.6 or iTunes 9.0, Apple releases updates that solve problems or add functionality. Updates are free, and you should always install them.

 **LET ME TRY IT**

Installing Updates

By default, your Mac checks for updates on a weekly basis and downloads the updates automatically. When Mac OS X has downloaded updates, it notifies you that they are ready to be installed. If you don't want to wait for the weekly check, you can click the Apple menu and click Software Update any time. To install an update, follow these steps:

1. When an update notification such as the one in Figure 13.2 displays, click the Install button.

Figure 13.2   *If you are curious about what the update includes, click Show Details.*

2. If licensing information displays, click Agree.

3. Enter you password in the dialog box that opens and click OK.

You can never install an application or an update without confirming that it is okay to do so by filling in this dialog box. This is one of OS X's many safety features.

4. When the installation is finished, you may have to restart the computer or simply click OK and then Quit.

Upgrading to New Versions of Mac Applications

Whereas updates are free, upgrades are not. When you upgrade the Mac operating system (OS), you automatically get upgrades for all the free programs included with the operating system, such as Mail, Address Book, Safari, and so on. Generally, Apple offers two types of upgrades—an upgrade of the operating system only, and an upgrade of the operating system plus the iLife suite of applications. For Snow Leopard, the operating system upgrade is $29; the Snow Leopard and iLife upgrade combination, called the Mac Box Set, is $169. Upgrading your software is a matter of personal preference and finances.

Backing Up with Time Machine

How would you like to be in the *Four Percent Club*? It's the exclusive club made up of all Mac owners who back up their Macs. The one-time membership fee is as low as $65, the price of a 500GB USB external drive from newegg.com. Membership benefits include perpetual peace of mind, uninterrupted sleep, and a complete backup of your entire system. Who could resist such a deal? Join today!

I'm sorry—did I lose you with that introduction? Here's the translation: Statistics show that only 4% of Mac users back up their systems. This is *unbelievable* when you can buy an external hard drive for as little as $65 and use Mac's stellar backup application, Time Machine, to back up your entire computer. In the days before Time Machine, it might have been somewhat daunting to figure out how to back up your system and then remember to do it on a regular basis, but that's all ancient history. Time Machine is so simple and so automatic that you can literally "set it and forget it." There is absolutely no excuse for not using Time Machine to back up your system.

Creating Full Backups

A second hard drive is required for use with Time Machine. The second hard drive should be larger than the hard drive you're backing up, and it should be formatted for a Mac. (Many new drives come formatted for Windows only.) For most users, a 500GB drive should be adequate.

As soon as you install or plug in the additional drive, Mac OS X asks you if you want to use it to back up with Time Machine. Click Use as Backup Disk. The Time Machine pane of System Preferences opens and the backup starts immediately. Time Machine backs up everything on your hard drive, all your data and preferences, all the other users' data and preferences, all your applications, and the operating system.

Okay, let's reread the previous paragraph and notice that it takes only *one* click on your part to set up Time Machine. That, dear reader, is how Time Machine has consigned all other backup programs to ancient history.

The first back up can take hours, but you can continue to work during that time. You may notice some slowness, but only during this initial backup. As long as the drive is attached to the Mac, Time Machine checks your computer for changes every hour and backs them up. It keeps multiple backups of your system, allowing you to restore from a particular date or time.

Eventually your backup drive will fill up and Time Machine will start deleting the oldest backups to make room for the newest backups.

Restoring Data

Time Machine can restore single or multiple data files, entire folders, applications, or the entire system to the Finder. Additionally, it can restore an item to iPhoto, an entry to the Address Book, or an item to Mail.

 **LET ME TRY IT**

Restoring a Deleted File to the Finder

Let's say that you have a folder in Finder that is missing a file. Maybe you deleted the file thinking you didn't need it any more, and you also emptied the trash. Time Machine has a copy of the file that you can restore. Here's how you do it:

1. Open the Finder, open the folder where the file used to reside, and then open Time Machine from the Dock or the Applications folder. The folder you selected in Finder now appears in Time Machine with windows of multiple backups behind it.

If you don't really know where the file used to reside, just open Time Machine and perform a search as instructed in step 2.

2. From this point, you have multiple ways to look for the files: click a Finder window, click a date in the date line on the right, click the flat arrow that is pointing away from you, or perform a search in the Spotlight search box.

3. When you think you have found the file you want to restore, select it and press the Spacebar to view the content of the file.

4. If the file you found is the one you want to restore, click Restore in the bottom-right corner of the screen. The Finder window appears to travel in time and makes a landing on the desktop with the file restored to its original location.

> To restore items to iPhoto, Address Book, or Mail, open the application first and then open Time Machine.

Restoring the Hard Drive

Hard drives rarely last a lifetime. Eventually they crash. Sometimes they fall victim to a catastrophic event before they have time to crash. Either way, you should expect to restore your hard drive at some point in the future and be prepared for it. Follow these steps to restore the hard drive:

1. Connect the drive that holds the Time Machine backup and insert the Snow Leopard installation DVD in the DVD drive.

2. Double-click the Install Mac OS X icon.

3. Click Utilities in the menu bar and click Restore System from Backup.

4. Click Continue. Click your Time Machine disk and then click the most recent backup in the list. Sit back and wait. When the backup is complete, your Mac will work just as it did before.

Being Diligent

If you use an external drive for Time Machine's backups and you unplug it, Time Machine cannot perform its backups; however, the next time you plug in the drive, Time Machine starts backing up again. It does this automatically without your prompting. So the only thing you have to do to keep your backups current is keep the drive plugged in. If that's a problem for you, consider buying the more pricey, wireless Apple Time Capsule. It costs $299, but it holds 1TB of data, and it's also a Wi-Fi base station.

Having Fun and Getting Creative

This chapter is your entertainment guide for using DVD Player, Front Row, QuickTime Player, and iTunes.

14

Watching Movies, Listening to Music, and Playing Games

When there's time to have some fun, Mac OS X provides some very good audio and video entertainment applications. This chapter tells you how to watch movies on DVD Player or Front Row, look at YouTube videos on QuickTime Player, and listen to music in iTunes or Front Row. Macs are very short on games that come with the system, but this chapter does show you how to play a game of chess with a friend or with your Mac.

Watching Movies and Videos

Did your two-year-old who loves all your remote controls somehow open the drive on your $300 DVD player and break it? No problem. Just pop a DVD into your Mac and enjoy. You have two different programs you can use to play DVDs: DVD Player and Front Row. Take your pick—they have the same controls and produce the same quality. You might prefer Front Row, however, because it has a remote.

Using DVD Player

By default, when you insert a DVD in the DVD drive, Mac OS X launches DVD Player and begins playing the DVD immediately. The video plays in full-screen mode. To display the controls, as shown in Figure 14.1, point to the bottom of the screen. Use the mouse to click the controls.

Figure 14.1 *You can hide controls when you are not using them.*

If you click the Exit Full Screen button, you see the video in a window and the onscreen remote control is visible (see Figure 14.2). Use the mouse to click the controls on the remote. When you are finished, click the eject button in the onscreen controls and press Cmd-Q to quit DVD Player.

Figure 14.2 *Use this virtual remote when viewing in less than full-screen mode.*

By default, the DVD Player launches when you insert a video DVD. To change what happens when you insert the disc, open System Preferences, click CDs & DVDs, and select a different option for When You Insert a Video DVD.

Using Front Row

Front Row is an entertainment center that plays movies, iTunes, podcasts, TV shows, and displays your photos from iPhoto. Although you can start Front Row from the Applications folder, the easiest way to start it is to point the remote control at your Mac and press the Menu button on the remote. How cool is that? (You still remember where you put that mysterious, little, white gadget that came with your Mac, don't you?)

When you start Front Row, a menu displays with all the options for the different types of entertainment Front Row provides. If you want to use Front Row to watch a movie instead of DVD Player, launch Front Row first and then insert the DVD. If the DVD has been played previously, a menu displays with options to resume playing, start from the beginning, eject the disk, and go to the DVD menu. Otherwise, Front Row starts playing the movie immediately.

Use the remote control to navigate the current DVD's menu as well as the Front Row menus. If you press the Menu button while the movie is playing, the movie's menu displays. Press the Menu button again and a Front Row menu with DVD options displays. Press Menu again and the Front Row main menu displays. Once more, and Front Row quits.

Using QuickTime Player

QuickTime Player is yet another application that plays movies, but not the movies that you view with DVD Player or Front Row. You use QuickTime Player to view short videos like you see on YouTube. Like me, you probably have friends who send you funny and interesting videos in email messages. To play one of these videos, double-click the file and, if the video is in a format it can read, QuickTime Player opens automatically with the file loaded and ready to play. Click the Play button to play the video. To quit QuickTime Player, press Cmd-Q

Even short videos that QuickTime Player can open may not play if they use a compression/decompression format that QuickPlayer cannot process. Quick-Time Player reads these formats: QuickTime Movie (.mov), MPEG-4 (.mp4 and .m4v), MPEG-1, 3GPP, 3GPP2, AVI, and DV.

Attaching Your Mac to a TV

Say your two-year-old has destroyed your DVD player—there is one other possibili-ty for you. You can connect your Mac to a TV and watch your movie on the TV screen. Ah! It sounds so easy, but many things Influence whether this will work cor-rectly. You must take these things into consideration: the type and age of the Mac you have determines which adapter you must purchase; the type of video ports you have on your TV also determines what type of adapter you must purchase; the type of adapter you use determines what kind of video cable you must use. For example, if you have a Mac Pro (with ATImX1900 XT), a MacBook Pro, a Mac mini, or a Power Mac G5, you can purchase an Apple DVI to Video Adapter to connect the DVI port on your computer to any S-video or RCA enabled device, such as a TV or VCR. On the other hand, if you have an iMac with Intel Core Duo, a MacBook (except for the 2.0GHz Intel Core 2 Duo with the white case that came out in Jan-uary 2009), or a 12-inch PowerBook G4, you have to purchase the Mini-DVI to Video Adapter.

Then there's the whole issue of sound. One recommendation is to use a Mini-plug to RCA splitter cable to connect from your speaker output on the computer to the RCA audio inputs on the television.

If you understand all this audio/video jargon and you have the expertise to con-nect video components, then this might be a snap for you. If not, then I suggest you just buy a new DVD player. Of course, you have to hook that up, too!

Listening to Music with iTunes

iTunes is a media player, the front door to the iTunes Music Store, a music CD burner, and the central location for synchronizing your Mac with your iPod or iPhone. To launch iTunes, click its icon in the Dock or simply insert a music CD. iTunes opens automatically due to the preference set in the CDs & DVDs pane of System Preferences.

The first time you open iTunes, you have to agree to the License Agreement. Then the iTunes Setup Assistant opens. You can click Next on each screen and finally click Done. When finished, you will have agreed to use iTunes to handle audio content from the Internet and to let iTunes search your Home folder for MP3 and AAC music files you already have. When the assistant closes, iTunes opens in a window, as seen in Figure 14.3.

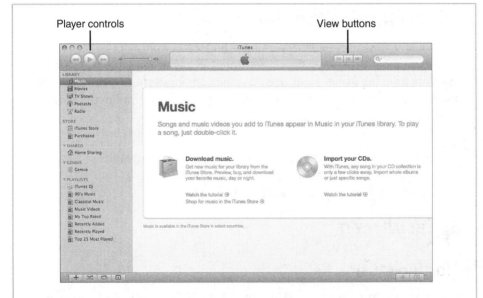

Figure 14.3 *If the Setup Assistant finds music, it lists it in the right pane instead of the informational screen.*

The design of iTunes is very similar to the design of the Finder window. It has a list of sources in the Sidebar and a viewing pane on the right. When you first start using iTunes, if you click any source in the Library, the viewing pane displays introductory information and links to more information or tutorials, but once you add items in the sources, the right pane displays the items. Use the controls at the top to play items.

In addition to the onscreen controls, you can use the F7 through F9 keys on new keyboards to control the play of tracks.

Using the View buttons in the toolbar, you can display items for certain sources in a list, a grid, or cover flow view. The default view for Music is the Grid view, which displays icons. Additionally, when you're viewing Music, a third pane for the Genius sidebar displays. To hide or show the Genius sidebar, click View in the menu bar and click Hide Genius Bar or Show Genius Bar.

 TELL ME MORE   **Media 14.1—A discussion about Using the Genius**
Access this audio recording through your registered Web Edition at
my.safaribooksonline.com/9780789743916/media.

Adding Music to the Library

You can add music to your library by importing tracks from a CD, by purchasing albums or single tracks from the iTunes store, by downloading the free Single of the Week from the iTunes store, or by downloading music from the Internet. When you download music from the iTunes Store or from another Internet site, iTunes adds it to its Library automatically.

 SHOW ME   **Media 14.2—A video about Importing Music**
Access this video file through your registered Web Edition at
my.safaribooksonline.com/9780789743916/media.

 LET ME TRY IT

Importing Music

Every time you insert a music CD in your disk drive, iTunes asks if you want to import it. iTunes wants you to have all your favorite music in one place and at your fingertips, so it's persistent. Even if you have already imported a CD, if you insert it again, iTunes asks if you want to import it. (Click Do not ask me again if you regularly insert CDs just to play them.) To import music from a CD, follow these steps:

1. Insert the CD in the optical drive.

2. To import *all* the tracks on the CD, click Yes for the import question. iTunes works through the tracks, marking a completed track with a check mark in a green circle. If you don't want to import all the tracks, skip this step and go to step 3.

3. If you want to select the tracks to import, click No for the import question. Then uncheck the tracks you don't want, and click the Import CD button (in the lower-right corner).

4. If the track names import as Track 01, Track 02, and so on, select them, click Advanced in the menu bar, and click Get CD Track Names.

You must be connected to the Internet to get track names because iTunes gets them from http://www.gracenote.com.

5. Click the eject button in the Sidebar beside the CD's name to eject the CD.

 SHOW ME   Media 14.3—A video about Downloading Cover Art
Access this video file through your registered Web Edition at
my.safaribooksonline.com/9780789743916/media.

If you import a track you don't want, you can select the track and press the Delete key. A confirmation dialog box opens (unless you have previously selected Do Not Ask Me Again). Click Remove and then click Move to Trash. Note that you can't delete tracks listed in the source called Recently Played, Recently Added, or Top 25 Most Played.

If you just want to play a CD, you can click No to the import question if it displays. The name of the CD shows up in the Sidebar under Devices, it is selected, and the tracks display in the right pane. To play a track, double-click it. When you finish playing the CD, you can eject it by clicking the eject button in the Sidebar beside the CD's name.

Creating and Using Playlists

If you are playing tracks in your Music source, iTunes plays the first track you select and continues playing the next tracks until you stop it or it gets to the end of your list. If you click the Repeat button, before you play the first track in your list, iTunes plays all the tracks in your list and then starts over. If you click the Shuffle button, iTunes plays your tracks in random order.

If you click the Repeat button while a track is playing, iTunes repeats that track.

Essentially, all the tracks in your Music source make up a playlist, but you can create smaller playlists and include only the tracks you select. You might create a playlist for a party, one for exercising, one with only country music, and so on. You can simply listen to your playlists on iTunes or burn them to a CD for use in a CD player.

To create a playlist, click the + button (under the Sidebar). A new playlist called untitled playlist appears at the bottom of the Playlists category in the Sidebar. Type a name for the list and press Return. Drag songs from the Library to the list. To play a playlist, select it in the Sidebar and double-click the first song.

The iTunes DJ playlist is a live mix—that is, each time you select it, iTunes chooses songs randomly in the source you select. If you don't like the mix, click Refresh and iTunes chooses songs again.

Burning a Music CD

The great thing about burning your own CDs is that you get to choose your own songs to include from different artists and albums that span all genre and all eras. Instead of Elvis's Greatest Hits, you can have My Favorite Hits.

 **LET ME TRY IT**

Burning a Playlist to a CD

A playlist can include more tracks than will fit on a CD, so you may have to adjust the number of tracks that you include in a list before burning the disc. When a playlist is selected, the total size of the list displays in the status bar. To burn a playlist to a CD, follow these steps:

1. Select the playlist in the Sidebar.

2. Make sure the check boxes for the tracks you want to include are checked.

3. Click the Burn Disc button. A dialog box opens, as shown in Figure 14.4.

Burn Settings

CD Burner: HL–DT–ST DVDRW GWA4080MA

Preferred Speed: [Maximum Possible ⬍]

Disc Format: ⦿ Audio CD
          Gap Between Songs: [2 seconds ⬍]
          ☐ Use Sound Check
          ☐ Include CD Text
   ◯ MP3 CD
   ◯ Data CD or DVD
       Data discs include all files in the playlist. These
       discs may not play in some players.

⑦   (Cancel) (Burn)

Figure 14.4 *iTunes selects the format based on the type of tracks you have selected.*

4. Click the Burn button and insert a blank CD as instructed. The progress displays at the top of the window. When finished, the name of the CD, which is the same name as the playlist, displays under Devices in the Sidebar.

Listening to Radio

iTunes can access lots of live, streaming radio broadcasts. To listen to one, click Radio in the Library category of the Sidebar, click the disclosure triangle beside a stream, and double-click a radio station to connect to. The name of the station appears in the box at the top. Additional information about the name of the song, show, or artist may appear below it. To disconnect from the station, click the Stop button in the toolbar controls.

Listening to Music in Front Row

The advantage of using Front Row to play music is that, unlike iTunes, which accesses only *your* music, Front Row accesses all music on the hard drive, including music stored in other users' iTunes folders. To listen to music, select Music from the Front Row menu and press the play button on the remote. Select a category such as Playlists, Albums, Songs, Genre, and so on, and press the Play button again. Select the song and press the Play button. To back up through the menus one level at a time, press the Menu button. Press the Menu button enough times, and you quit Front Row.

Acquiring and Playing Podcasts

A podcast is an audio or video recording that has multiple episodes released over time. Using iTunes, you can download a single episode or subscribe to the series, in which case, iTunes automatically downloads new episodes when they become available. To select podcasts for downloading, click Podcasts in the Sidebar and click the Podcast Directory button. Browse through the podcasts and double-click one you want. Click Get to download a single episode or click Subscribe. To unsubscribe, click Podcasts in the Sidebar, click the podcast in the right pane, and click the Unsubscribe button.

You can play a podcast in iTunes or Front Row. To play one in iTunes, click Podcasts in the Sidebar, double-click the podcast series in the right pane that you want to play, and double-click the episode you want to play. In Front Row, select Podcasts from the menu, select the podcast series you want to play, and press the play button on the remote. Then select the episode you want to play and press the play button on the remote again.

SHOW ME   Media 14.4—A video about Playing Podcasts in Front Row
Access this video file through your registered Web Edition at
my.safaribooksonline.com/9780789743916/media.

Playing Games

When it comes to fun and games, Mac is heavy on fun, but, unfortunately, light on games. Only one game comes with Snow Leopard and that is—no, not Solitaire—Chess.

To launch Chess, open the Applications folder and click the Chess icon. A 3D wooden board with wooden pieces displays, and you can start playing the game immediately. You are the white pieces. Drag the corner of the board to rotate it in space to give you a better view.

To start a new game, click Game in the menu bar and click New. Select the players (Human vs. Computer, Human vs. Human, or Computer vs. Computer), select the variant, and click Start. Various menu options allow you to take back a move, see a hint for your next move, see the last move, and see a log of the game. To quit Chess, press Cmd-Q.

A large number of games are available for downloading from the Apple site. Just click the Download link at http://www.apple.com and then click the Games category. Many files listed are demos or shareware, but a few freeware programs appear in the list as well. To download a game, click the Download button. For easy access, move the game from the Downloads folder to the Applications folder.

This chapter shows you how to use Photo Booth, iPhoto, and Comic Strip in some very creative ways.

15

Being Creative with Photos

Mac OS X Snow Leopard gives you so many ways to be creative with photographs. Unless you're a professional photographer, you have every application that you could possibly want—all included in Snow Leopard. This chapter covers some of the most creative things that you can do, such as creating self-portraits with special effects in Photo Booth and using iPhoto to create slideshows with music and transitions, photo books, photo calendars, and greeting cards.

Making Self-Portraits in Photo Booth

When Photo Booth opens, you see your own face staring back at you. Just like in the old photo booths that used to be in every dime store, you can pose and take your own picture. (If you ever took your picture in one of those photo booths, call me, and we'll reminisce about the good ole days.) To launch Photo Booth, click its icon in the Dock. To close it, click the red Close button in the title bar.

Taking Pictures and Movies

The iSight camera, built into all Macs that can run Snow Leopard, takes still photos as well as movies. Obviously, it's not like using a handheld camera because you really can't point it at subjects too easily, and the resolution is low (72 pixels/inch), but it's great for taking pictures or videos of yourself that you might use on the Internet. For example, you might want to take a picture of yourself to use as your Account Picture or as an avatar on a discussion forum. Additionally, you might want to video a message that you want to send to someone or post on a website.

To take a still picture of yourself (and anyone else who can crowd in beside you), click the red Shutter button. A countdown allows you to get ready. Look into the camera and smile. Your portrait appears as a thumbnail in the pane at the bottom. Click the x in the corner if you want to delete the photo.

To shoot a movie, click the Movie Clip button (the third button from the left that has a strip of film as its icon) and then click the red Shutter button. Watch the countdown and then start performing when you see the elapsed time counter. Click the Stop button when finished. Your movie appears as a thumbnail in the pane at the bottom. You also can delete a movie by clicking the x in the corner.

If you click a photo or movie in the bottom pane, it displays in the upper pane. Return to picture-taking mode by clicking the Shutter button.

Click the Effects button to apply special effects before you take a picture or a movie. Use the scroll buttons to view the effects, click the one you want, and then click the Shutter button.

 TELL ME MORE Media 15.1—A discussion about Using Special Effects
Access this audio recording through your registered Web Edition at
my.safaribooksonline.com/9780789743916/media.

Sending Photos and Movies to iPhoto or Email

To send photos or movies to iPhoto, select the items in Photo Booth and click the iPhoto button as shown in Figure 15.1. iPhoto opens and imports the items into a single event. To email items, select them and click the Email button. Mail opens with a new message and the items display full size in the body of the email. Right-click the items and click View as Icon if you prefer.

Figure 15.1 *Select the photos across the bottom that you want to send to iPhoto or email.*

Creating and Exporting Slideshows

You can quickly create a slideshow on-the-fly—one that you show once and don't care to save—but if you invest time customizing a slideshow, you will probably want to save it. You can customize a slideshow by selecting a theme, background music, special effects, and transitions.

iPhoto provides six themes for you to choose from: Classic, Ken Burns, Scrapbook, Shatter, Sliding Panels, and Snapshots. The Ken Burns theme uses an effect that gives motion to still photographs by panning and zooming. (Ken Burns is an Emmy-winning director and producer of documentary films noted for his use of the effect.) The names of the other themes give some clues to what they are like.

 **LET ME TRY IT**

Creating a Slideshow

The Classic and Ken Burns themes are the most customizable, allowing you to set your own transition effects—the way one slide leaves the screen and the next slide appears. The other themes use preset transition effects that you can't change. To create and customize a slideshow, follow these steps:

1. Open iPhoto and select the source(s) with the photos you want to use.

2. Click the Add button (under the Sidebar) and click Slideshow.

3. Type a name and click the Create button. The name of the slideshow appears in the Slideshows category in the Sidebar.

4. Drag the photos in the browser at the top of the screen to put them in the order you want.

5. Click the Themes button in the toolbar, click a theme, and click the Choose button.

6. Click the Preview button to view the theme. Click the Preview button again and repeat steps 5 and 6 until you find a theme you like.

7. Click the Music button. Click the Source pop-up button and click a source. Selecting iTunes may give you access to the most tracks. Click the name of the song you want and click the Apply button.

8. Click the Settings button. A dialog box opens that has a tab for All Slides and a tab for This Slide, as shown in Figure 15.2. Select the options you want and close the dialog box.

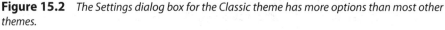

Figure 15.2 *The Settings dialog box for the Classic theme has more options than most other themes.*

9. If you want to apply special effects to an individual slide or the same effect to several slides, select the thumbnails of the slides, click the Settings button, and click This Slide. The Classic and Ken Burns themes also have more options to choose from on this pane. You can select a different display duration and a different transition for the slide. You also can turn the Ken Burns effect on and off. Click the effects that you want and close the dialog box.

10. Click the Play button and enjoy the show. To watch the slideshow any time, select the slideshow in the Sidebar and click the Play button.

To share your slideshow, you can export it as a movie. Select the slideshow in the Sidebar and click the Export button. Select as many sizes as you want. The iTunes option is selected by default, and I recommend you keep the check mark for this option. Click the Export button and click OK. The export may take several minutes, but when it is finished, iTunes opens with the Movies source selected. Your new slideshows appear in this category.

Designing and Publishing a Photo Book

Which is better—old-fashioned albums or iPhoto photo books? A photo book takes up less room on the shelf; it's lighter in weight; it's much more professional looking; and it's more permanent. I vote for iPhoto photo books.

iPhoto books come in these bindings and sizes:

- **Hard cover with book jacket**—13×10 inches and 11×8.5 inches

- **Soft cover**—11×8.5 inches, 8×6 inches, and 3.5×2.6 inches

- **Wire bound**—11×8.5 inches and 8×6 inches

Each book has a minimum of 10 sheets and ranges in price from $10 to $50. For a large or extra-large book, you probably need between 40 and 80 high-resolution photos. For a small or medium book, you can have no more than two photos per page, so you need 20 to 40 pictures. You can use lower resolution photos in smaller size books.

LET ME TRY IT

Creating a Photo Book

Many websites offer photo books that you can create using their templates, but creating a photo book in iPhoto produces a more customized book. You have so many more choices of layout, colors, fonts, and so on. Additionally, the price to print a book from iPhoto is comparable to the prices at other websites. To create a photo book, follow these steps:

1. Open iPhoto and select the photo source(s). You don't have to use all the photos you select, and you can add even more photos later if you need them. I like to have lots of *material* to work with when I'm creating a book because once I get into it, I never know where the creative muse will take me.

2. Click the Add button (under the Sidebar) and click Book. The dialog box shown in Figure 15.3 opens.

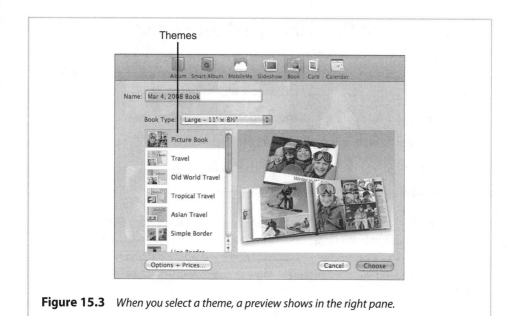

Figure 15.3   *When you select a theme, a preview shows in the right pane.*

3. Type a name, select a book type, select a theme from the Sidebar, and click the Choose button. Click OK if an instructional dialog box opens. The photos from your sources display as thumbnails in the browser at the top of the screen, and the cover page is in view as shown in Figure 15.4. The book's name displays under Keepsakes in the Sidebar.

4. Drag the thumbnails in the browser to put them in the order you want. Think of the "story" you want to tell in your book and arrange the pictures in that order.

If you don't want a photo that appears in the browser, select it and press the Delete key. The photo still exists in its original source.

5. At this point, you could click the AutoFlow button and *all* the photos would flow onto pages in your book. If you don't intend to use all the photos you brought into the book, this is not a good method to use. Also, realize that you pay extra for each additional sheet in the book (above 10). Instead of using AutoFlow, you can drag photos to each page manually.

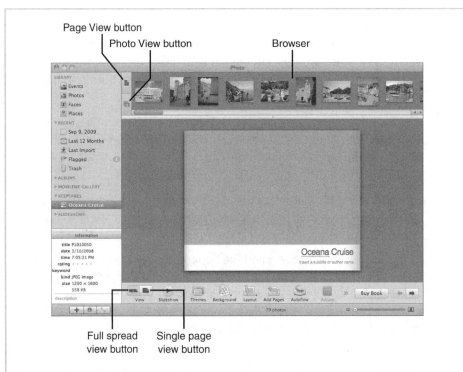

Figure 15.4   *Click the Page View button to view pages when you want to add, delete, or move pages in the book.*

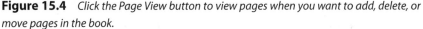

When dragging photos to a frame on a page, you don't have to select a photo that matches the orientation of the frame. The frame changes to match the orientation of the photo you drag to it. Also, you can use a photo in a book more than once.

6. Whether or not you use AutoFlow, you can go to each page and click the Background button to select a color. Additionally, you can click the Layout button to select the number of photos on a page and then drag thumbnails to the frames on the pages. If you used AutoFlow, changing the page layout could delete photos or produce empty frames that you need to fill.

Move to the next or previous page with the Next or Previous button.

7. Click the button in the browser to view pages if you want to add, delete, or move pages. To add a page, click the button for single page view or the full spread view (see Figure 15.4), and then click the Add Pages button to add a page or two after the current page. To delete a single page or two-page spread, select the page or spread, press the Delete button, and click OK. To move pages or spreads, drag them in the browser.

8. Click in the text boxes, selecting all default text when necessary, and type your own titles, comments, and descriptions. When working in small text boxes, use the slider in the bottom-right corner of the window to enlarge the view.

9. As a final check, scroll through the pages to make sure you have photos in all frames and text in all text boxes. Also, be sure to check the spelling (click Edit, Spelling, Show Spelling and Grammar).

10. When you are finished designing the book, you can just keep it in iPhoto and view it as a slideshow, or you can click the Buy Book button. Warning dialog boxes appear if you have any empty photo frames, any photos with low resolution, or any text boxes with default text in them. If no problems are found, you are connected with an ordering page. If you don't have an account, you can set one up and then continue with your order.

When designing a book, you might find the following information and tips helpful:

- Settle on the book's theme and size before adding text. If you change the theme or size after adding text, you could lose some of it.

- Use the full spread view to make sure the layouts of two facing pages are compatible.

- Photos that have been placed have a check mark on the thumbnail.

- A photo with a resolution that is too low displays an exclamation point in a yellow triangle. Either replace the photo or use the photo at a smaller size.

- To remove a photo from a frame, click it and press the Delete key. The photo still remains in the browser.

- You can change the stacking order of photos in a layout by right-clicking a photo and clicking Move to Front or Send to Back.

- To crop and position a photo in a frame, click the photo. Drag the sizing slider to crop the photo, and then drag the photo to display the portion of the photo that you want in the frame.

- If you don't like the caption for a photo, click the photo on the page or in the browser and type a new title for it in the information pane.

- To set the font type and font size for all text elements in a book, click the name of the book under Keepsakes in the Sidebar and then click the Settings button. Select the font and size for each element and click OK when finished.

- To show or hide page numbers in the book, click the name of the book under Keepsakes in the Sidebar and click the Settings button. Select or deselect Show Page Numbers and then click OK.

> If you don't see the Settings button in the toolbar, your screen resolution and the iPhoto window size have conspired to hide the button from view. Click the double-arrow to the right of the Adjust button and click Settings.

Creating Other Keepsakes

Once you master creating a photo book, you can apply many of the same methods and principles to creating a calendar, a greeting card, or a postcard. The cost to print a 13×10.4-inch 12-month calendar is $19.99; greeting cards are $1.99 each; and postcards are $1.49 each.

 SHOW ME   Media 15.2—A video about Creating a Calendar
Access this video file through your registered Web Edition at
my.safaribooksonline.com/9780789743916/media.

 **LET ME TRY IT**

Creating a Calendar

Obviously, you are going to need at least 12 photos to create a calendar—one for each month. But unless you have very high resolution photos, you should select two or three dozen photographs. To create a calendar in iPhoto, follow these steps:

1. Select the photos you want to include and click the Add button.

2. Click Calendar, type a name, select a theme, and click Choose. The dialog box shown in Figure 15.5 opens.

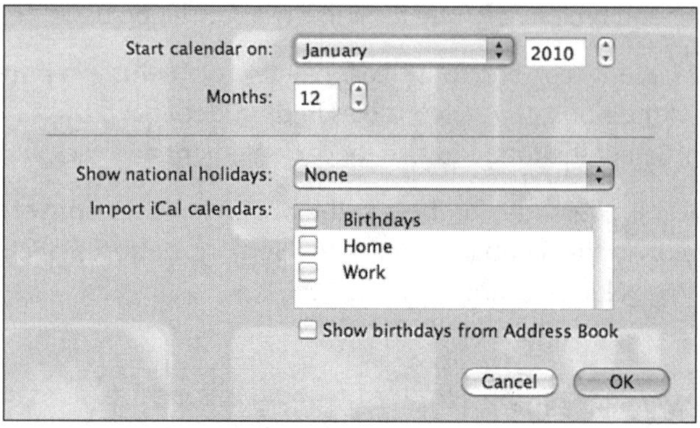

Start calendar on: [January ▴▾] [2010 ▴▾]

Months: [12 ▴▾]

Show national holidays: [None ▴▾]

Import iCal calendars:
☐ Birthdays
☐ Home
☐ Work

☐ Show birthdays from Address Book

(Cancel) (OK)

Figure 15.5 *If you import birthdays from the Address Book, you can delete the ones you don't want.*

3. Specify your choices and click OK.

4. Click OK again if an instructional dialog box opens. Use AutoFlow to place the photos or design the pages individually using the Layout button.

5. Drag a picture to a calendar date, or click a date, type text, and then click the x to close the window.

6. When you are finished, click the Buy Calendar button to connect with the ordering page.

 SHOW ME   Media 15.3—A video about Creating a Greeting Card
Access this video file through your registered Web Edition at
my.safaribooksonline.com/9780789743916/media.

 LET ME TRY IT

Creating a Greeting Card

iPhoto provides templates for the major holidays and for special occasions, such as birthdays and birth announcements. Additionally, you can use one of the many generic templates to create a card for any occasion. To create a greeting card in iPhoto, follow these steps:

1. Select the photos you want to include and click the Add button.

2. Click Card. Type a name for the card, select a type from the Sidebar, select a card in the right pane, and click Choose.

3. Use the Color, Design, and Orientation tools to design the card.

4. Click in the text boxes, selecting all default text when necessary, and type your own text.

5. When you are finished, click the Buy Card button to connect with the ordering page.

Using Comic Life

I'm disappointed that I don't have enough space in this book to cover the comic strip–creating application called Comic Life. You don't hear much about this program, and you may think it has no practical application for anyone but comic strip writers, but I like it because it allows you to add text to your photos. You can put a funny quote on a picture, export it to iPhoto, and make a humorous greeting card with it. Don't miss the free video that shows you how to do this. I think you'll find it well worth your time, and it might spark a few ideas for projects that you can create on your own.

 SHOW ME   Media 15.4—A video about Using Comic Strip
Access this video file through your registered Web Edition at
my.safaribooksonline.com/9780789743916/media.

This chapter covers some of the in's and out's of creating a simple movie in iMovie.

16

Making Your Own Movies

iMovie is a great little video production program for home movies, YouTube videos, and other nonprofessional videos. It's part of the iLife '09 suite that comes on every new Mac and also in the OS X Snow Leopard upgrade box version. You can import your video footage, edit out the parts you don't want, add transition effects, include titles and credits, build a great audio track, and output your finished movie in various formats. I cover all these basic features in this chapter, but iMovie can do more. As you get proficient with iMovie, you may want to go to the next level and learn how to use themes, adjust the video saturation, add sound effects and voiceovers, use audio fade in and fade out, apply special effects to video, add cutaway shots, use the green screen effect, and so on.

Getting Started

To launch iMovie, click the iMovie icon in the Dock. The first time you open the application, a welcome screen displays. Uncheck Show This Window When iMovie Opens and click Close. The program window is shown in Figure 16.1.

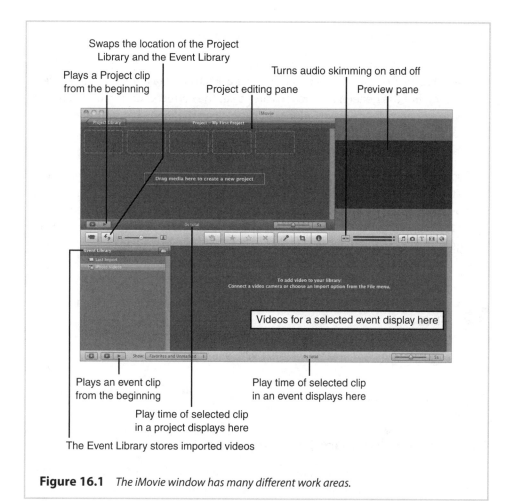

Swaps the location of the Project
Library and the Event Library

Turns audio skimming on and off

Plays a Project clip
from the beginning

Project editing pane

Preview pane

Drag media here to create a new project

Videos for a selected event display here

Plays an event clip
from the beginning

Play time of selected clip
in an event displays here

Play time of selected clip
in a project displays here

The Event Library stores imported videos

Figure 16.1 *The iMovie window has many different work areas.*

SHOW ME   Media 16.1—A video about Overview of iMovie Window
Access this video file through your registered Web Edition at
my.safaribooksonline.com/9780789743916/media.

Adding Video to the Events Library

The main thing you need to make a movie is some video footage. You can import video directly from your camcorder or camera. Each camera or recorder is a little different, but the general instructions are to set the correct output mode in the device, connect the device to your Mac, click File in the menu bar, and then click Import from Camera. If you have problems, refer to the iMovie Help article titled "If iMovie doesn't recognize your camcorder."

If you don't have a video camera, you might have some videos stored on your Mac that you can import. Look for files with an extension of .mov. If you don't have any movies on the hard drive, then you can record a movie in Photo Booth. See Chapter 15, "Being Creative with Photos," for instructions. Photo Booth saves its recordings in the Photo Booth folder, located in the Pictures folder, which is located in your home folder.

 SHOW ME Media 16.2—A video about Importing Video from the Hard Drive
Access this video file through your registered Web Edition at
my.safaribooksonline.com/9780789743916/media.

 **LET ME TRY IT**

Importing Video from the Hard Drive

Whether you import from a camcorder or from a file on a disk drive, the video file comes into iMovie and resides in the Event Library as a new event or as part of an existing event, depending on the settings you make at the time of import. iMovie stores events in the library in date order, with the most recent date at the top. You can import video stored on your hard drive by following these steps:

1. Click File in the menu bar, click Import, and then click Movies. A Finder dialog box opens, as shown in Figure 16.2.

The first time you import a movie, a dialog box presents a choice of Large or Full for the size before the Finder opens. Click OK to select the default (Large).

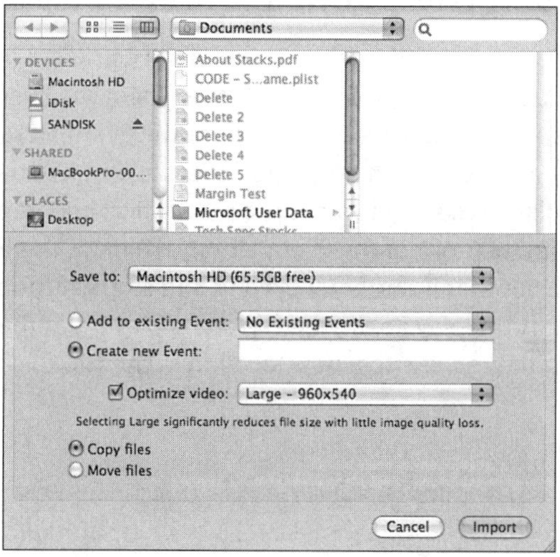

Figure 16.2 *If you are importing from a camcorder, this dialog box has an option to check for stabilization.*

2. Navigate to the location where you know the video is stored. (If it's in Photo Booth, the location is Pictures\Photo Booth.) Click the file to select it.

3. Click Create New Event and type a name for the event or click Add to Existing Event and select the event from the pop-up menu.

4. Select an option for Optimize Video and select either Copy Files or Move Files. I recommend Copy Files, which is the default setting.

5. Click Import. The video is added to the Event Library in the left pane, and the frames of the clip display in the pane to the right.

Each continuous video that you import into an Event is called a *clip*. When you select an event in the left pane, the frames of all its clips show in the right pane. The clips in your events are the raw materials you use to build your movie projects.

Playing Clips in the Event Library

Once you get videos imported into the Event Library, you can view them in the Preview pane in the upper-right corner. Select an event in the Event Library. The clips for that event display in the pane to the right of the Event Library. Press the Spacebar to start playing the clips and press the Spacebar when you want to stop playing. As the clips play in the Preview pane, a red vertical line travels through the clips in the pane to the right of the Event Library. Think of this line as the "clip cursor." It marks the spot that is currently playing and stops at the spot where you stop the play. If you start the play again, the clip starts playing at the point of the red line. You can drag the red line to a new location in the clip to change the starting point.

To play an event clip from the beginning, click the clip and then click the Play button (see Figure 16.1) or press the \ key. Click the button or press \ again to stop the play.

Creating and Playing a New Movie Project

The Project Library, in the upper-left pane, is the storage area for all the video projects you have created. The projects may be finished, or they may be works in progress. iMovie lists projects in alphabetical order. Using the button in the upper-left corner, you can toggle this pane between displaying all your projects and editing a specific project.

To create a new project, click File in the menu bar and click New Project. Type a name for the project and select an Aspect Ratio setting. Select a Theme and click Create. The Project Library pane toggles to edit mode and the new project opens in the pane.

The default choice for Theme is None. While you are learning to use the program, I don't recommend that you use a Theme because Themes do some things automatically, and this could give you a false sense of what *you* are doing versus what the Theme is doing.

The next thing you want to do is add clips to the project. You do this by dragging clips from an event into the project editing pane and dropping them in the order in which they should play. Use one of the following methods to add clips:

- **To add a complete clip**: Click the source in the Event Library that contains the clip you want to add. To select the entire clip, Option-click it in the right pane. A yellow border surrounds the entire clip. Drag it to the Project editing pane.

- **To add a portion of a clip**: Click the source in the Event Library that contains the clip and then click the clip in the right pane to set the yellow border. Drag the handles on either end to include more or less of the clip. This is tricky because you want to get just the right part. You may have to view the clip in the Preview pane a few times to determine where the handles should be. Move the pointer through the clip to skim through it. You may want to click the button to turn off audio skimming while you are doing this. (Refer to Figure 16.1.) Once you have the correct portion selected, drag it to the Project editing pane.

To save the project, click… wait, there is no Save command for projects. iMovie saves each project automatically with every change you make.

When you have added video clips to a project, you can play the project in the Preview pane. Drag the red vertical line to any starting point and press the Spacebar. Press the Spacebar again to stop the play. Click the play button (shown in Figure 16.1) or press the \ key to play the project from the beginning and also to stop the play.

Trimming and Splitting Clips

Trimming a clip means cutting some frames off at the beginning or the end, while splitting a clip means cutting a clip in the middle. Sometimes, instead of selecting a portion of an event to drag into a project, you may prefer to add an entire clip and then trim it in the project. To trim a clip in the project, click the clip, move the handles on each end of the yellow border where you want them, click Edit in the menu, and click Trim to Selection. When you edit a clip in a project, you don't change the original source.

One reason you might want to split a clip in the middle is to add a transition, apply a special effect, or delete a portion of the clip that you don't want. To split a clip, click the clip to select it. Move the handles at the beginning and the end of the yellow border to the locations where the clip should split, click Edit in the menu bar, and click Split Clip. If the first handle is at the beginning of the clip, or the second handle is at the end of the clip, the clip will only split into two pieces. If both handles are somewhere in the middle of a clip, the clip will split into three clips.

If you change your mind, click one of the clips, click Edit in the menu bar, and click Join Clip.

Adding Transitions between Clips

A transition is an effect, like fading to black, that signals a major change in the movie. It tells the viewer that the scene is going to change to some place else, that a dream sequence is over, that a flashback in time has ended, and so on.

You add a transition between clips in the project so if there is no break in the clip where you want a transition, you have to split the clip, as described in the previous topic. To add a transition, click the Transition Browser button to display all the transitions available in iMovie. Drag the transition that you want to use to the Project editing window and drop it between the two clips (see Figure 16.3).

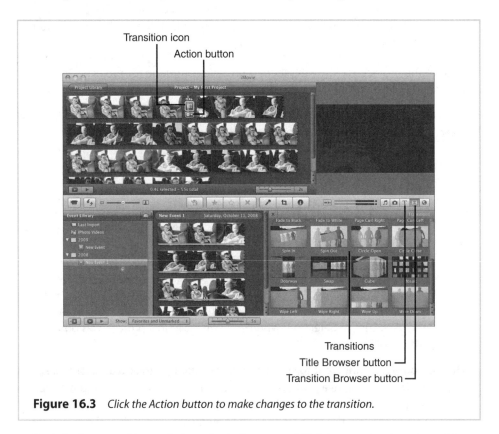

Figure 16.3 *Click the Action button to make changes to the transition.*

By default, a transition only lasts for half a second. To increase the duration of the transition, point to the icon between the clips, click the Action button (see Figure 16.3), and click Transition Adjustments. Type a larger number for the transition. If you just want this transition to have the new duration, uncheck the Applies to All Transitions option and click Done.

Adding Titles

Typically, you use titles at the beginning of a movie and for the credits at the end, but you can include titles within a movie as well. You can superimpose a title over the video or make a title an individual clip.

 SHOW ME Media 16.3—A video about Inserting Titles
Access this video file through your registered Web Edition at
my.safaribooksonline.com/9780789743916/media.

 LET ME TRY IT

Inserting Titles

iMovie provides many different types of title clips that you can use. Many contain action or additional graphics. Additionally, you can customize almost all the title clips by selecting the font, font size, and font color you want to use. To add a title clip to a movie, follow these steps:

1. Click the Titles Browser button (see Figure 16.3).

2. Drag the title you want to the Project pane, dropping it before, after, or between clips.

To superimpose the title, drag it from the Title Browser and drop it on top of a clip in the Project pane.

3. Click the background you want to use. The title displays in the Preview pane.

4. Select the default text in the title and type the text you want.

5. If the button is available in the Preview window, click Show Fonts to open the dialog box shown in Figure 16.4.

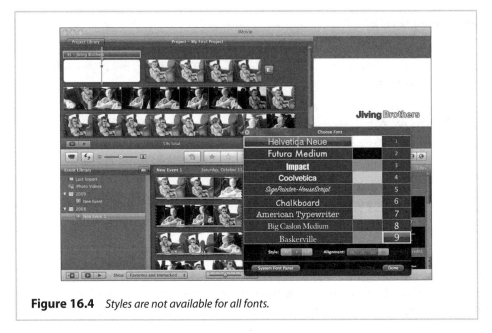

Figure 16.4   *Styles are not available for all fonts.*

6. Select a font, a color, a size, a style, an alignment and then click Done.

7. Click Done.

Sharing and Exporting Movies

When your masterpiece is finished, you have several ways to share the movie. You could send it to the Media Browser so it is available for you to access in other programs such as iWeb. You could publish it to iTunes, where you could view it with iTunes or Front Row. You could put it on a DVD by sending it directly to an iDVD project (see Chapter 18, "Making Your Own DVDs") so you could give discs to your friends. You could export it to the Finder in .m4v format so you could send it in an email message. You could send the movie to YouTube or your MobileMe Gallery so everyone in the world would have a chance to see it. When you become more knowledgeable, you might want to export it using QuickTime so you can set the frame rate, key frames, compression type and quality, data rate, and so on. If you are using Apple's professional audio and film-industry suite, Final Cut Studio, you can export to Final Cut XML format.

To perform any of these tasks, click Share in the menu bar and take your pick. I think you can figure it out from there.

If you make any changes to the project after you have published it to iTunes, YouTube, MobileMe Gallery, or Media Browser, iMovie reminds you that you need to publish the project again. An out-of-date reminder displays in the title if you have published to some applications, such as iTunes and YouTube.

 TELL ME MORE   Media 16.4—A discussion about Keeping Projects Up to Date

Access this audio recording through your registered Web Edition at my.safaribooksonline.com/9780789743916/media.

This chapter introduces you to the basic steps of
making your own recording in GarageBand.

17

Making Your Own Audio Recordings

GarageBand is the application you use to make your own audio recordings. It's included in the iLife '09 suite that comes on every new Mac and in the box upgrade of OS X Snow Leopard. You can make audio tracks for voices, music played by real instruments that are connected to your Mac, and music played by software instruments included in GarageBand. Additionally, you can mix and tweak the tracks until you have just the result you want. If you are an aspiring country singer looking to make your own demo CD to send to Nashville, you might want to look for a more sophisticated program than GarageBand, but for the musical hobbyist or a budding podcaster, GarageBand is full of features that will keep you busy and entertained. In addition to recording music, you can use GarageBand to teach yourself to play a guitar or the piano, write music, and even create ring tones.

Getting Started

GarageBand requires the use of a large amount of your system's resources; therefore, you should close all other applications when you are using GarageBand. To launch GarageBand, click its icon in the Dock. When the Welcome screen opens, click Close. (You see this screen only the first time you open GarageBand.)

Before you do anything else, you need to limit the number of instruments GarageBand can use because it's quite possible that you or GarageBand could create a song that is too complex to play on your Mac. Click GarageBand in the menu bar and click Preferences. Click the Advanced tab and select 8 from the Real Instrument Tracks pop-up menu and also from the Software Instrument Tracks pop-up menu. Select 10 Sampled, 5 Other for Voices per Instrument and close the window.

Creating a Magic GarageBand Project

Even though you might not burn a professional CD using GarageBand, the application is still relatively complex for a beginner, especially one who isn't musically inclined or who's never mixed sound tracks before. If that describes you, don't skip this chapter because GarageBand has a feature especially for you—it's called Magic GarageBand. With this feature, you can create an instrumental recording just by selecting a musical genre. Then sit back, wait for the magic, and join in the fun.

 **LET ME TRY IT**

Creating a Magic Instrumental Recording

When you use Magic GarageBand, you can select from several musical genres for your new song. Additionally, you can select the instruments that a song uses and even play one yourself. Follow these steps to create a Magic GarageBand song:

1. Click Magic GarageBand in the GarageBand window.

2. Click the genre you want, such as Roots Rock, and click Choose. The curtain opens and the instruments appear onstage (see Figure 17.1).

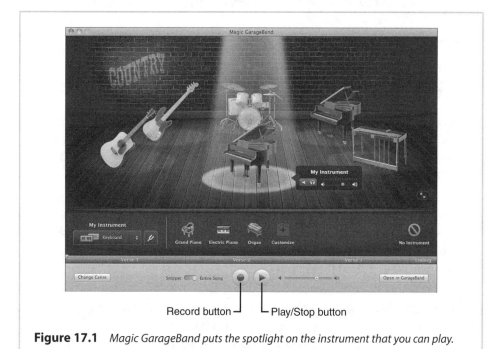

Figure 17.1 *Magic GarageBand puts the spotlight on the instrument that you can play.*

3. When the control buttons appear at the bottom of the screen, click the Play button to listen to the song that GarageBand created for you.

4. While the music is playing, you can play along. Your instrument is the piano in the middle of the stage. Click the button with the tuning fork on it to display the keyboard. After you've practiced a little, click the Record button to record what you play on the piano. Click the Record button again to stop recording.

5. Click the instrument on the far right of the stage. (The yellow spotlight shines on that instrument when it's selected.) This instrument is playing the melody. Click a very different instrument in the bar under the stage to hear the change in the music. Select other instruments on stage and change them until you have a mix of instruments you like.

6. To try a different genre, click Change Genre, select the genre, and click the Audition button.

7. When you are finished, click the Open in GarageBand button to see the tracks. If your eyes glaze over at this point, you're done.

8. Click File in the menu bar and click Save As. Type a name for the song and click Save.

9. To send the song to iTunes, click Share in the menu bar and click Send Song to iTunes.

10. Close the window when finished.

Creating a Voice Project

Showing you how to use GarageBand like a pro is not within the scope of this book, but I do want to show you how to work in GarageBand *without* using the Magic option. One simple type of recording you can make, even if you don't play an instrument, is a voice recording.

To make a voice recording, you could use the internal microphone on your Mac, but for best results, you might want to connect a good USB external microphone. If you connect an external microphone, click GarageBand in the menu bar and click Preferences. Click the Audio/MIDI tab. Select your device from the Audio Input pop-up menu and close the window.

 SHOW ME   Media 17.1—A video about Creating a Voice Project
Access this video file through your registered Web Edition at
my.safaribooksonline.com/9780789743916/media.

LET ME TRY IT

Creating a Voice Project

After you have all your equipment connected and configured, you are ready to create a new voice project. When you create the new project, you will have to make settings for Tempo, Signature, and Key if you will be singing. If you will be speaking, these settings don't matter. Follow these steps to create a voice project:

1. Click New Project in the GarageBand window, click Voice in the right pane, and click the Choose button.

2. Type a name for the recording and select a location where you want to save the file. (The Where option defaults to GarageBand.)

3. If you will be singing, select the options for Tempo, Signature, and Key.

4. Click Create. The window shown in Figure 17.2 opens.

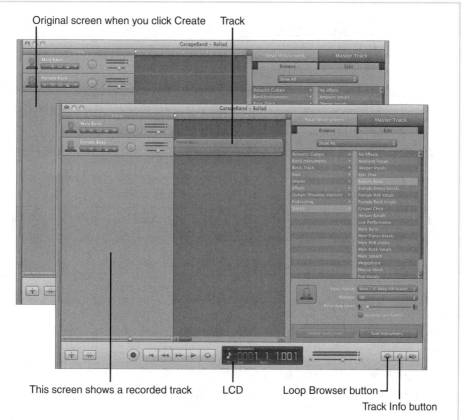

Figure 17.2 *When you record a track, the recording shows in the right pane of the project window.*

Recording the Track

When you create a Voice project, GarageBand assumes that you want to record a song and it gives you two tracks to start with—a male track and a female track. Both tracks are just alike.

If you intend to use both tracks (produce a duet, in other words), turn on the Metronome to hear the beat (click Control, Metronome) and turn on Count In (click Control, Count In) so that the second singer can come in on the same beat as the first singer.

 SHOW ME   Media 17.2—A video about Recording a Voice Track
Access this video file through your registered Web Edition at
my.safaribooksonline.com/9780789743916/media.

 **LET ME TRY IT**

Recording a Voice Track

Each minute of a stereo audio recording exported with CD quality sound uses about 10MB of disk space. So before you start recording, you might want to display the recording time in the LCD control. To keep track of the time, click Control in the menu and click Show Time in LCD. Then when you are ready to start recording the track, follow these steps:

1. Click the track for your voice, click the Record button, and begin speaking or start belting out your song.

2. When finished, click the Record button and click the Stop button.

3. Repeat steps 1 and 2 for the second track if you want to record a duet with someone else's voice or even your own.

4. Click File in the menu bar and click Save to save your work.

5. To send the song to iTunes, click Share in the menu bar and click Send Song to iTunes.

6. Close the window when finished.

You could use a vocal recording like this for podcasts, but check out GarageBand's Podcast feature instead. It has more options for podcasting.

Playing the Recording

To hear your recording, click the control button to go back to the beginning, and then click the Play button. You'll hear a little reverberation in your voice because GarageBand sets that effect by default when you create a voice project. If you were speaking on your recording instead of singing, you probably will want to remove the effect. To remove reverberation, click the Track Info button (refer to Figure 17.2), click the Edit tab, and move the slider for Master Reverb to zero.

If you are knowledgeable, click an empty slot in the Edit pane and add any effect that you want to tweak—Distortion, Amp Simulation, Tremolo, AUPeak Limiter, and so on.

 TELL ME MORE   Media 17.3—A discussion about Setting Effects
Access this audio recording through your registered Web Edition at
my.safaribooksonline.com/9780789743916/media.

Adding and Deleting Tracks

Perhaps you don't want one of the default tracks that GarageBand gives you. To delete it, click the track to select it (it turns blue), click Track in the menu bar, and click Delete Track. To add a track, click Track in the menu bar, click New Track, select the type of track, and click the Create button.

If you have a track that you have modified in the Edit pane, as described in the preceding section, you might want to duplicate the track so that the new track has the same effects. To duplicate a track, click the track to select it, click Track in the menu bar, and click Duplicate Track. GarageBand adds a new, empty track with the same effects.

Adding Loops

GarageBand has a library of prerecorded music files, called *loops*, that you can add to your projects. The Loop Browser, displayed by clicking the Loop Browser button (refer to Figure 17.2), displays the loops for all real and software instruments, all genres (Rock, Country, Jazz, and so on), and all moods (Grooving, Relaxed, Dark, and so on). When you select all the preferences you want in the top of the browser, the loops that qualify display below. To listen to a loop, click it. To add a loop to a project, drag the loop to an empty space in the middle pane, and GarageBand creates an appropriate track for it. To extend the length of the loop, point to the upper-right corner of the loop, as shown in Figure 17.3, and drag to the right.

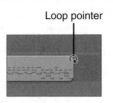

Loop pointer

Figure 17.3   *Wait until you see the loop pointer before you drag the loop.*

Exporting a Recording

To export a recording, click Share in the menu bar and click Export Song to Disk. For CD quality, do not select Compress; if you don't need CD quality, click Compress and select the encoder and the quality. Then click Export. Type a name for the file, select a location, and click Save.

If you are looking for both quality and smaller file size, you can use the compression bitrate of 128 kbps with MP3 Encoder and get near-CD quality and only use one MB per minute. If you choose Variable Bit Rate, the encoder uses different bitrates for different parts of the song; the quality is not quite as good, but the file may be smaller.

18

Making Your Own DVDs

iDVD is the application that burns your home movies to DVD with stunning-looking menu layouts that may rival or exceed what you see on commercially produced DVDs. I've rented some movies that had terrible menus, and I knew I could have done a better job with iDVD!

In addition to movies, iDVD also can burn DVDs that contain slideshows with background music, as well as a special DVD ROM section with the actual movie and photo files that a computer user could copy.

Getting Started

In iDVD you work on a *project*. You save the project just as you would save a word processing document, but the project file itself is not the real product of iDVD; the burned DVD is. Think of the project as the workspace that you use to create the structure and content of a DVD that you want to burn.

The structure of the DVD is made up of a main menu and usually additional submenus. Adding a movie or slideshow to a menu adds an option to the menu that links to the content. iDVD calls these options *buttons*. Figure 18.1 shows the structure and the corresponding menus for a DVD that uses a theme called *Bands*.

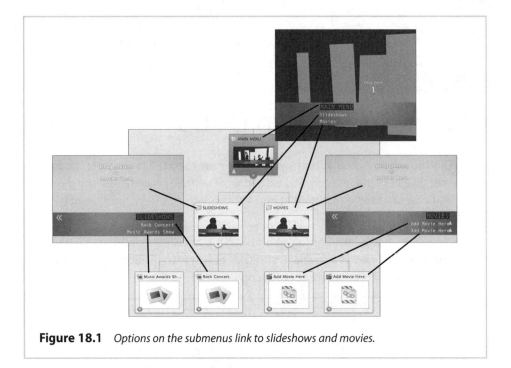

Figure 18.1 *Options on the submenus link to slideshows and movies.*

Creating a Magic iDVD Project

Instead of building an iDVD project step by step, I'm going to show you how to create a project using the Magic iDVD feature. This feature works like a setup assistant to guide you through the process of creating a DVD.

 SHOW ME   Media 18.1—A video about Creating a New Project with Magic iDVD

Access this video file through your registered Web Edition at
my.safaribooksonline.com/9780789743916/media.

 **LET ME TRY IT**

Creating a New Project with Magic iDVD

Using the Magic iDVD feature, you can select a theme and specify the files you want to use for slideshows and videos. The Magic feature does the rest for you—creating menus and adding special effects. To create a new iDVD project, follow these steps:

1. Click the Applications icon in the Dock, click iDVD, and click the Magic iDVD button. The window shown in Figure 18.2 opens.

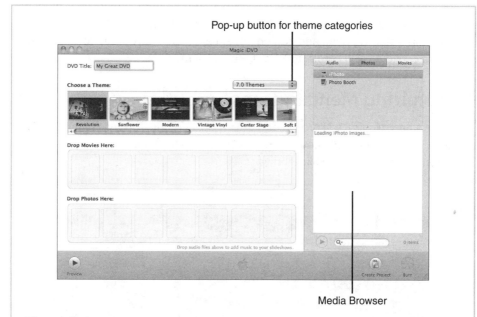

Pop-up button for theme categories

Media Browser

Figure 18.2 *Drag and drop media, and iDVD Magic does the rest.*

2. Type a title for the project and select a theme. (To see all the possible themes, select All from the Theme pop-up menu.)

3. Click the Movies tab in the Media Browser and drag movies to the drop areas for movies on the left.

4. Click the Photos tab in the Media Browser and drag events, albums, or slideshows to the drop areas for photos on the left.

> Additionally, you can drag individual photos to a drop area either by selecting them at one time in the Media Browser or by dragging them individually to the same drop area.

5. Click Audio in the Media Browser, select a song, and drag it to a slideshow you have already placed. Drop the song on top of the slideshow icon.

6. Click the Play button to preview your DVD. The preview shows what the DVD will look like when it's played after it's been burned.

7. Click the Close button in the window to end the preview.

8. Click the Create Project button.

Enhancing a Project

The DVD that Magic creates for you is good enough to burn immediately, but you also have the option of customizing it even more. By working with the Magic iDVD project as a starting point and adding enhancements to it, you can get an idea of how to create an iDVD project without the use of Magic.

Customizing Menu Buttons and Titles

Create a new Magic iDVD project or open an existing one. The DVD's main menu opens in the window, as shown in Figure 18.3. By default, the main menu has two buttons on it: Movies and Slideshows.

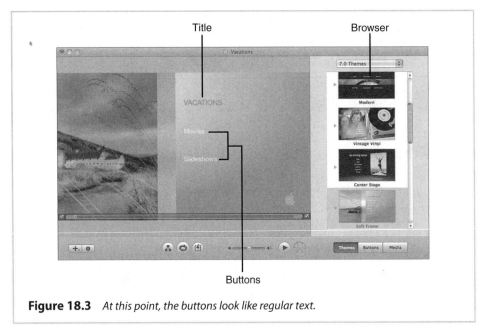

Figure 18.3   *At this point, the buttons look like regular text.*

To personalize the DVD, you can change the appearance of the buttons, the text, and the font attributes. For example, you might want to change "Movies" to "Vacation Movies." To change the text of an option, click it one time. Then click it again to select the text. Type the new text and select a font, font style, and font size. If you change the font, style, or size, make the same changes for all buttons on the menu.

Selecting the text of a button is very tricky. If you click too fast, the submenu opens and you have to click the arrow button to go back. Here's a little trick I use. I click the button; then I move the pointer away from the button and back again before I click the second time. Works like a charm!

SHOW ME   Media 18.2—A video about Adding Graphics to a Button
Access this video file through your registered Web Edition at
my.safaribooksonline.com/9780789743916/media.

 **LET ME TRY IT**

Adding Graphics to a Button

To give a button a little pizzazz, you can add a graphic element. The buttons can have underlines, bullets, a frame, and so on. To add a graphic element to a button, follow these steps:

1. Click the button one time to select it and then click the Buttons button in the browser.

2. Click the pop-up button at the top to select a category—Bullets, for example—and select a graphic.

3. Press Cmd-I to open the Inspector window, as shown in Figure 18.4.

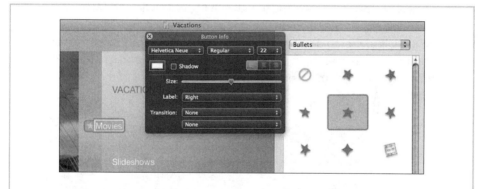

Figure 18.4   *The Inspector window allows you to make changes to the button.*

4. Drag the Size slider to change the size of the graphic.

5. Click the Label pop-up button and select a position for the label.

6. Click the Transition pop-up button and select a transition effect.

7. Click the Close button to close the Inspector window.

To maintain consistency, make the same changes in font and graphic appearance to all buttons on a menu. Preview the DVD to see how you like your modifications.

The title that Magic gives the main menu is the name of the project. You can change the text of the title using the same method you use to change the text of a button. The title is not a button, though, so you can't add a graphic element to it.

Adding a Submenu

To add a submenu to any existing menu, go to the menu, click the Add button, and click Add Submenu. A new button appears below the existing buttons on the menu, and it is selected so you can easily change the text of the button. This new button links to the submenu. (If you have modified buttons on the menu previously, you'll need to modify the new button to match.)

Configuring a New Submenu

Double-click a new button that you have added to a menu to go to the new submenu. The submenu has a title, but it doesn't match what you typed as the name of the button on the previous menu so you'll want to edit the title.

On the new submenu, you need to add the buttons that link to the content. Click the Add button and click Add Movie or click Add Slideshow, as shown in Figure 18.5. A new button appears on the menu with the instruction *Add Movie Here* or *Add Slideshow Here*, depending on the kind of button you added. Click the Media button in the browser to display the Media Browser. Click the Photos tab for slideshows or the Movies tab for movies. Select a movie or a source from iPhoto and drag it to the new button on the menu. Change the text of the button to something appropriate.

Figure 18.5   *Click the Add button to add a submenu, movies, or slideshows.*

If you preview the DVD at this point, you see that the buttons actually play a portion of the movie or the slideshow in a thumbnail in a continuous loop. If you prefer, you can change the button to show a still image. Click the movie or slideshow button to select it and click it again. Then click Still Image.

Editing Drop Zones and Menu Backgrounds

Drop zones are areas on a menu that can display slideshows, movies, or still photos, but that's not really their purpose. They are there for visual interest only—eye-candy on the menu, if you will. If you think about the way the menus for most commercial DVDs look, you'll remember that part of the movie usually plays over and over again when you are on the main menu before you press the button on your remote to play the movie. Basically, that's a drop zone.

If you build a DVD from scratch, the drop zones are empty, but if you use Magic iDVD to create the DVD, it fills drop zones with the files that you put on the DVD. That's not a bad choice actually, but you can change the drop zone by clicking the Media button to open the Media Browser, selecting a movie from the Movies pane or a source from the iPhoto pane, and simply dragging it to the drop zone. What you drag there replaces the default.

To add a movie, photo, or slideshow to the background of a menu, drag the appropriate source from the Media Browser. Don't get carried away, though; sometimes a drop zone is really all the eye-candy you need.

Adding Sound to a Menu

One final personal touch you can make to a menu is selecting the background music. A Magic iDVD plays default music that goes with a particular theme, but you can override the default music by adding different music to the menu. Click the Media button to open the Media Browser and click the Audio tab. Drag an audio file or a playlist and drop it on a blank space on the menu's background. Preview the menu to hear your music.

Adding a ROM Section

If you want to include the actual files, movies, or photos that you have used on the disc so that a computer user can access them, you can put them in a ROM section on the disc. These files are not accessible from a DVD player, but you can navigate to them when the DVD is loaded in an optical drive in a computer.

 SHOW ME   Media 18.3—A video about Adding Files to the DVD ROM Section
Access this video file through your registered Web Edition at
my.safaribooksonline.com/9780789743916/media.

LET ME TRY IT

Adding Files to the DVD ROM Section

When you add files to a ROM section, why not make them easier to find by putting them in folders? For the photos that make up your slideshows, you can create a folder called Photos. Or create a folder for each slideshow and name the folders with the same names you gave to the slideshows. For the videos, create a folder called Videos. If you want to include files that aren't really part of the DVD project, create folders such as Extra Photos or Uncut Videos, and so on. To add files in a ROM section on the DVD, follow these steps:

1. Click Advanced in the menu bar and click Edit DVD-ROM Contents.

2. Click the New Folder button. A new folder named *untitled folder* displays in the window.

3. Click the folder and then click it again to select the text. Type a name for the folder and press the Return key.

4. Click the Add Files button. Navigate through the Finder and select the files you want to add. Click Open. Click the disclosure arrow beside the folder name to see the files listed.

5. Repeat steps 2–4 to create another folder and add other files to it.

6. Close the window when finished.

Burning the Disc

When the DVD is just the way you want it, click File in the menu bar and click Save. Then you are ready to burn it. The burning process takes a few hours—longer if you continue to work while the disc is burning. Click the Burn button, insert a blank DVD, and wait patiently.

Use the Disk Utility application in the Utilities folder (in the Applications folder) to completely erase a disc if you need a blank disc.

TELL ME MORE   **Media 18.4—A discussion about Erasing a Disc**
Access this audio recording through your registered Web Edition at
my.safaribooksonline.com/9780789743916/media.

This chapter tells you how to use iWeb to create a personal, noncommercial website.

19

Creating a Website

iWeb is a very good website creation application for people who want to create a great looking site but don't really know much about HTML, XML, XHMTL, Javascripts, and so on. The application uses templates, drag and drop, and some ready-made widgets to make things easy for you. Websites you create with iWeb can include text, photos, movies, music, podcasts, RSS feeds, web widgets, hyperlinks, your latest Tweets, a YouTube video, and even Google AdSense.

Many third-party tools, HTML snippets, and Javascripts are available on the Internet to perform additional functions in iWeb, such as adding metadata for search engine optimization or changing the font attributes of the navigation menu.

iWeb is a part of the iLife '09 suite that comes on all new Macs, and it's intended for personal use. In other words, it's adequate to design a personal website. If you need to design a commercial site, you should consider a more robust, professional web designing application—or better yet, contact my son at 323Design.com.

Opening iWeb and Creating a New Site

The iWeb icon is not in the Dock by default, so to open the program, you must open the Applications folder and click iWeb. The first time you open iWeb you are given the opportunity to sign in or join MobileMe. You can click Don't Show Again and then click No Thanks for this dialog box. Then the dialog box shown in Figure 19.1 opens.

Figure 19.1   *Click a template in the sidebar to see the different page designs in the right pane.*

Select a theme collection from the pop-up menu, click a theme, click a template in the right pane, and click Choose. The window shown in Figure 19.2 displays the page you created and a sidebar. The sidebar shows the names of all the sites you create and the pages in each site. Notice that iWeb has already started building a navigation menu for you. As you add more pages, iWeb adds the names of those pages to the menu.

By default, iWeb names your websites "Site," "Site 2," and so on, and it uses the name of the template for the page name (for example, Welcome, About Me, Photos, and so on). You should rename the site so it is more indicative of the content, and you can rename pages at your option. To rename the site or a page in the site, click the name in the sidebar and then click it again to select the text. Type the new name and press Return. The name of the site changes in the sidebar and in the Site Publishing Settings you see in the right pane when the site is selected. (I explain these settings later in the chapter.)

Navigation menu

Inspector button

Figure 19.2   *The template uses default text and photos.*

Once you open iWeb for the first time and create the first site, if you want to create additional sites, click File in the menu bar and click New Site. The new site displays in the sidebar under the last site you created.

For knowledgeable web designers who are looking for the page named *index.htm,* iWeb creates this page automatically when you publish your site. You never see it in the sidebar.

Designing the Site

Notice that the templates iWeb provides are for specific uses—photos, albums, movies, blogs, and podcasts. Additionally, there is a generic blank page that you can use for whatever you wish and design however you wish. The photo template has the built-in capability of creating a slideshow from the photos on the page. If you use the album template, for each album you place on the page, iWeb automatically creates a photo page (with built-in slideshow capability) to display the pictures in that album. The new page is given the same name as the album.

SHOW ME   Media 19.1—A video about Creating a Blog Page
Access this video file through your registered Web Edition at
my.safaribooksonline.com/9780789743916/media.

Adding Pages

You can start customizing the first page immediately and add additional pages as
you need them, or you can add the other pages that you know you want in the
website and then go back and customize them.

To add another page to the site, click the Add Page button, click a page template
within your theme, and click Choose. iWeb automatically adds the new page to the
navigation menu at the top of the page.

> It's best to stick with the same theme for all pages in a website. Using different
> themes looks amateurish, and it confuses your visitors because different themes
> do different things with the navigation menu.

 LET ME TRY IT

Excluding Pages from the Navigation Menu

You can add as many pages to a website as you want, but you shouldn't include all
of them in the navigation menu if it causes the menu to wrap to a second line. This
isn't good form. If your menu wraps because of long page names, just shorten the
names, but if the problem is that you have 20 pages, then you need to exclude
some pages from the menu and create links to them from other pages. To exclude
a page from the navigation menu, follow these steps:

1. Select the page in the sidebar and click the Inspector button (see
    Figure 19.2).

2. Click the Page Inspector tab (if necessary) and click Include Page in
    Navigation Menu to remove the check.

3. Close the window.

 SHOW ME   Media 19.2—A video about Hyperlinking Pages in
Your Website
Access this video file through your registered Web Edition at
my.safaribooksonline.com/9780789743916/media.

 **LET ME TRY IT**

Hyperlinking Pages in Your Website

Let's say you have created four movie pages on your site. Instead of including all of them in the navigation menu, create another page that *is* in the menu and create hyperlinks on that page to the four movie pages. Here's how you set up a hyperlink between two pages in your website:

1. Select the text, photo, or shape that will be the hyperlink.

2. Click the Inspector button and click the Link Inspector tab (if necessary).

3. Click Hyperlink (if necessary) and click Enable as a Hyperlink, as shown in Figure 19.3.

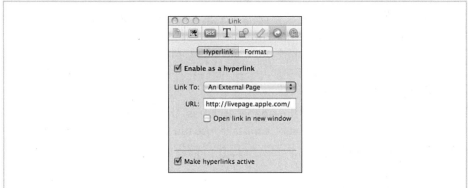

Figure 19.3 *When you create a hyperlink, it is active immediately, unless you uncheck the option at the bottom.*

4. Click the Link To pop-up button and click One of My Pages.

5. Click the Page pop-up button and click the name of the page you want the hyperlink to open.

6. If the link is text, click the Format tab to set the colors and add or remove underlines.

7. Close the Inspector window when finished.

Hyperlinking to External Pages and Files

Using the same basic steps listed previously, you can create a hyperlink to an external page—that is, a page on another website. Instead of selecting One of My Pages in step 4, select External Page and then type the URL of the page. Click Open Link in New Window if you don't want people to leave your website when they click the link.

Additionally, you can create a hyperlink to a file. Let's say that you want a visitor to be able to download a registration form for a family reunion from your site. You can accomplish this by creating a hyperlink to a file, usually a PDF file. Using the same steps listed previously, click File in step 4 and then specify the filename. When a visitor clicks the link, the file opens, and he can save it to his computer.

Moving and Deleting Pages

The order of pages in the sidebar corresponds to the order of the pages in the navigation menu. If you want to rearrange the order of pages, drag a page to a new position in the sidebar. The navigation menu automatically updates to reflect the new order. The page at the top of the list in a site is the Home page, but it doesn't have to be named "Home."

To delete a page, select it in the sidebar and press the Delete key. No confirmation dialog box opens, so if you make a mistake, use the Undo Delete Page on the Edit menu to get the page back.

Editing Pages

To customize the pages in your website, you need to replace the default text in the text boxes and replace the default photos with your photos and movies. You aren't constrained to the number of photos or the number of text boxes that appear on a template page by default; you can add and delete photos and text boxes to accommodate your design.

Additionally, you can customize just about anything on a page using the Inspector. You'll have to explore these possibilities on your own. Just click any item and then click the Inspector button to see what you find.

Adding Graphics and Videos

You can drag photos from the iPhoto pane of the Media Browser to a *media placeholder* on any page that has such a placeholder. (If you don't see the Media Browser, click the Show Media button in the toolbar.) Additionally, you can open the

Finder and drag graphic files from any location to the media placeholders. Once a photo is placed, use the Inspector to crop and reposition it within the cropped space.

To add a new media placeholder to a page, you must copy an existing placeholder and paste it. To copy a media placeholder, first point to it to be sure it is a media placeholder. The tag *This image is a placeholder…* displays if it's a true media placeholder. Click to select the placeholder, right-click it, and click Copy. In the sidebar, click the page you want to paste it on, click Edit, and then click Paste. If you want to paste it on the same page, be sure that nothing is selected on the page when you click Edit, Paste.

If you want to place photos on a page without dragging them to a media placeholder, you can, but then you won't have the options that are available to you in a media placeholder. For example, the photos will not play as a slideshow.

Yet another way to add a graphic to a web page is to insert it in a text placeholder where text can wrap around it. To insert a photo in a text placeholder, drag the graphic to the text placeholder and use the black pointer to point to the place in the text where you want to insert the graphic. Press the Cmd key to set the cursor in position. Drop the graphic and then release the Cmd key.

When you place photos on your web pages, iWeb works in the background to reduce the resolution of the photos so that your pages load faster. If you want visitors to your site to be able to download your photos to their computers at a higher quality (to print, for example), you can set the download resolution size to a higher quality. This gives you the best of both worlds—a fast page and high-quality photos that visitors can download. On a photo page or album page, click the Inspector button and click the Photo Inspector tab (if necessary). Click the Photo Download Size pop-up button and select a higher resolution.

If you want to add a video to a movie page, click the Movies tab in the Media Browser or open the Finder and drag the video to the placeholder. To prepare a video for your webpage, first export the video using QuickTime so that it has the optimum compression, quality, and size, but most importantly so that it is prepared for streaming on the Internet. See Chapter 16, "Making Your Own Movies," for instructions on exporting a video.

Adding Your Own Text

All template pages contain default text in *text placeholders*. To edit text in a placeholder, select the page that has the default text, click the text placeholder to select it, select the text, and type the new text or paste text that you have copied from another source.

SHOW ME   Media 19.3—A video about Formatting Text

Access this video file *through your registered Web Edition at*
my.safaribooksonline.com/9780789743916/media.

Formatting Text

The template that you are using for the web page determines the format for the text in a particular placeholder. You can use the default formats, or set your own formats, including the font, font size, and font attributes, such as bold, italic, and so on. To format text, follow these steps:

1. Select the text.

2. To add emphasis to text, click Format in the menu bar, click Text, and click Bold, Italic, or Underline.

3. To align the text, click Format in the menu bar, click Text, and click Align Left, Center, Align Right, or Justify.

4. To change the font or its attributes, click Format in the menu bar and then click Font, Show Fonts. In the Collection list, select Web. Select a Family, Typeface, Size, and other attributes from the Font window. Close the window when finished.

Almost all computers have the fonts in the Web collection. If you use that really cool font called Zebra Gothic for your text—you know, the one that you and only three other people downloaded from a now-defunct website—when your friend John visits your website, he's not going to see the Zebra Gothic. He didn't download it to his computer, so his computer will use something like Times New Roman or Arial. This usually causes text to wrap in unattractive ways you didn't intend or anticipate. So if you want your website to look the same to a visitor as it does when you design it, use Web fonts.

To add an additional text placeholder, click the Text Box button in the toolbar and type the new text. Then resize and drag the text box to the location on the page where you want it to appear. To delete a text box or text placeholder, select it and then press the Delete key.

Adding Special Buttons and Widgets

Using the Insert menu, you can add buttons and widgets to your pages. For example, to add an email button on the current page, click Insert, Button, Email Me. To add a Google Map widget, click Insert, Widget, Google Maps. Then type the address and click Apply. After you add these elements, you can drag them into the positions that you want.

Deleting Web Page Elements

To delete almost any element on a page—a placeholder, widget, graphic, and so on—select it and press the Delete key. Because almost all elements on web pages are contained in placeholders that occupy fixed spaces on the page, when you delete an element, nothing else on the page rearranges. Of course, after you delete an element, you may want to rearrange the page yourself, and you can do so by dragging placeholders to any location on a page. Just be careful that you don't overlap placeholders. The placeholder on the bottom might have a function, such as a hyperlink, that would be rendered unusable after you publish the site.

> You cannot delete the navigation menu or any part of it.

Publishing the Site

When you finish the site, you can publish it to your computer or network or to a server on the Internet. If you publish to a server on the Internet, iWeb gives you two options: the MobileMe server (for subscribers only) or an FTP server. You use the FTP server option if you pay for website hosting from a provider such as GoDaddy or 1and1.

 TELL ME MORE   Media 19.4—A discussion about Using a Web Host for Your Domain
Access this audio recording through your registered Web Edition at
my.safaribooksonline.com/9780789743916/media.

To publish the site, click the site in the sidebar. Click the Publish To pop-up button and select the correct option for you:

- If you select MobileMe, add your contact email address if you have an Email button on your site. Enter your URL if you have a Subscribe button on your site. Select Make My Published Site Private if you want to limit access to your site, and then specify a user name and password.

- If you select FTP Server, fill in the FTP server settings and the website URL.

- If you select Local Folder, specify the folder's location. It's a good idea to publish a website to a folder on your local computer so you can test it before you "go live."

Click the Publish Site button in the toolbar at the bottom and click Continue. When finished, click Visit Site Now or click OK.

After you publish a website, all the icons for the site and its pages turn blue in the sidebar. If you add pages or make changes to pages, those pages turn red to indicate you have not published them.

index

B

D

E

Q–R

U

X–Y–Z